3/19

DATE DUE

PRINTED IN U.S.A.

40610

ADHD Medications

The Story of a Drug

Painkillers: History, Science, and Issues
Victor B. Stolberg

Antipsychotics: History, Science, and Issues
Jeffrey Kerner and Bridget McCoy

Steroids: History, Science, and Issues
Joan E. Standora, Alex Bogomolnik, and Malgorzata Slugocki

Vaccines: History, Science, and Issues
Tish Davidson

ADHD Medications

HISTORY, SCIENCE, AND ISSUES

Victor B. Stolberg

The Story of a Drug

 GREENWOOD™

An Imprint of ABC-CLIO, LLC
Santa Barbara, California • Denver, Colorado

Library of Congress Cataloging-in-Publication Data

Names: Stolberg, Victor B., author.
Title: ADHD medications : history, science, and issues / Victor B. Stolberg. Description: Santa Barbara : Greenwood, [2017] | Series: Story of a drug | Includes bibliographical references and index.
Identifiers: LCCN 2017027300 (print) | LCCN 2017029382 (ebook) |
    ISBN 9781610697262 (ebook) | ISBN 9781610697255 (hardcopy : alk. paper)
Subjects: | MESH: Attention Deficit Disorder with Hyperactivity—drug therapy |
    Drug Therapy—history | Drug-Related Side Effects and Adverse Reactions
Classification: LCC RC394.A85 (ebook) | LCC RC394.A85 (print) |
    NLM WS 350.8.A8 | DDC 616.85/89061—dc23
LC record available at https://lccn.loc.gov/2017027300

ISBN: 978–1–61069–725–5 (print)
        978–1–61069–726–2 (ebook)

21 20 19 18   2 3 4 5

This book is also available as an eBook.

Greenwood
An Imprint of ABC-CLIO, LLC

ABC-CLIO, LLC
130 Cremona Drive, P.O. Box 1911
Santa Barbara, California 93116-1911
www.abc-clio.com

This book is printed on acid-free paper ∞

Manufactured in the United States of America

This book discusses treatments (including types of medication and mental health therapies), diagnostic tests for various symptoms and mental health disorders, and organizations. The authors have made every effort to present accurate and up-to-date information. However, the information in this book is not intended to recommend or endorse particular treatments or organizations, or substitute for the care or medical advice of a qualified health professional, or used to alter any medical therapy without a medical doctor's advice. Specific situations may require specific therapeutic approaches not included in this book. For those reasons, we recommend that readers follow the advice of qualified health care professionals directly involved in their care. Readers who suspect they may have specific medical problems should consult a physician about any suggestions made in this book.

It is my pleasure to dedicate this book to my family, particularly my wife, Marie Rose, and our two sons, Victor and George, for their encouragement, support, and, most of all, tolerance during my work on this project.

Contents

Contents

Series Foreword

Many books have been written on recreational drug use—its medical consequences, history, impact on the criminal justice system, and many other important facets of this complex issue. But recreational illegal drugs are not the only drugs Americans use.

In fact, while approximately 10 percent of Americans are illicit drug users, a staggering 70 percent of Americans regularly take at least one prescription drug. And almost everyone has taken at least one prescription or over the counter (OTC) medication at some point in their lives. There are hundreds of therapeutic drugs to address all manner of physical and psychological conditions and diseases, from destroying harmful bacteria to relieving pain to managing feelings of anxiety or depression. These drugs can have a powerful impact on the human body, but they can have larger economic and societal effects as well. Prescription and OTC drugs are a multibillion dollar industry, and the abuse of certain prescription medications has become a major public health concern.

Yet, despite these medications' prevalence, importance, and potential for abuse, few books have been written about them. This series, *The Story of a Drug*, aims to tell the untold tale behind many of these drugs. Each volume in the series explores a major class of drugs, examining them from a variety of perspectives, including medical, economic, legal, and cultural.

To maximize clarity and consistency, each book in the series follows the same format. Each begins with a fictional case study to illustrate the significance of the book's subject matter, highlighting key concepts and themes that will be explored elsewhere in the text. Chapter 2 provides an overview of the drug class, including discussion of different subtypes or major divisions, as well as basic information about the conditions or diseases such drugs are meant to treat. The history and evolution of these drugs are discussed in Chapter 3. Chapter 4 explores how the drugs work in the body at a cellular level, providing necessary information on body systems and mechanisms of action as needed. Chapter 5 examines the large-scale impacts of such substances on the body and how such effects can be beneficial in different situations and for different applications. Dangers such as side effects, drug interactions, misuse, abuse, and overdose are highlighted in Chapter 6. Chapter 7 focuses on how the drugs is produced and distributed as well as touching upon regulatory and other legal issues. Chapter 8 addresses professional and popular attitudes and beliefs about the drugs as well as representations of such drugs and their users in popular culture. Finally, chapter 9 speculates on the drugs' possible future, including emerging controversies and trends in research and use.

Each volume in this series also features a glossary of terms and a collection of print and electronic resources for additional information and further study.

It is our hope that the books in this series will not only provide valuable information but also spur informed discussion and debate about these drugs and the many issues that surround them. For instance, are antibiotics being overprescribed leading to the development of drug-resistant bacteria? Should antipsychotics, usually used to treat serious mental illnesses such as schizophrenia and bipolar disorder, be used to render inmates and elderly individuals with dementia more docile? Do schools have the right to mandate vaccination for their students, against the wishes of some parents?

As a final caveat, please be aware that the information presented in these books is no substitute for consultation with a licensed health care professional. These books do not claim to provide medical advice or guidance.

—Peter L. Myers, PhD
Emeritus member, National Addiction Studies Accreditation Commission
Past President, International Coalition for Addiction Studies Education
Editor-in-Chief Emeritus, *Journal of Ethnicity in Substance Abuse*

Preface

This work reviews much of what is known about Attention Deficit Hyperactivity Disorder (ADHD) and ADHD medicines. It covers the history of ADHD, the etiology of ADHD, the symptoms of, the major variants of, and the usefulness of various treatments, including chiefly that of the varied ADHD medicines and of the related nonpharmacological supportive approaches.

The first chapter of this book presents a case history of ADHD in the life of one individual and his family. This selection is intended to present a more intimate feeling of how ADHD can play out in the lives and experiences of an individual with ADHD and of their families and close associates. ADHD very often persists into adolescence and adulthood as it does in our case study. Without diagnosis and treatment, an individual with ADHD, like the one in the opening chapter, is highly likely to experience inner difficulties in school and in other areas of their life. Earlier initiation of treatment not only helps the individual perform better in academic and work settings but can also help to avoid the feelings of anxiety and depression typically associated with the difficulties often experienced by those with ADHD, including the unpopularity with their peers, and conflicts with parents, teachers, and other figures of authority.

Treatment with an ADHD medication commonly produces substantial benefits for over two thirds of individuals with ADHD. These respective ADHD medicines, when taken in the dosages prescribed, do not tend to result in addiction, but rather significantly decrease such a likelihood. Treatment with an ADHD medicine is not intended to cure ADHD, but rather to reduce the occurrence of negative symptoms.

The second chapter provides a formal introduction to ADHD and various treatment approaches, including, of course the use of respective ADHD medications, both the stimulants and the nonstimulant medicines. It will also review many of the varied alternative ways used to help individuals with ADHD. There is no single factor currently believed to cause ADHD, although several environmental factors may contribute to it. The third chapter presents a historical discussion of ADHD and of the development of the many medicines used to help treat individuals with ADHD. Next, an overview of the science of how respective ADHD drugs work is presented along with coverage of their varied effects and applications. Attention will then also be given to some of the risks associated with the use and misuse of ADHD medicines, including their abuse potential and possible overdose concerns. We will then explore some of the issues around the production, distribution, and regulation of these medicines, particularly focusing on the use of clinical trials and of drug scheduling. Discussion will include some of the social dimensions around ADHD and medicines used to treat it. What the future holds for ADHD medicines is difficult to predict, but they have become increasingly prevalent and are likely to continue to be for the foreseeable future.

The basic tenet of this book is to expand the general discussions related to issues around the condition of ADHD and, more directly, of the use of ADHD medicines. This work is not intended to dismiss or to negate the prevailing views, but rather to sit alongside the positivist perspective and to contribute to a more comprehensive and nuanced understanding of the phenomena around ADHD medicines.

Acknowledgments

I would like to take this opportunity to acknowledge my family, particularly my wife and our two young sons, for their ongoing support and forbearance during my time on this project. I would like to heartedly thank the former series editor, my dear friend and colleague for nearly three decades, Dr. Peter L. Myers. His continued steadfast support and unwavering friendship has been a solid base for much of my professional career, but also for my own personal growth and development. I would also like to thank all the staff and consultants behind the scenes at ABC-CLIO for bringing this work to completion. Chiefly, I would like to thank Maxine Taylor, senior acquisitions editor for Health/Wellness and Psychology at ABC-CLIO for steering me through this journey.

Most importantly, I would like to sincerely acknowledge all of those individuals who are struggling with ADHD, particularly those with whom I have had the pleasure of interacting with both professionally and personally. Further, the hard work and dedication of so many individuals working with individuals with ADHD and their families established a platform upon which I could build this project.

Chapter 1

A Case Study: Driven by Fire

All individuals with Attention Deficit Hyperactivity Disorder (ADHD) will not have the same experiences, nor will they all have the same reactions to the use of respective ADHD medications. Some individuals with ADHD will be prescribed a particular ADHD medicine, begin to use it and find, perhaps within a short period of time, that it makes a tremendous difference in how they feel and function. Other individuals may be administered the very same medication but experience far less satisfactory results or even experience adverse side effects. However, it is quite possible that if those individuals tried using other ADHD medications, they might experience much more favorable results. We will briefly consider a fictitious case study of an individual with ADHD to explore some of the many varied types of interactions that can occur in the course of searching for ways to help that person through the course of his or her life, both with and without the use of ADHD medications.

INTRODUCTION

Anthony G. is a white male, now aged 42 years. He is 5 feet 10 inches tall and weighs about 187 pounds. Anthony had a somewhat difficult childhood; he was always getting into trouble and had few childhood friends—a phenomenon that is shared in common with many children who have untreated ADHD. He was not diagnosed with ADHD until at a relatively late age, which means that he did not begin to receive appropriate treatment for this serious neurodevelopmental disorder until he was older than most individuals who initiate treatment for ADHD. The fact that Anthony had ADHD as a child should not be too surprising. In fact, the Centers for Disease Control and

Prevention (CDC) estimates that 13 percent to 20 percent of children in the United States aged 18 or younger have some form of mental disorder, of which ADHD is the most common.

Anthony G. has a long, convoluted personal history, as is often the case for an individual with ADHD, particularly if diagnosis and treatment are delayed. We will review his life story through three major phases, respectively that of his early childhood, his adolescent years, and, finally, his college and adulthood experiences.

EARLY CHILDHOOD

Anthony G. was born prematurely, and from his very earliest days, both of his parents realized that there was something quite different about him. In fact, his mother said that even while he was in the womb, he was overly active, rolling over and over, kicking for extended periods of time; she recalls it as a rather difficult pregnancy. She also admits that she smoked cigarettes daily and drank alcohol beverages regularly during the pregnancy; both of these maternal choices have been associated with a considerably greater risk for the subsequent development of ADHD among their offspring. Anthony was his mom's second child, but the first with her present husband, who, not surprisingly as it turns out, was later diagnosed with ADHD himself. Octavio, Anthony's father, in recounting his own personal dysfunctional family history, revealed many characteristics indicating that both his father and mother, Anthony's paternal grandparents, probably also had ADHD. The fact that Anthony's father and both of his grandparents probably also had ADHD should not be too surprising when it is well understood, as will be discussed somewhat in more detail in Chapter 2 and elsewhere later as well in this work, that ADHD tends to run in families and that it, accordingly, has a high likelihood of being passed on genetically. Anthony was a precocious, very active child, but, despite his blatantly obvious behavior problems and associated difficulties, it would be several more years before he was finally diagnosed with ADHD.

Unfortunately, missing a young child's diagnosis for ADHD can lead to a cascading series of adverse impacts that can not only limit the successes of an individual but also potentially result in very severe consequences for the individual, his or her family, and society at large. When a family like Anthony's does not fully understand what is going on with a troubled child at an early age and, consequently, when that child is not able to learn the compensatory skills required to effectively manage and to live with ADHD, it can have devastating consequences on the course of that individual's life trajectory, not only in the immediate short term but later as well.

The effects of not diagnosing and thus of not properly managing and treating ADHD can be very severe for the individual and for his or her family. The likelihood of negative consequences such as criminal justice involvement, addiction, and suicide is much greater among individuals with untreated ADHD. In this regard, those who are incarcerated, as Anthony briefly was, are much higher among individuals with untreated ADHD than in the general population, particularly for those persons with longer-term sentences. Similarly, somewhere from 20 percent to 50 percent of adults with ADHD also meet the diagnostic criteria for an alcohol or other type of drug disorder. The incidence of death from suicide is thought to be almost five times higher among adults who had ADHD as children. Fortunately, for Anthony, he was eventually diagnosed with ADHD, but it was yet some time before that actually was accomplished.

Problems at Home

Anthony was always a very active child. His mother, Ruthie, says that she remembers him as being "all over the place." Ruthie had an older daughter, Anthony's half sister Margaret. Ruthie says that from the very beginning, Anthony was a much more active child than Margaret ever was. At the age of one, Anthony crawled undaunted into the ocean; at the age of two, he was diving into the open water. Anthony was tiny and very agile as a toddler; he was an adept climber and would smash anything that he could get his hands on. Anthony was always on the go, constantly fidgeting, always grabbing any object in sight, and usually breaking it. The family was unable to keep any knickknacks in their house. In the twinkling of an eye, he could be climbing to get on top of the refrigerator or other obstacle, and, not infrequently, getting hurt. Individuals with ADHD, like Anthony, have more than their fair share of accidents and generally are much more likely than individuals without ADHD to make numerous visits to hospital emergency rooms.

Anthony would tend to squirm down out of the reach of others and then he would typically do whatever he wanted to do. It was extremely difficult to make a telephone call at home with Anthony around as he would interrupt mercilessly. By the age of three, he had to be chased running widely through stores, whenever his parents dared bring him out. At the age of four, Ruthie remembers a horrifying experience of watching Anthony darting across a parking lot narrowly missing moving cars as he went running straight ahead to the store. After a few failed attempts, it was too embarrassing to go out to a restaurant with him. It often appeared to his parents and to other adults who knew him well that he did not seem to be listening to what was being said to him.

Another problem that Ruthie and Octavio had to contend with was Anthony's persistent tactic of lying. For many children with ADHD, such as Anthony, lying is often utilized as a coping mechanism. A lie can be used to cover up something that was forgotten to do, or to avoid criticism or punishment, and even as a way to avoid dealing with feelings of shame and guilt over repeated failures that individuals with ADHD tend to experience.

Anthony was a very restless child who would constantly tease his older sister, Margaret, without mercy. Anthony was as over talkative as he was hyperactive, chattering nonstop as he moved ceaselessly about. There was never any peace and quiet when Anthony was in the house.

Anthony would annoyingly not tend to stay with any activity for a very long period of time. He could pull all of his toys off the shelves and out of his toy boxes, play with them for a couple of moments, and then discard them and move rapidly on to something else. It was amazing at how fast he could get the living room or his bedroom, or anywhere else in the house for that matter, messy. He would sleep all night once he finally got to sleep, but the real problem was getting him to eventually fall asleep, which was routinely a battle of wills. Initially, Ruthie thought that the difference in behavior was maybe just because Anthony was a boy, but as time went on, she sensed that it was much more involved than simply that.

Problems at School

Anthony entered a preschool day care program when he was three years and seven months old. One of his preschool teachers soon thereafter described Anthony as "having ants in his pants." He was constantly on the move, never wanting to sit still or to rest; this created a continual battle with the staff at the preschool program who specifically wanted Anthony to lie down and take a nap during the day, as all of the other children there did without trouble. His overly active and energetic behaviors led him to be ridiculed and tormented by both the staff and other children at the day care program as he did not conform to their expectations and to the standard norms of behavior. Anthony was well aware, even at that rather young and tender age, that the day care workers were not happy with him being there and, thus not surprisingly, he started to say that he hated school and that he did not want to go back there ever again. Each morning it became a noisy struggle to get him up and dressed to go to the day care program. Eventually, the director of the day care called Anthony's parents and told them that they must remove him from the program.

Kindergarten was a brand new opportunity for Anthony to start over again in school. It was a new school, with new teachers, new classmates, and so forth.

However, his general behavioral profile had not improved very much. Anthony was still overly active; he was constantly getting out of his seat, very distractible, interrupting the class, and having extreme difficulty in concentrating on his work. His work, when even done, was sloppy, and his desk was usually rather messy and extremely disorganized. The school would call his parents complaining about his behavior at least once a month and often would do so more frequently than that.

Anthony says that he always felt like he was an impostor in school. He felt that he had to work harder than everyone else in his class did, which many individuals with ADHD can readily identify with. Anthony barely passed and got through kindergarten, but he could not keep up with his classmates the next year when he entered the first grade, in spite of his good intentions and his evident high intelligence. Most individuals with ADHD, like Anthony, tend to be of average to above average intelligence. He would routinely tend to blurt out answers in class. Nevertheless, he was held back in the first grade and struggled with each subsequent grade after that. He was frequently reduced to tears when he could not finish his classwork properly as most of the other students did with apparent ease. It could take him four hours to complete what was normally supposed to be 20 minutes of homework; trying to explain how to do the homework was usually very frustrating as he would be continually distracted by seemingly irrelevant stimuli. His handwriting was awful compared to that of his class peers, and that never really improved.

Anthony's mother at least, who does not have ADHD, was always more patient with Anthony than his father, who would tend to overreact when trying to get Anthony to focus more on his homework assignments. Octavio, Anthony's father, who it turned out also has ADHD, would quickly become overwhelmed when trying to assist Anthony with his homework and he would start yelling at him. Anthony would sit and blankly stare at a writing assignment for hours, unable to get his thoughts down on paper, even though they were in his mind, and if given the opportunity, he could easily say what he wanted to write, but he could not readily write it out.

Reading was something that always seemed to take far longer for Anthony than it did for most of the other students in his classes. He would read a paragraph and then skip ahead; he would, therefore, usually miss many of the key points discussed therein. He would almost never read directions and, not surprisingly, regularly make many careless mistakes in his schoolwork. He would rush to complete assignments and exams fast and, even if it was something that he really knew well, usually make numerous careless errors. He would almost never go over answers to check them again, even when instructed to do so and given plenty of extra time specifically to do so.

Anthony was also very forgetful, and he would constantly misplace things, such as regularly leaving his lunch box at school and continually losing his sweaters, hats, gloves, and so forth. Almost every week his parents had to remind him to look for his "lost" belongings in the school's lost and found box. The school's janitors all knew Anthony and his misplaced property very well.

In middle school, Anthony began experiencing more serious academic difficulties. He could not pass most of his subjects as he easily had previously in elementary school as he could not seem to consistently turn in homework assignments on time and he often forgot to study for upcoming examinations. These academic requirements are far more difficult for an individual with ADHD to comply with than they are for most other students. Students like Anthony can easily get lost and slip through the cracks in large, unresponsive school districts. In a large urban school district, like Anthony's was, the school personnel have a much harder time getting to know all of the students and to consider their individual needs, let alone being familiar with the parents of most of the members of such a large student body. In these types of settings, it is much more difficult to keep track of the academic progress of individual students, and it is also far less likely that the parents will be notified if a student is struggling to keep up. Anthony was essentially pushed forward through the grade levels despite demonstrating serious academic deficits in many key areas.

High school was a particularly challenging time for Anthony with his untreated ADHD. Despite his apparent intelligence, he got mostly C and D grades while he was in his high school courses. Individuals with ADHD have a notoriously difficult time dealing with transitions, even good ones like moving on from middle school to high school. Many of the other high school students considered Anthony to be stupid and essentially a troublemaker. Accordingly, it is probably not very surprising that Anthony thoroughly hated going to high school and again, as it had been earlier, that he did not have many friends.

Behavioral Interventions

Anthony's parents knew that there was a serious problem with his behaviors, but they were somewhat confused over what to do about it, what it was caused by, and, most importantly, how to try and fix it. They certainly recognized that there had been a serious problem for some time, but they switched between blaming the school and its teachers, blaming Anthony, and, not uncharacteristically, blaming themselves for being bad parents. When Anthony was five and a half years old, his parents took him to see a pediatrician. The doctor clearly saw Anthony's high activity level and his difficult-to-control nature, so, being relatively unaware and uniformed about ADHD, which was not uncommon for physicians at the time, he advised Anthony's mother and father to take some parenting classes.

The recommendation to take parenting classes did not help Ruthie and Octavio's self-esteem as parents, but it only added to their feelings of having not served Anthony appropriately. Nevertheless, the parenting classes, as well as several self-help parenting books they stumbled upon, did teach Ruthie and Octavio several basic behavioral techniques that they tried, with some limited success, to implement with Anthony. They had to learn how to be more patient, more persistent, and certainly how to be more creative in how they responded to Anthony's rapidly changing behaviors. They learned that consequences generally were most effective in changing Anthony's behavior when they were imposed immediately following the breaking of the rules. Ruthie and Octavio were essentially taught how to give immediate and positive feedback for the behaviors that they wanted to encourage and, at the same time, how to ignore or redirect those behaviors that they wanted to discourage. These basic behavioral management strategies at least permitted them to minimally cope with Anthony and his difficult-to-deal-with behaviors.

Behavioral interventions are, however, often most effective when they are used in combination with ADHD medications. Nevertheless, they can be very useful even if ADHD medications are not administered, as was the case with Anthony at the time. Behavioral therapy, such as cognitive behavioral therapy (CBT), or behavior modification programs can assist by both diminishing unrealistic expectations and helping to build up a repertoire of relevant coping skills, such as increased organizational skills. Some individuals with ADHD can learn to function appropriately even without their taking ADHD medications, particularly if they acquired coping skills through behavior therapy or other approaches. Many of these simple behavioral techniques actually did seem to help improve Anthony's functioning somewhat. For example, his parents bought a "This Week" erasable board that could be used to break down tasks by the day of the week that they needed to be completed by. All of this information could be written down on one page that they mounted on the front door of their kitchen refrigerator. This simple approach greatly helped a scattered individual like Anthony to keep on track for seeing and reaching the bigger picture. It also helped his parents help him move progressively toward obtaining his manageable goals.

ADOLESCENCE

Adolescence, in most Western societies at least, can be a very trying time for many young people and for their parents and other family members as well;

this certainly was the case for Anthony, as it frequently is for many adolescents with untreated ADHD and for their families as well. Living with an undiagnosed ADHD condition can lead to years of low self-esteem and to pervasive feelings of shame until the long-awaited diagnosis can hopefully shed some light as to why things were so hard for them for so long, and then work can finally begin on making the difficult changes.

Festering Troubles

Anthony moved out of his parents' house when he was 18 years old after dropping out of high school, yet within six months of doing so, he had obtained his GED. Anthony said that he left school because of the persistent teasing and bullying from his peers about his being "stupid." He then started temporary work as a remote customer service representative, working mainly on a commission basis. However, he lost that job a few short months later after smoking marijuana and thus failing a urine drug test at work. Anthony was very surprised at the several months–long fruitless job search that followed his loss of that first job. He estimates that he applied for about 70 to 80 different positions; about a dozen of the companies trying to fill those positions called him in for an interview, but then his lack of academic skills, such as his poor penmanship and difficulties following instructions on job applications, a not uncommon report from individuals with ADHD, resulted in these potential offers rapidly being taken off the table. Anthony once secured a position as a pizza delivery person, but his pattern of driving too fast and thus of accumulating multiple speeding violations led to his driver license revocation and then, of course, to the sudden loss of that particular job. Once Anthony succeeded in getting another job, he would often soon impulsively quit—a characteristic very commonly reported among adults with ADHD. Keeping steady employment was a major shortfall for Anthony during that phase of his life.

Anthony said that he felt inferior, hopelessly disorganized, and undisciplined at that time. He had gotten used to feeling tired before he even got out of the bed, dreading the challenges that he knew the new day would inevitably bring. He was constantly exhausted with the pervasive worrying about the impending obligations coming and that he would have to navigate his way through. Individuals with ADHD, like Anthony, often either overestimate or underestimate how long it will take to complete something. When he overestimated what it would take to finish some task, Anthony would frequently become paralyzed by the projected impending demands and, after anguishing over it, would eventually just give up and quit.

Anthony began getting into fights while abusing drugs, and he was arrested three times. These kinds of scenarios are not uncommon among individuals with ADHD; in fact, about 75 percent of children with ADHD consistently present with behavioral symptoms of defiance and aggression. After Anthony was incarcerated for 18 months, he finally realized that things seriously had to change. The incidence of ADHD among inmates in prison is about eight times higher than it is for that of the general adult population; estimates for the number of prisoners with ADHD range from 21 percent to 45 percent. It is, of course, also worth remembering the point here that the United States represents only about 5 percent of global population but that it incarcerates about 25 percent of the world's prisoners. Anthony completed a rehabilitation program at a halfway house after being released from jail. He was one of the more than a half million individuals who are released from U.S. federal and state prisons each year. In fact, the total number of state and federal prison releases has more than tripled in the last 30 years. This tidal wave of releases comes after the country has waged a war on illegal drugs for many decades, which created tougher enforcement and stricter laws that led to an explosion of incarcerations and a mushrooming ex-offender population. Nearly half of all released inmates are arrested again within eight years, either for a new offense or for frequently violating the conditions of their release.

While Anthony was completing his time in the halfway house program, a counselor there noticed his hyperactive behavior. Anthony was having prob-lems with many of the other residents in the program, particularly as a conse-quence of his tendency to talk excessively and frequently interrupt the conversations of others. He also exhibited extreme difficulty waiting in lines and waiting his turn in small group activities. Anthony was as a consequence becoming somewhat demoralized. The counselor himself had been diagnosed with ADHD a few years earlier and was taking the ADHD medicine, Adderall. The counselor said that much of Anthony's behavior reminded him of his own untreated ADHD symptoms, particularly in his being disorganized, easily frustrated, and taking longer time than others on completing many tasks. The counselor mentioned this observation in a team staff meeting at the reha-bilitation program and the psychiatrist working there agreed to evaluate Anthony. The psychiatrist, fortunately, was well acquainted with ADHD, and his initial observations of Anthony who tended to fidget while seated and his difficulties with concentrating convinced the psychiatrist to conduct a more thorough, comprehensive diagnostic assessment. This formal assess-ment soon led to Anthony, finally at the age of 36, receiving a diagnosis for ADHD of the predominantly hyperactive/impulsive subtype. Anthony's situa-tion is certainly different from others as most children with ADHD are diagnosed either in early childhood or in elementary school. Individuals like Anthony who is extremely bright are more likely to reach adolescence or young adulthood without getting a formal diagnosis.

Once Anthony was diagnosed with ADHD, he was finally able to begin receiving appropriate treatments. It is generally recognized that the more culturally relevant a particular diagnosis is to an individual and to his or her family, the more likely the individual and his or her family is to seek and maintain getting help for the condition. Fortunately, Anthony and his family by this time were relatively well informed about the nature of ADHD and the respective treatment approaches, including the administration of ADHD medications. From this perspective, Anthony was predisposed to seek specific treatment for his ADHD, including the use of respective ADHD medications.

Medications

Many specific medications have been employed in treating the symptoms characteristic of ADHD in most individuals. Certainly, ADHD drugs should be considered in formulating an individualized plan for the comprehensive treatment and management of ADHD. These medications should not be regarded as either a panacea or a pariah but rather as part of the broad arsenal of tools available to help support individuals and the families of those living with this neurobiological condition.

There has been considerable speculation for some time now on the possible relationships existing between the taking of various drugs, particularly many of the respective ADHD medications, on learning and on memory. The psychostimulant amphetamine (Dyanavel XR), for example, not only stimulates arousal and activity, but it also is known to potentiate the functioning of the catecholamines at the neuronal synapses, which will be discussed further in a later chapter and that is highly relevant for both learning and memory. There has also been speculation for a considerable time over the possibility of the existence of a specific memory molecule. In this regard, it is well recognized that the neurons are very active synthesizers of particular proteins and that neuronal stimulation, which is essential for learning and memory, produces a change in the structures of certain respective proteins. The administration of several psychostimulant ADHD medications, like amphetamine (Dyanavel XR), after learning a task has been demonstrated in animal studies to significantly help to reduce the incidence of amnesia.

After Anthony was diagnosed with ADHD, he began to finally receive appropriate treatments. ADHD medications can do wonders when they are properly used in the right dosages. However, they can be dangerous if they are used improperly. An ADHD medicine regimen should not be started unless the individual and his or her family are totally comfortable with the decision. Before initiating the use of ADHD medications, Anthony researched the medications online and read as many of the latest studies on them that he could find. He wanted to make a scientifically informed decision, not an emotionally driven one, which is far too common among the parents of children with ADHD and related conditions. His physician assured him that if the initial ADHD medicine did not work right or if it produced any unacceptable side effects, the dosage could be reduced or that particular medicine could be discontinued. Anthony decided that a trial of the use of an ADHD medicine made sense for him.

Anthony's initial course of pharmaceutical treatment, as it is for most individuals diagnosed around his age, consisted of a prescription for an ADHD psychostimulant medicine. The first medicine that Anthony's doctor prescribed for him was the very popular methylphenidate hydrochloride (Ritalin) tablet, initially in the 5 mg dose, but as this showed little therapeutic effect, he was then switched the next week to the 10 mg dose and then soon thereafter to the 20 mg dose. However, Anthony was noticeably more active, and he also demonstrated more aggressive behavior while on the various doses of methylphenidate hydrochloride (Ritalin), so his doctor then switched him to another popular psychostimulant ADHD medicine, which is the typical therapeutic course of action.

The second ADHD medicine that was prescribed for Anthony by his doctor to treat his ADHD was the extended release formulation of the dextroamphetamine sulfate oral capsule, which was initially granted approval by the Food and Drug Administration (FDA) to be marketed under the trade name of Dexedrine on August 2, 1976. Anthony again progressed from the 5 mg capsule of dextroamphetamine sulfate (Dexedrine) quickly through the 10 mg capsule and then on to the 15 mg capsule of dextroamphetamine sulfate (Dexedrine). Unfortunately, Anthony once again appeared to be far more active than desired, and he also consistently exhibited more aggressive behaviors while taking the dextroamphetamine sulfate (Dexedrine) capsules.

A typical course of action often taken in searching for effective treatment options for an individual like Anthony who did not achieve satisfactory results with selected psychostimulant ADHD medications but, rather, had atypical responses would normally be to try one of the second-line nonstimulant ADHD medications, such as the norepinephrine specific reuptake inhibitor (SNRI) atomoxetine hydrochloride (Strattera) or the synthetic cyclic primary amine amantadine hydrochloride (Symmetrel). However, Anthony's psychiatrist had learned that Anthony had a paternal aunt who was taking the selective serotonin reuptake inhibitor (SSRI) fluoxetine (Prozac) for bipolar depression and decided to try Anthony on this antiobsessive ADHD medicine. Almost as soon as Anthony started taking his fluoxetine (Prozac), he calmed down and was less disruptive and far more attentive. Although he was initially prescribed the 120 mg dose of fluoxetine, it was quickly evident that he did better while on the 20 mg dose, which particularly helped reduce his anxiety levels. He had finally found an ADHD medicine that helped him to control his ADHD symptoms.

COLLEGE AND ADULTHOOD

The staff at the halfway house where Anthony was living helped him to enroll in a local community college, and they also assisted him in applying for state and federal financial aid. There was a special support program at the community college for individuals who were in the various halfway programs in the area. Anthony entered the community college through this route. Once Anthony was accepted at the community college, he was referred to the Disability Support Services Office for assistance related to his ADHD.

By working with the Disability Support Services Office, Anthony learned that he had the right to reasonable accommodations in his college classes. He found that by accessing the services available through the Disability Support Services Office, he could get tutors, readers, note takers, extra time on tests, and, what he found most helpful, testing in a separate quiet setting without distractions. He also learned how to use some of the various types of assistive technology, like computers that he could speak to, which would help him to write out his class essays and term papers. They advised him on finding selected professors who were more familiar with needs of students with a disability and who posted their class notes online. Anthony could then download the notes for the next class and read them ahead of time and mark up the relevant points with different color highlighters or pens for emphasis, and thus he was able to focus more on the lecture and achieved much more retention and mastery of the course material.

Challenges

For individuals with ADHD who are college students, as Anthony was, there can be a common set of challenges. To be successful in college, or in almost any other endeavor for that matter, it can be very helpful if they organize their lives in ways that make it more likely that they will use the time available to effectively study and to meet their other demands. It is generally advised that individuals with ADHD study away from home or their dormitory as there are typically too many distractions in these venues. A quite study room in the library or similar facility is often desired by some; on the other hand, there are some individuals with ADHD who like the stimulation of a far more active environment to help keep them from zoning out. Anthony found that the café in the Student Center had the best ambiance for him to focus his study efforts. Scheduling a set time and day for studying specific subjects can help to build a regular study routine. Anthony found that he did better, and could pay attention better, when he took classes with small enrollments, which afforded him plenty of opportunities for class discussions; he, like many other individuals with ADHD, was more likely to get bored and distracted if he was in large lecture classes.

The typical individual with ADHD will generally be faced with a plethora of problems in many areas of their life. There is no doubt that many of the challenges that face the typical individual with ADHD can be an awful lot to handle. It almost goes without saying, of course, that individuals with ADHD all have different needs and will face their own unique set of challenges. Some of these differences will tend to be somewhat similar to those of other individuals with ADHD, but others may not. However, regardless of the challenges faced, we have come a long way in developing a better understanding of ADHD and in learning ways to effectively manage it. It is of utmost importance that a thorough assessment and an accurate diagnosis be performed and that an individualized plan of treatment, usually including the use of ADHD medications, be formulated to best address the symptoms and other associated needs of each individual.

Strategies

There are many different strategies that individuals with ADHD have found to be helpful. The range of strategies used can be rather large, but they essentially relate to practices to promote optimal health and to build on one's strengths and not to obsess with deficits.

Behavioral therapy helped teach Anthony how to monitor his own behaviors. He was taught how to utilize his strengths and how not to get bogged down in his failures. Many individuals with ADHD, like Anthony, obsess over their own personal faults, but this does not help. Anthony had to learn how to savor his successes. Individuals with ADHD typically tend to quickly forget their successful moments. This tendency to minimize victories may relate to their tendency to hyper-focus, which can function both constructively or destructively. It is a destructive characteristic when it causes individuals to excessively obsess over problems, whether real or imagined problems. Obsessing with one's shortfalls is a common reaction among individuals with ADHD. Fortunately, Anthony's counselor at the halfway house was trained in metacognitive therapy (MCT) and was able to work with him on reducing this self-criticizing tendency. MCT, originally developed in the 1990s to treat generalized anxiety disorder, is a psychotherapeutic approach that targets persistent negative thought processes and maladaptive rumination and offers a viable alternative to standard CBT for treating individuals with ADHD and related issues. Anthony learned how to use various MCT techniques, including verbal reattribution and detached mindfulness exercises, which helped him to move past the pattern of holding on to negative attributions.

By focusing on what works well for him, Anthony learned how to concentrate on his strengths and, consequently, how to make those areas even stronger. He knew that he was great at starting projects but not so good at getting them finished. He was encouraged by his therapist to partner with someone who is good at the small details and in bringing them all together and closing them out. He also found an app for his cell phone that let him assign an amount of time for each task that he needed to complete so that he would not get stuck on a particularly troubling one and going down what he used to humorously refer to as a "rabbit hole."

Once Anthony learned a simple yet a highly effective strategy of breaking large tasks up into smaller ones, he became much more successful at completing them. For example, a basic task like reading a chapter or studying for an exam is best done through breaking them up into a series of small blocks of time. This is partially explained at least by the fact that our brains are not well designed for long units of time directed at concentrated effort. Cyclic brain wave changes throughout each day make it more difficult for individuals to maintain focus for more than 90 minutes to 120 minutes at a time before their brain switches to a less alert phase. Accordingly, it is generally recommended that larger tasks should be broken up into more manageable blocks of up to 90 minutes maximum with about 15-minute breaks in between for optimal performance results.

Anthony's physician also recommended, after checking his blood work, that he take Omega-3 fish oil supplements. Studies have indicated that many individuals with ADHD have lower levels of Omega-3 fatty acids in their blood compared to individuals without the disorder and that the associated lipid imbalances from this are a factor associated with ADHD and related neurodevelopmental disorders. Zinc nutritional supplements have also been frequently recommended for reducing symptoms of hyperactivity and impulsivity but not for those of inattentiveness, in individuals with ADHD. Iron, vitamin C, and magnesium are other nutritional supplements sometimes recommended for improving symptoms of ADHD. Anthony was also instructed to eat a well-balanced diet, which is good solid advice for anyone. Accordingly, he successfully adjusted his diet to include plenty of fruits and vegetables, sufficient complex carbohydrates, and some lean protein.

Anthony had always been active, if not hyperactive, but it was only after he took up running as an adult that he felt more balanced. Exercise, such as running, helps to modulate ADHD by increasing the levels of dopamine and norepinephrine, two natural neurotransmitters in the brain that serve to help regulate the attention system. Regular physical activity, like Anthony's running, helps to improve the tone of the locus coeruleus, a region of the brain that when more efficient helps to make us less easy to startle and thus less likely to react disproportionately to stimuli; consequently, we tend to become less irritable and anxious. Further, regular physical activity has been shown in clinical studies to increase the volume of the prefrontal cortex in adults, which serves to improve executive function, a critical need for anyone living with ADHD. Executive function refers to organizing, planning, and executing tasks efficiently; these are areas that individuals with ADHD often struggle with.

PITFALLS AND PROMISES

There are both many pitfalls and promises that are often associated with the experiences of an individual with ADHD. This certainly is the case with Anthony. Many individuals with ADHD can be highly creative and very successful, as we will explore further in Chapter 8. However, before most people with ADHD can reach their full potential, they must first learn how to cope and manage themselves within the normative range of behaviors acceptable to their society. Toward this end, it is generally only after a diagnosis is made that the challenges can be defined and a course of action designed to help them master the brain-based obstacles that individuals with ADHD typically encounter, particularly with respect to the realms of the self-regulation of behavior.

One characteristic that Anthony shares in common with many other individuals who also have ADHD is the issue of easily becoming overwhelmed. In particular, many adults with ADHD have trouble planning, and when they start to try doing so, they often become too stressed and too overwhelmed to get started on anything. These individuals often have many thoughts and ideas racing through their minds at once, and, understandably, this can make it rather difficult to maintain proper focus, which, in turn, can lead to feelings of anxiety. They typically will become lost in negative thoughts attributing their inability to get things done to some personal character flaw or other personality problem. This phenomenon is referred to as attribution theory, where one looks for internal attributes to explain behavior. Thus, Anthony would not only feel overwhelmed, but he would also feel that something was wrong with him as a person. This has been explained by the fact that the amygdala tends to take over and drain resources from the prefrontal cortex, which is a part of the brain that helps us to think clearly and make rational decisions. Anthony had to learn how to keep it simple, to use stress relaxation techniques, such as controlled breathing exercises, to stop the stress response from kicking in. Anthony found that making a list of his ideas and then identifying which ones were the most important to do soon and which ones could wait helped to reduce much of his sense of being overwhelmed. Many individuals with ADHD, including Anthony, sometimes have a hard time in filtering out stimuli from their environments; it is not necessarily that they cannot focus, but that they tend to focus on irrelevant stimuli. Anthony found that using background noise, like listening to soft classical music, helped him to reduce the attack of multiple stimuli that can foster a sense of being overwhelmed. While a cluttered work environment can overwhelm some individuals, Anthony found that he was comforted by having piles of papers around his study area and that being able to readily pull out an assignment that he was working on helped to reduce the dread of being overwhelmed with projects to complete.

Many individuals with ADHD, like Anthony, complain of having restless nights and waking up thoroughly exhausted in the mornings. Sometimes individuals report that it is their racing brain that keeps them up at night. Sleep deprivation certainly affects our ability to focus, to concentrate, and to regulate our emotions, all of which are common problems for many individuals with ADHD. Many ADHD medications, particularly the psychostimulant medications, can create adverse side effects impacting sleep; on the other hand, many adults with ADHD find that their taking the last daily dose of their ADHD medicine about 45 minutes before bedtime helps to slow down their buzzing brain. Studies have suggested that drinking coffee or other caffeinated beverages too close to bedtime can play a role in preventing their getting a good night's sleep. Shutting off or at least dimming the lights for a couple of hours before actually going to bed can be helpful as well. Anthony learned the hard way that when he stopped checking e-mails and talking or texting on his cell phone in bed, he had more restful nights; these types of behaviors can be sleep traps that interfere with maintaining our own natural daily rhythms of our body that help us to have a good restful sleep. Simple relaxation techniques, like focusing on breathing in and out and consciously tensing and relaxing various muscle groups, can also help to slow down our brains. Sticking to routines as to when, where, and how for going to bed and in waking up can help also.

Some adults with ADHD can focus very intently on something that they enjoy or that they find interesting at that point in time; this ability is commonly referred to as hyper-focus. On the other hand, these same individuals often have to struggle to pay attention to tasks that they find uninteresting and even boring. The trouble is that many of the simple tasks that are routinely necessary for success in our everyday lives can be regarded as uninteresting and even dull, like remembering to renew our driving license before it expires. Many individuals with ADHD, like Anthony, tend to put off what they tend to regard as boring tasks in favor of pursuing other activities that they find to be far more enjoyable. Anthony has a particular difficulty in filling out forms and other documents carefully and completely; he typically rushes to get through them; this has repeatedly caused problems for him both in work environments and at school as well as in his personal life.

Fortunately, it is never too late to change things. Now that Anthony knows that he has ADHD and is learning how to manage it, he can try to repair his damaged relationships with his parents, other family members, friends, and associates. He is particularly interested in repairing his fractured relationship with his parents, hoping that he can restore their trust in him. He is well aware that he has acted irresponsibly in the past and that he has hurt them numerous times; he cannot change the past, but now that he is getting treatment for his ADHD and learning how to live with it, he is optimistic that he can reestablish a healthy relationship with them.

Anthony is actually a success story as less than half of all adults with ADHD who are aged 45 or more never seek any kind of treatment for their ADHD and only about 25 percent have ever tried taking an ADHD medicine. Treating ADHD later in life, even if not detected at an earlier age, can make a tremendous difference in one's quality of life; it certainly did for Anthony. He successfully finished college and has been working steadily ever since. He recently got married and has his first child on the way. Life is good for Anthony now and getting better every day as he learns how to better handle the challenges of living with his ADHD. Anthony's story shows us that it is never too late to embrace life with ADHD without letting it define who you are or what you can do. For Anthony, as for many other individuals, ADHD medications played a vital part in him getting himself and his life together and, consequently, in being able to live a full and satisfying life.

Chapter 2

What Are ADHD Medications?

This chapter provides a more formal introduction to attention deficit hyperactivity disorder (ADHD), to various approaches taken to treat it, and to the types of medications drawn upon to treat it. In order to gain a better understanding of ADHD, it is necessary to review the core symptoms of the disorder and how a diagnosis is made as well as note the genetic and biological basis of the condition along with mention of its incidence and prevalence and of some of the closely related conditions. The varied treatment approaches generally applied to ADHD must be recognized, particularly the respective types of medications used to help individuals with the disorder as well as recognition of other substances and alternative and complimentary ways of helping people with ADHD.

UNDERSTANDING ADHD

ADHD is now understood to primarily be a neurobiological behavioral disorder that is characterized by developmentally inappropriate and chronic problems related typically to impulsivity, inattention, and, in some cases, hyperactivity. Thus, at a very fundamental level, ADHD is essentially considered to be a brain-based disease; therefore, a better understanding of brain anatomy and physiology associated with attention and its dysfunction is essential to gain a better understanding of this disorder. The center of executive control, particularly that of directed attention, as well as of the ability to manage emotions or, at least, to delay emotional responses, lies in the dorsolateral prefrontal cortex of the human brain. ADHD is now recognized to primarily be a result of weakened prefrontal cortex activity in the neural circuits responsible for regulating behavior and attention, rather than as was previously thought as a condition stemming from pervasive hyperarousal. The frontal cortex sends signals to other regions of the human brain in order to permit us to be able to process and perform any task. If the transmitted signal is weak, as is usually the case in individuals with ADHD, then attention can easily be directed elsewhere. This lack of focus can manifest in myriad problems, including with the neurodevelopmental disorder now known as ADHD. Accordingly, many neurotransmitters have been implicated in ADHD, and it is also clear that no single neurotransmitter is responsible for the development of ADHD.

A behavioral disorder is recognized as a persistent condition in which an individual exhibits a continual pattern of abnormal behaviors that consist of an array of specific factors, such as their unusual and contextually inappropriate actions, words, and the ways they respond to certain types of situations. A behavioral disorder ordinarily causes severe and continual problems in an individual's daily-life activities, like those displayed at home, school, and work. In children, a behavioral disorder, such as ADHD, generally results in their daily behaviors severely interfering with their academic and social progress; in adults, employment and intimate personal relations are often adversely impacted.

ADHD can have an adverse impact on academic, personal, familial, vocational, and societal functioning, including impairing relationships with family, friends, teachers, supervisors, and colleagues. It can present as a highly diverse disorder, which can manifest differently in individuals of different ages or who differ in other critical ways. The primary characteristic of ADHD is that of a repeated pattern of inattention and/or impulsivity and/or hyperactivity that substantially interferes with normal development and functioning.

There are different levels of how ADHD affects someone. There are some individuals who have mild levels of ADHD, while there are others who can have more severe symptoms. Those with mild symptoms may only have minor problems with areas like organization, while others may suffer more pervasive dysfunctionality.

There are also different types of ADHD. However, there is no general consensus as to what the specific subtypes are; many professionals feel that there are three ADHD subtypes, while other experts assert that there are more. One well-respected psychiatrist, Daniel G. Amen (1995, 2013), for example, has described seven or more specific ADHD subtypes. These include the Classic ADHD subtype, the symptoms of which he feels are associated with low levels of the neurotransmitter dopamine; the Inattentive ADHD subtype is characterized by individuals who have trouble focusing, are introverted, and tend not to be hyperactive and is more common among females; the Over focused ADHD subtype is characterized by having difficulty changing attention, excessive worrying, being oppositional, and argumentative, which appears to be related to low levels of both dopamine and serotonin as well as high levels of activity in the anterior cingulate; the Limbic ADHD subtype seems to be a combination of the characteristics of the Classic ADHD subtype along with being depressed and is also associated with low levels of dopamine and serotonin and an over active limbic system; the Temporal Lobe ADHD subtype is characterized by having symptoms of the classic subtype and temporal lobe issues such as difficulties with learning, memory, and having temper outbursts, and it seems to be associated with low levels of GABA (gamma-amino butyric acid); the Anxious ADHD subtype is characterized by having symptoms of the Classic subtype and high levels of anxiety resulting in difficulties focusing, and it seems to be associated with low levels of both dopamine and GABA and with low prefrontal cortex activity; and, finally, the Ring of Fire ADHD subtype is characterized by mood swings and being easily distracted, and it seems to be associated with low levels of both serotonin and GABA and, in general, an overly active brain.

Symptoms of ADHD

There are many behavioral symptoms that are routinely associated with ADHD, but ADHD affects different individuals in many different ways. One individual may present with issues of inattentiveness but not generally be either impulsive or hyperactive, while another person might show clear signs of hyperactivity yet not be easily distracted. Further, most individuals who are hyperactive also tend to be impulsive. As an individual grows and develops, the symptoms of ADHD may change as well. Some symptoms, depending on the individual, may get worse, while others may get better. Many children with the predominantly hyperactive/impulsive presentation or with the combined presentation discover that as they become teenagers, their symptoms of excessive locomotor activity decline and are replaced by a pervasive sense of internal restlessness. At any rate, the three core symptoms of ADHD are inattention, hyperactivity, and impulsivity.

Inattention. Inattention, or the inability to attend to tasks in a developmentally appropriate way is a hallmark characteristic of ADHD. Individuals with the inattentive type of ADHD symptoms are characterized by the inability to concentrate on a specific task or to pay attention; they often appear not to be listening. Disorganization is another common feature of this cluster of ADHD symptoms, such as routinely losing materials. According to the *Diagnostic and Statistical Manual of Mental Disorders*, fifth edition (*DSM-5*), children up to and including the age of 16 years must exhibit six or more of nine specific diagnostic criteria of inattention, consistent with their developmental level, for at least six months to the extent that they negatively impact their academic and social activities, while individuals aged 17 years and up (i.e., adolescents and adults) must exhibit at least five of these symptoms of inattention. Examples of these inattentive symptoms include things like often being easily distracted, lacking persistence, often seeming not to listen when spoken directly to, and often having trouble organizing tasks and activities. Students with these types of inattentive symptoms of ADHD often do not finish homework or chores; they typically will rush through assignments and tend to make careless mistakes. Girls with ADHD tend, in general, to present more with the predominantly inattentive type of symptoms, while boys, generally, exhibit the predominantly hyperactive/impulsive presentation or the combined presentation.

Hyperactivity and Impulsivity.   The inability of an individual to regulate his or her activity level in developmentally appropriate ways is a common, but not essential, symptom of ADHD; this is what is referred to as hyperactivity. Hyperactivity, as associated with ADHD, typically manifests itself with the excessive and inappropriate locomotor activity, such as fidgeting, talkativeness, running about, or tapping. Difficulty with self-regulation is a core symptom of ADHD that most typically manifests in individuals who exhibit the inability to inhibit their behaviors in developmentally appropriate ways; this is what is typically referred to as impulsivity. Impulsivity, as associated with ADHD, typically refers to the impetuous behaviors that appear to erupt spontaneously without forethought; these outbursts sometimes can have a high potential to cause harm to the individual. This impulsiveness may stem either from the inability to delay gratification or simply from the desire to attain immediate rewards. Impulsivity appears to be associated with expression of the Delta-FosB transcription factor, which is found in the nucleus accumbens, a part of the brain related not only to impulsive behaviors but also to reward evaluation. The manifestations of impulsivity are characterized with a tendency toward hasty, heedless action. The hyperactivity and impulsivity symptoms are lumped together under the same subtype in the *DSM-5*. According to the *DSM-5*, again, children up to and including the age of 16 years must exhibit six or more of nine specific diagnostic criteria of hyperactivity and impulsivity, consistent with their developmental level, for at least six months to the extent that they negatively impact their academic and social activities; while individuals aged 17 years and up (i.e., adolescents and adults) must exhibit at least five of these symptoms of hyperactivity and impulsivity. Examples of these hyperactive and impulsive symptoms include things like often being unable to play or take part in leisure activities quietly, talking excessively, and interrupting or intruding on others. Further, individuals with high levels of impulsivity are at greater risk for developing many associated problems, such as eating disorders.

Diagnosing ADHD

Unfortunately, ADHD is not an easy condition to diagnose. It is not usually easy to tell if someone does or does not have ADHD. There is no single questionnaire, blood test, brain scan, or other single medical exam that can prove that a particular individual has or does not have ADHD. It is largely a subjective diagnosis made by a professional who collects opinions of others who know the individual, like family members, teachers, or colleagues, and other sources of information. The number of ADHD diagnoses has been sharply rising for some time. In 1990, there were slightly over 900,000 diagnosed cases of ADHD in the United States, but by 1995, the total number had increased to over two million. According to the Centers for Disease Control and Prevention (CDC), diagnoses for ADHD in children increased by around 42 percent from 2003 to 2011. At any rate, as ADHD is recognized to be a neurodevelopmental disorder, several of the inattentive and/or hyperactive and impulsive symptoms must have been present prior to the time when the individual reached the age of 12 years. Further, several of the inattentive and/or hyperactive and impulsive symptoms must be present within two or more settings, such as at home, school, and work; when with relatives or with friends; and in other settings. It is also essential that these respective ADHD symptoms must interfere with, or at least reduce the quality of life of, the individual's academic, vocational, or social functioning. It must also be remembered that a diagnosis of ADHD is highly correlated with having an average to above average intelligence.

The overall average age of receiving an ADHD diagnosis among U.S. children is seven years. However, children with more severe ADHD tend to be diagnosed at younger ages. Accordingly, eight years is the average age of diagnosis for U.S. children reported as having mild ADHD; seven years is the average age of diagnosis for U.S. children reported as having moderate ADHD; and, five years is the average age of diagnosis for U.S. children reported as having severe ADHD.

There is an array of various medical tests that can be used to support a diagnosis of ADHD, even though they are not sufficient in and of themselves to make a diagnosis. A diagnosis of ADHD, for instance, can be underpinned by functional magnetic imaging abnormalities in the dorsolateral prefrontal cortex, the inferior frontal cortex, and the striatal and parietal regions of the brain. Some clinicians prefer to use positron emission tomography (PET) scans that assess activity, blood flow, and glucose metabolism in the brain, while others use single photon emission computed tomography (SPECT) imaging that uses less radiation than PET scans and also evaluates brain activity and blood flow patterns. These are but a few examples of some of the many approaches that can be of help in making a diagnosis of ADHD.

Genetic/Biological Basis of ADHD

ADHD is now recognized to be a highly heritable condition, with genetic alterations identified in noradrenergic and dopaminergic neural pathways. However, it must be acknowledged that no individual can actually inherit ADHD; this is because we can only inherit a predisposition for conditions like ADHD. The proclivity that is very heritable for ADHD only gives an individual a greater susceptibility for the symptoms to develop, whether or not they are ever expressed is a somewhat different matter. In fact, it is the interplay between many variables, including the biological, genetic, and psychosocial factors that interact and combine to produce ADHD in any one individual. The environmental factors, including the respective life experiences of an individual, will ultimately determine if the genetic proneness is ever expressed or not expressed. For example, it has been suspected that if a young child plays video games too much, then there may be a greater likelihood that the genes that predispose an individual to ADHD will actually be expressed and that the child will develop ADHD. On the other hand, if that same child did not excessively play video games, even though the predisposing genes were inherited, ADHD may never develop.

Genetic research has identified considerable support for the genetic/biological basis of ADHD. At least two specific gene sites have already been implicated in identifying the genetics of ADHD; these include the dopamine transporter gene (DAT1) located on chromosome r and the D4 receptor gene located on chromosome 11. Other genes are also no doubt involved as well, including some that influence serotonin. Twin studies also support the notion of a genetic basis for ADHD, with a higher concordance in monozygotic than in dizygotic twins. For example, if one fraternal twin has ADHD, then about 29 percent of their twin siblings will also have it, while if one identical twin has ADHD, then about 81 percent of their twin siblings, who have an identical genetic makeup, will also have it. Further, biological parents of individuals with ADHD have a higher incidence of ADHD than do adoptive parents.

It is now generally thought that if one parent has ADHD, there is about a 30 percent probability that each of their children will have ADHD. While if both parents have ADHD, the probability rises to over a 50 percent chance (some estimates are as much as 85% to 90%) for each of their children. With these types of odds, it is quite possible that either all children or no children in a particular family could inherit ADHD. Similarly, looking at the siblings in a family, if one of the children has ADHD, then there is about a 30 percent probability that each of the other brothers or sisters in the family unit will have the disorder as well. However, if the sibling in question with ADHD is an adult, then the odds of another of his or her adult siblings also having ADHD increases to greater than 40 percent. As we next look at the incidence and prevalence rates for ADHD in a general population, we can see that these ADHD family probability rates are much higher, indicating, in the very least, that ADHD does tend to run in families.

INCIDENCE AND PREVALENCE

The prevalence rates of ADHD can vary depending on numerous factors, such as age, gender, cultural background, and comorbidities. The prevalence rate for ADHD refers to the estimated number of individuals who are dealing with ADHD at any given time, while the number of new cases diagnosed in a year is considered to be the incidence rate. It is estimated that there are approximately 6.4 million children, adolescents, and adults in the United States who have been diagnosed with ADHD, which would be about 11.4 percent of the population. However, the true rate of ADHD diagnosis is estimated to be around 7.8 percent, with the difference largely attributed to misdiagnosis, which is typically more frequent in younger children. Different subpopulations would, of course, be expected to have variable prevalence rates. For example, it is thought that approximately 25 percent of adults who are in treatment for a substance use disorder could be diagnosed with ADHD. Prevalence rates vary considerably in different countries; for instance, the prevalence rate among grade school–age children in the United Kingdom is less than 1 percent, considerably lower than in the United States.

An extrapolation of the prevalence of ADHD can be calculated for respective countries based on the incidence rates in the United States, the United Kingdom, Canada, and Australia against the total population of the respective country. This method does not take into account any genetic, environmental, sociocultural, racial, or other differences that might exist in a respective country. Nevertheless, these extrapolations can be interesting in considering the scope of ADHD around the world. For example, based on this approach, it can be extrapolated that the prevalence of ADHD in countries could be around 12.922 million in India, 2.893 million in Indonesia, 2.234 million in Brazil, 1.931 million in Pakistan, 1.747 million in Russia, 1.715 million in Bangladesh, 1.273 million in Mexico, 1.046 in the Philippines, 1.003 in Vietnam, and 1 million in Germany.

Children and Youth

The average global prevalence rate of ADHD is estimated to be between 5.3 percent and 7.1 percent in children and adolescents. According to the CDC, 9.5 percent of all children between the ages of 3 years and 17 years were diagnosed with ADHD by 2015. Many of these six million children and youth will need treatment and continuing professional support. At any rate, ADHD is certainly the most common behavioral disorder and the most common psychiatric diagnosis made for children and youth in the United States. The type of ADHD symptoms that are most prominent tends to vary with age and other circumstances. Preschoolers and younger elementary school students are most commonly noted to exhibit symptoms of hyperactivity, while later in elementary school and through middle school, students are more likely to be found to exhibit symptoms of inattention. Boys are about two to three times more likely than girls to have an ADHD diagnosis. The condition is most common among boys who are firstborns. Girls with ADHD are more likely to be over talkative rather than hyperactive, to daydream frequently, and to be anxious and over emotional. Adolescents may manifest hyperactivity primarily by fidgeting and by experiencing feelings of impatience and jitteriness.

Adults

In the past, many of those familiar with ADHD believed that children and adolescents with ADHD would generally outgrow it. However, this is no longer the consensus in the field as considerable research has indicated that, in fact, the disorder routinely continues on into adulthood. Although the estimates vary and there are valid questions as what criteria to use, it has been reported that anywhere between 15 percent and 65 percent of children and adolescents who were diagnosed with ADHD will continue to experience symptoms of the disorder lasting into, at least, young adulthood. Further, it generally thought that about 80 percent of adolescents who received ADHD medications as children will continue to need them through adolescence, and that about 50 percent or more will continue to need them as adults. In fact, many clinicians report that about half of individuals diagnosed with ADHD will have symptoms that persist through adulthood. The average global prevalence rate of ADHD is estimated to be between about 2.5 percent and

3.4 percent in adults. An estimated 4.4 percent of adults aged 18 years and over in the United States have ADHD. According to the National Institute of Mental Health (www.nimh.nih.gov), 8.1 percent of the U.S. adult population will experience ADHD at some point in their lives. In adults, ADHD can affect individuals at work, school, home, and/or in social settings. However, symptoms of ADHD may impact adults differently than they do children and youth. For most individuals with ADHD, the symptoms of hyperactivity and impulsivity usually taper off as they get older. On the other hand, the majority of adults with ADHD suffer with the inattentive types of symptoms, such as difficulties with planning, completing tasks, and managing time, along with issues of forgetfulness, disorganization, and unreliability. Among middle-aged and older adults, symptoms of anxiety and depression tend to increase as the occurrence of ADHD symptoms rise. Adults with ADHD tend to experience greater difficulties in crucial life areas than their peers who are not so affected, such as persistent problems with unemployment, low educational attainment, and poor interpersonal relationships.

Related Conditions

There are numerous other conditions that are related to ADHD. There are varied factors that can cause symptoms that can be easily mistaken for ADHD. Hyperactivity, for instance, is indeed a hallmark of ADHD, but it can have many other causes other than ADHD as well. In fact, young children are normally very active and, developmentally, often have a short attention span. Changes at puberty, in both males and females, can create symptoms of hyperactivity in normal teenagers. Varied other conditions can manifest with symptoms of hyperactivity. For example, children who are having problems at home, including those who are victims of sexual abuse, as well as those suffering from emotional conflicts, can present as hyperactive. Hyperactivity may be exhibited by children and adolescents who are bored at school, some may be gifted and talented, while others may have a specific learning disability. Certain food colorings and preservatives, such as allura red (FD&C Red No.40), quinolone yellow (D&C Yellow No. 10), sodium benzoate, sunset yellow (FD&C Yellow No. 6), and tartrazine (FD&C Yellow No. 5), have been implicated as possibly increasing hyperactive behaviors in children. Individuals with thyroid disease can also appear to have symptoms like those with ADHD; while an over active thyroid gland can cause one to be inattentive and/or hyperactive, an underactive thyroid gland can cause one to appear unfocused and lethargic. Individuals abusing certain psychoactive substances, such as some of the central nervous system stimulant drugs like cocaine or methamphetamine, can exhibit symptoms of hyperactivity and/or distractibility that could easily be mistaken for ADHD. Accordingly, many conditions that can cause symptoms that appear similar to those stemming from ADHD must be ruled out before an accurate diagnosis for the disorder can be made. Some of these myriad related conditions include hearing problems, vision problems, psychiatric problems, and undetected seizures to name just a few more of the possibilities.

There are a variety of factors, other than genetics, that have been identified as a cause of ADHD. One of the most common, perhaps, is an unrecognized head injury, particularly to the frontal regions of the brain. If a human brain, particularly that of a baby, is deprived of oxygen for too long or exposed to some toxic substance, then symptoms of ADHD are more likely to be observed. Low oxygen levels, whether from the umbilical cord being obstructed during birth, or in a premature baby with underdeveloped lungs, or in someone who drowned, clearly result in decreased overall brain activity. Fetal exposure to alcohol, tobacco, or other drugs is well documented to increase the risk of ADHD as well as of learning disabilities and other problems. Exposure to other toxic substances, such as lead, mercury, molds, pesticides, food additives, colorings, preservatives, and so forth have also been implicated. Infections in the brain, such as encephalitis or meningitis, can create harmful inflammation that could damage brain tissue. When other psychiatric problems are comorbid with ADHD, it is impossible to say which, if either, came first. For instance, we know that there is a high incidence of diagnoses for antisocial personality disorder among individuals with ADHD, but there is considerably more difficulty in establishing if one disorder did or did not cause the other.

ADHD TREATMENT APPROACHES

Management of ADHD should ideally consist of a multimodal, individualized treatment approach, which for many, but not necessarily all, individuals includes the administration of ADHD medications. This multimodal treatment strategy may, in addition to pharmacological therapy, consist of behavioral therapy, psychoeducation, and perhaps even more holistic strategies, such as those considering lifestyle and dietary interventions.

Many varied forms of cognitive and behavioral therapies and counseling are routinely used to treat individuals with ADHD. The consistent provision of structured practical assistance, such as helping a young child to complete school work or to organize tasks, helps the child learn to self- monitor his or her own behaviors. Assisting a child in learning how to think before talking or acting is a worthwhile counseling goal. Establishing very clear rules and clear, reasonable expectations of behavior and consistently sticking to structured routines are also highly advisable for helping individuals with ADHD. Psychoeducation and counseling can also be very useful in helping adults to learn more about ADHD and how to deal with it and, further, helping them to develop planning and organizational skills and consistently implementing them into their daily routines. ADHD coaching has become a highly viable treatment option in helping adults. These ADHD coaches can help individuals to improve their personal repertoire of coping skills related to areas like scheduling, organization, goal setting, building confidence and self-esteem, and maintaining an attitude of persistence.

For preschool-aged children, that is those four years to five years old, nearly one in two individuals with ADHD in that age group receive no behavioral therapy, and around one in four are treated only with medication. It is considered the best practice to provide behavioral therapy first before medication in this age group. Further, less than one in three children and adolescents aged 6 years to 17 years old receive both behavioral therapy and medication. The best practices suggest that for individuals in that age range, they should be provided with both treatment approaches. According to the CDC, about 7 out of 10 children who were diagnosed with ADHD in the United States were, in fact, taking medication for it in 2011 to 2012.

Behavioral and Cognitive Approaches

Behavioral therapy is widely recognized as an effective sphere of ADHD treatment; ADHD medications alone are often not enough to address the comprehensive therapeutic needs of someone with ADHD. There are myriad therapeutic modalities that can be considered as behavioral and cognitive approaches. An overarching commonality behind these behavioral and cognitive treatment approaches is to help furnish the individual with the appropriate social and psychological supports needed to address the respective symptoms creating problems in his or her life. Individual psychotherapy is a commonly employed approach. Cognitive Behavioral Therapy (CBT) is perhaps one of the best known and most widely used psychotherapeutic approaches that is added along with the use of medication to construct an effective treatment strategy for individuals with ADHD, particularly for adults. CBT essentially focuses on the individual's thoughts and behaviors based on the assumption that someone with ADHD has both positive and negative beliefs that arise from inaccurate thought processes. This approach is intended not only to provide the individual with specific skills that can be used to avoid the negative behaviors and thoughts but also to learn assorted strategies to help him or her cope with and even eliminate the adverse consequences. Individuals are taught how to avoid high-risk situations as well as how to better understand how their respective choices can lead to either positive or negative results. The late Albert Ellis developed a form of CBT that is now known as Rational Emotive Behavioral Therapy; it was formerly referred to as Rational Emotive Therapy and before that as Rational Therapy; this variant of CBT focuses on helping individuals to resolve behavioral and emotional problems by reducing catastrophic thinking, which is characterized by negatively distorted perceptions of things, usually regarding them as more horrible, awful, or unbearable conditions than they really are.

Another variant of behavioral and cognitive therapies is the contingency management approach, which is most typically used with children and adolescents with ADHD and related conditions; in this approach, individuals might earn points under a voucher system for demonstrating more attentive, restrained, nonhyperactive behaviors. The vouchers could be used to "purchase" privileges or items that reinforce a healthy, responsible lifestyle, such as a specified period of leisure time. Direct contingency management requires considerable intervention by trained professionals, such as teachers or therapists who can closely monitor the implementation and effects of this approach. A simple reward system can also be established at home. The utilization of these sorts of motivational incentives can hopefully serve as positive reinforcement for maintaining an appropriate, balanced set of behaviors, rather than the inappropriate ones typically associated with someone who has ADHD. The ideal goal of these sorts of approaches is, of course, to help the individual with ADHD learn how to monitor and control his or her behavior on his or her own. Strategies to improve this self-control include self-evaluation, self-instruction, and problem-solving techniques. The individual is taught how to evaluate specific situations, to contemplate his or her actions, as well as what the possible consequences of these actions might be and then to respond accordingly.

Dynamic psychotherapy is another variant of behavioral and cognitive therapy that is founded on the assumption that all symptoms arise from deep, underlying unconscious psychological conflict. The primary objective of dynamic form of psychotherapy, in this case, is to assist the individual with ADHD to be more aware that such conflicts exist as well as to encourage the learning of adaptive coping strategies as part of a healthier way to address such intrapsychic conflicts in the future.

Group psychotherapy can also be a highly effective component of ADHD treatment as it particularly helps to address the social stigma that is typically associated with the loss of control and other displays of inappropriate behaviors typical of individuals with ADHD. Members of psychotherapeutic groups generally benefit from the opportunity of hearing other members of the group who share their similar experiences and feelings. Knowing that other individuals feel and experience things in a manner comparable to them helps them learn to normalize and reduces the commonly reported sense of isolation that is so typical among individuals with ADHD. This group approach, accordingly, is particularly helpful in refining social skills, in increasing self-esteem, and in promoting a sense of success.

Multimodal family therapy, also referred to as multidimensional family therapy, is another therapeutic approach that can be helpful in treating individuals and family members of those with ADHD. Albert Lazarus introduced multimodal therapy as an approach rooted in social learning theory. Multimodal therapy is a comprehensive and theoretically based approach that considers seven discrete but reciprocally interactive personality dimensions, or modalities; these are, respectively, Behavior, Affect, Sensation, Imagery, Cognition, Interpersonal Relationships, and Drugs/Biology (hence the multimodal therapy acronym, BASIC ID). This psychoeducational strategy encourages professionals to improvise and to individualize brief therapies to the respective individual. Family therapy is based on working therapeutically with family members to help them to explore and improve family relationships and processes in order to promote the mental health of individual members as well as that of the entire family unit. Howard Liddle developed multidimensional family therapy as a multiple systems–oriented approach to help integrate myriad developmentally focused therapeutic techniques in order to emphasize the integral relationships between affective, behavioral, cognitive, and environmental inputs. It is thought that all of these factors influence someone with ADHD and that this multifaceted approach to therapy could be an effective method to better address so many varied issues.

There are numerous other behavioral and cognitive approaches to therapy that could potentially be used in helping individuals and families suffering with the impacts of ADHD. Relaxation exercises, guided imagery, and varied other complementary therapeutic techniques, some of which will be discussed later in this chapter, could potentially be of assistance to someone with ADHD. For example, Eye Movement Desensitization and Reprocessing (EMDR) therapy is yet another therapeutic approach that could be employed as it is designed to lessen stress by having individuals process the meanings of events with the context of their own autobiographical memory. EMDR relies on eliciting distressing memories, but immediately distracting the patient with directed physical stimuli, like having them follow the tip of the therapist's finger or gaze. As the distressing memory is consciously verbalized, the patient is instantly told to notice any ideas or feelings that arise; the therapist encourages any positive associations and reinforces them with repeated eye movement practice.

Medication Approaches

The use of medications to treat ADHD is generally recommended, and while medications alone do not address the underlying reasons that an individual develops ADHD, the use of these medications can help to more effectively keep negative symptoms under control while other supplementary treatment approaches are implemented. Examples of first-line medications that may be prescribed as part of a treatment approach to ADHD include central nervous system stimulant medications, such as amphetamine (Dyanavel XR, Evekeo), dextroamphetamine (Dexedrine), and methylphenidate (Ritalin). Antidepressant medications, like the tricyclic antidepressants (TCAs), such as amitriptyline (Elavil), desipramine (Norpramin), and nortriptyline (Pamelor); the selective serotonin reuptake inhibitors (SSRIs), such as fluoxetine (Prozac), fluvoxamine (Luvox), paroxetine (Paxil), and sertraline (Zoloft); and bupropion (Wellbutrin) may also be used in treating ADHD, as can a synthetic cyclic primary amine, like amantadine (Symmetrel), or a noradrenergic specific reuptake inhibitor, like atomoxetine (Strattera). In other circumstances, other classes of drugs can also be used to reduce symptoms of ADHD; these include the antihypertensive medications, such as the alpha 2 agonists like clonidine (Kapvay) and guanfacine (Intuniv); the beta blockers, such as atenolol (Tenorim), nadolol (Corgard), and propranolol (Inderal); the anticonvulsant medications, such as carbamazepine (Tegretol) and valporic acid (Depakote); the eugeroics, like modafinil (Provigil) and armodafinil (Nuvigil); the monoamine oxidase inhibitors (MAOIs), such as moclobemide (Amira), phenelzine (Nardil), and tranylcypromine (Parnate); the antipsychotics, like clozapine (Clozaril), haloperidol (Haldol), olanzapine (Zyprexa), pimozide (Orap), quetiapine fumarate (Seroquel), risperidone (Risperdal), and thioridazine; and cholinergic agents, like nicotine. Other types of substances are occasionally used as well.

The choice as to which ADHD medicine to use, or not to use, depends on an array of factors including the individual's personalized symptom profile, his or her age, comorbidities, if any, other health issues, side effects experienced, risks of addiction and diversion, as well as his or her personal and familial preferences for or against medication. Of the roughly 6.4 million children currently diagnosed with ADHD in the United States, approximately half are on some type of ADHD medicine. In addition, prescriptions to adults in this country diagnosed with ADHD increased 53.5 percent from 2008 to 2012;

the greatest increase was among females between the ages of 26 years and 34 years, which rose by 86 percent.

ADHD medications mainly work by altering brain chemistry, specifically the levels of the respective neurotransmitter substances. Dopamine, norepinephrine, and serotonin are the primary neurotransmitter substances that have been associated with ADHD and are generally targeted by respective ADHD medications.

MEDICATIONS USED TO TREAT ADHD

A wide array of medications is used to treat individuals with ADHD. The central nervous system psychostimulant drugs are, by far, the most commonly used medications to treat ADHD, but many other nonstimulant medications are also routinely used for relief of ADHD symptoms; these nonstimulants include amantadine (Symmetrel), some of the TCAs, bupropion, atomoxetine (Strattera), some of the antihypertensive medications, some of the beta blockers, some of the antiobsessive medications (i.e., SSRIs), some of the anticonvulsant medications, some of the MAOIs, some of the eugeroics, some of the antipsychotic medications, and some cholinergic agents, among myriad other substances. When available, the IUPAC (International Union of Pure and Applied Chemistry) name of each respective ADHD medicine will be provided since this system provides an internationally recognized standard nomenclature system.

Central Nervous System Stimulants

Psychostimulants, also referred to as central nervous system stimulant drugs, are typically the initial class of ADHD medications prescribed, and for many individuals, they often provide the most effective pharmacological treatment. The amphetamines and methylphenidate are the two major types of psychostimulant drugs used as ADHD medications and there are also some formulations that combine multiple drugs. Psychostimulant drugs are easily abused and many of them have a high-risk potential for addiction; abuse of these substances can result in elevated blood pressure, hyperactivity, insomnia, irritability, elevated blood pressure, cardiac irregularities, psychosis, and possibly even death from convulsions, over exhaustion, or cardiac arrest. The central nervous system psychostimulant drugs are so called as a class since they generally produce enhanced awareness, decreased appetite, less sleepiness, and increased locomotor activity.

Psychostimulant drugs are derived from many sources, some occur naturally in various plants and others are synthesized in the laboratory. Caffeine, for instance, occurs naturally in more than 60 different plant species, not just in coffee beans, but also in guarana berries, guarusa, and yerba mate. It is estimated that as many as 92 percent of adults in North America currently consume some form of caffeine on a regular basis. Caffeine, in moderate doses, stimulates the release of dopamine and other neurotransmitters while blocking the absorption of other neurotransmitters, such as adenosine, which is associated with relaxation and sleep. Caffeine, in high doses, is actually a toxic substance, but it takes about 150 mg to 200 mg of caffeine for every 2.2 pounds of body mass, consumed in a short period of time, to produce toxicity. That level of caffeine consumption would usually amount to somewhere between 75 and 100 cups of coffee for an average-sized adult. Regular use of caffeine has the potential to produce dependence and withdrawal symptoms. High doses of caffeine, around 600 mg/day, may help to control symptoms of hyperactivity. Caffeine is a methylated xanthine drug; closely related methylated xanthines that are also mild central nervous stimulants consumed regularly include theophylline in tea and theobromine in chocolate. Similarly, the leaves of the coca shrub, *Erythroxylon coca*, are used to make cocaine, the most powerful natural stimulant drug yet discovered, but not one recommended for treating individuals with ADHD. Coca leaves have been chewed as a mild stimulant for millennia, but cocaine, as first synthesized by Albert Niemann in 1859, has a much higher risk for creating dependency. The IUPAC name for cocaine is methyl(1R, 2R, 3S, 5S)-3-(benzoyloxy)-8-methyl-8-azabicyclo [3.2.1]octane-2-carboxylate. Numerous other central nervous system stimulant drugs have also been synthesized in the laboratory and have been found to have myriad therapeutic applications.

The main psychostimulant substances considered in this work as ADHD medications are amphetamine (Evekeo, Dyanavel XR), dextroamphetamine (Dexedrine), lisdextroamphetamine (Vyvanse), methamphetamine (Desoxyn), and methylphenidate (Ritalin). Other central nervous system stimulant drugs, for example, include those like dexfenfluramine (Redux), ephedrine (Bronkaid, Primatene), fenfluramine (Pondimin, Fen-Phen), methcathinone, phenmetrazine (Preludin), phenylephrine (Sudafed PE), phenylpropanolamine (Triaminic), and pseudoephedrine (Sudafed).

Amphetamines. The amphetamine class of ADHD stimulant medications includes all synthetic substances that are mainly direct releasers of the neurotransmitters dopamine and norepinephrine as well as reuptake inhibitors of both. It includes amphetamine itself as well as the closely related drugs dextroamphetamine (Dexedrine), lisdextroamphetamine (Vyvanse), and methamphetamine (Desoxyn).

Amphetamine Amphetamine (Evekeo, Dyanavel XR), also referred to as alpha-methylphenethylamine, is a potent central nervous system stimulant medicine. Amphetamine is a chiral compound which is a homologue of the naturally produced neurotransmitter phenethylamine. Amphetamine belongs to the amphetamines and derivatives class of organic compounds, which means that it is derived from 1-phenylpropan-2-amine. Amphetamine is available in different formulations, such as amphetamine sulfate and amphetamine aspartate monohydrate. The total molecular mass of amphetamine sulfate is 368.49 g/mol and that of amphetamine aspartate monohydrate is 286.32. The IUPAC name of amphetamine is 1-phenylpropan-2-amine. Amphetamine is prescribed not only to treat symptoms of ADHD but also for treating narcolepsy, a sleep disorder characterized by excessive daytime sleepiness and sudden attacks of sleep, as well as, for a limited period of time only, for addressing weight loss in obese individuals unable to lose weight, along with an exercise regime and a reduced caloric diet. The American Academy of Pediatrics recommends a twice- to thrice-a-day daily dosage for a short-acting amphetamine formulation, like that marketed under trade names such as Dexedrine or Dextrostat, with a recommended 5 mg to 15 mg twice a day or a 5 mg to 10 mg thrice a day prescribing schedule; a once- to twice-a-day daily dosage for an intermediate-acting amphetamine formulation, like that marketed under trade names such as Adderall or Dexedrine Spansule, with a 5 mg to 30 mg once a day or a 5 mg to 15 mg twice a day recommended prescribing schedule; and, a once-a-day daily dosage for an extended release amphetamine formulation, like Adderall-XR, with a 10 mg to 30 mg once a day recommended prescribing schedule.

Dextroamphetamine Dextroamphetamine (Dexedrine, Dextrostat, Liguadd) is the noncatecholamine, dextrorotary stereoisomer of the amphetamine molecule; it is a lipophilic, sympathomimetic amine and a slightly polar, weak base. Dextroamphetamine is a potent central nervous system psychostimulant medicine that is prescribed primarily for treating ADHD and narcolepsy, and it is also used off label for treating conditions such as depression and anxiety; it is also used by athletes, the military, and others as a performance enhancing drug, particularly for acceleration, alertness, and endurance, and as a cognitive enhancer, particularly for improving attention, episodic memory, inhibitory control, and working memory as well as recreationally as an euphoriant and as an aphrodisiac. It can be synthesized in adipate, saccharate, and sulfate forms. The total molecular mass of dextroamphetamine sulfate is 368.49 g/mol and that of dextroamphetamine saccharate is 480.55 g/mol. Dextroamphetamine, like amphetamine, belongs to the amphetamines and derivatives class of organic compounds. The IUPAC name for dextroamphetamine is (2S)-1-phenylpropan-2-2amine.

Lisdextroamphetamine   Lisdextroamphetamine dimesylate (Vyvanse) is a dextroamphetamine prodrug. Lisdextroamphetamine was created so that the pharmacologically active metabolite stimulant drug dextroamphetamine would be released and activated more slowly than when taken directly. Lisdextroamphetamine is prescribed primarily to treat ADHD in children aged 6 years to 12 years. The chemical structure of lisdextroamphetamine is composed of dextroamphetamine coupled with L-lysine, an essential amino acid; hence, lisdextroamphetamine is also called L-lysine-d-amphetamine. Following administration, lisdextroamphetamine is hydrolyzed during first pass through the liver or the intestines, and thereby it is converted into dextroamphetamine by means of cleavage of the lysine group. Lisdextroamphetamine belongs to the alpha amino acid amide class of organic compounds. The total molecular mass of lisdextroamphetamine is 455.49 g/mo. The IUPAC name for lisdextroamphetamine is (2S)-6-diamino-N-[(2S)-1-phenylpropan-2-yl]hexanamide.

Methamphetamine   Methamphetamine hydrochloride (Desoxyn) is closely chemically related to ephedrine and amphetamine and is a very potent sympathomimetic and central nervous system psychostimulant drug. Methamphetamine is prescribed primarily for treating ADHD and for exogenous obesity. Methamphetamine is rapidly absorbed and has high lipophilicity allowing it to easily cross the blood-brain barrier. Thus, unfortunately, methamphetamine is a commonly abused and highly addictive drug that can be relatively easily, but dangerously, produced by converting pseudoephedrine, which is available in several over the counter cold and allergy products, like that which is marketed under the trade names such as Sudafed. Methamphetamine belongs to the amphetamines and derivatives class of organic compounds. The IUPAC name for methamphetamine is (2S)-N-methyl-1-phenylpropan-2-amine.

Methylphenidate.   Methylphenidate hydrochloride (Ritalin) is a racemic mixture of a d-threo enantiomer and an l-threo enantiomer that is highly metabolized pre-systemically. Methylphenidate hydrochloride (Ritalin) is prescribed most commonly for treating symptoms of ADHD in children and for treating adults with ADHD and also for treating narcolepsy. Methylphenidate belongs to the phenylacetic acid derivative class of organic compounds, which means that it consists of a phenyl group substituted by an acetic acid at the second position. The IUPAC name for methylphenidate hydrochloride is methyl 2-phenyl-2-piperidin-2-ylacetate;hydrochloride. The American Academy of Pediatrics recommends a twice- to thrice-a-day daily dosage for a short-acting methylphenidate formulation, like that marketed under trade names such as, Ritalin, Methylin, or Focalin, with a recommended 2.5 mg to 20 mg twice a day to thrice a day prescribing schedule; a once- to twice-a-day daily dosage for an intermediate-acting methylphenidate formulation, like that marketed under trade names such as Ritalin SR, Metadate ER, and Methylin ER, with a 20 mg to 60 mg once a day or a 40 mg in the morning and 20 mg in the early afternoon recommended prescribing schedule; and, recommends a once-a-day daily dosage for an extended release methylphenidate formulation, like that marketed under trade names such as Concerta, Metadate CD, and Ritalin LA, with recommended prescribing schedules of 18 mg to 72 mg once a day for Concerta, and 10 mg to 60 mg once a day for either Metadate CD or Ritalin LA.

Combination Stimulant Formulations.   There are several formulations that combine more than one central nervous stimulant medicine with one or more other stimulants or with other types of medications. Many of these combination formulations exploit the fact that amphetamine exists as two enantiomers, respectively levoamphetamine and dextroamphetamine. Adderall is probably the best known and most widely used of these ADHD combination stimulant formulations; it is actually a combination of four different amphetamine salts; it consists, respectively, of 25 percent amphetamine sulfate, 25 percent dextroamphetamine sulfate, 25 percent dextroamphetamine saccharate, and 25 percent amphetamine aspartate monohydrate. Evekeo, another pharmacological combination product, consists of a racemic amphetamine sulfate with a 1:1 ratio of levoamphetamine and dextroamphetamine.

Nonstimulant Medications

As noted earlier, many nonstimulant medications are often prescribed for treating individuals diagnosed with ADHD. These include a wide array of medications such as amantadine (Symmetrel), some of the TCAs, bupropion (Welbutrin), atomoxetine (Strattera), some of the antihypertensives, some of the beta blockers, some of the antiobsessives, some of the anticonvulsants, some of the MAOIs, some of the eugeroics, some of the antipsychotics, and cholinergic agents as well as various other selected substances.

Amantadine.   Amantadine hydrochloride (Symmetrel) is a cyclohexyylamine used primarily as either an antiviral medicine or as an antiparkinsonian, but which is sometimes also used off label for treating symptoms of ADHD. Amantadine, also referred to as either 1-adamantylamine hydrochloride or 1-aminoadamantane hydrochloride, as noted is prescribed primarily as an antiparkinsonian or as an antiviral medicine; in the latter case, it is used to prevent

or treat respiratory infections caused by the influenza A virus. It also sometimes used for treating individuals with post-herpetic neuralgia (burning or
pain following a shingles infection). The IUPAC name for amantadine is ada-
mantan-1-amine.

Tricyclic Antidepressants.   The TCAs are medications usually prescribed
to treat depression and numerous other conditions, including eating disorders,
panic disorder, posttraumatic stress disorder (PTSD), obsessive compulsive disorder (OCD), and pain disorder; they are sometimes referred to as mood elevators.
The acute effects of the TCAs include reduction of the reuptake of norepinephrine and serotonin. The more commonly used TCAs for treating ADHD symptoms are amitriptyline (Elavil), desipramine (Norpramin), and nortriptyline
(Pamelor); other TCAs include amoxapine (Asendid), clomipramine
(Anafranil), doxepin (Sinequan), imipramine (Tofranil), protriptyline (Vivactil),
and trimipramine (Surmontil). The American Academy of Pediatrics recommends a twice- to thrice-a-day daily dosage, with a recommended 2 mg/kg to
5 mg/kg per day prescribing schedule for the TCAs like desipramine and nortri-
pyline. All of the TCAs noted earlier are approved by the Food and Drug
Administration (FDA) for treating unipolar depression.

Amitriptyline   Amitriptyline hydrochloride is a dibenzocycloheptene derivative TCA, which means that it consists of two benzenes connected by a cyclo-
heptene ring. Amitriptyline hydrochloride (Elavil) is a TCA medicine that
is usually prescribed to treat symptoms of depression as well as for treating
eating disorders, postherpetic neuralgia, and for preventing migraine headaches; it is also used off label for treating ADHD. The IUPAC name for
amitriptyline is 3-(5,6-dihydrodibenzo[2,1-b:2',1'-f][7]annulen-11-ylidine)-
N,N-dimethylpropan-1-amine.

Desipramine   Desipramine hydrochloride (Norpramin), also called desme-
thylimipramine, is an active metabolite of imipramine. Desipramine is a
dibenzazepine derivative TCA, which means that it contains a tricyclic
ring system with an alkylamine substituted on the central ring. The
IUPAC name for desipramine is 3-(5,6-dihydrobenzo[b][1]benzazepin-11-yl)-
N-metylpropan-1-amine. Desipramine is generally prescribed to treat symptoms
of depression; common off-label uses of desipramine include for treating neuropathic pain, insomnia, and, of course, ADHD.

Nortriptyline   Nortriptyline hydrochloride (Aventyl, Pamelor, Sensoval) is a
TCA medicine that is usually prescribed for treating symptoms of depression

as well as for treating panic disorders, postherpetic neuralgia, and as a smoking cessation aid; it is also used off label for treating ADHD. Nortriptyline hydrochloride is the N-demethylated active metabolite of amitriptyline. Nortriptyline hydrochloride is a dibenzocycloheptene derivative TCA, which means that it contains a tricyclic ring system with an alkyl amine substituted on the central ring. The IUPAC name for nortriptyline hydrochloride is 3-(5,6-dihydrobenzo[2,1-b:2',1'-f][7]annulen-11-ylidene0-N-methypropan-1-amine;hydrochloride.

Bupropion. Bupropion hydrochloride (Wellbutrin, Zyban), which used to be formerly known as amfebutamone, is a medicine prescribed mainly as an antidepressant and as a smoking cessation aid as well as sometimes being used off label to treat symptoms of ADHD, particularly appearing to be useful in helping individuals with comorbid aggression or chemical dependence. It is also the only medicine currently approved by the FDA for treating seasonal affective disorder (SAD). Bupropion also has mild anorexiant effects, which may help in weight loss. Bupropion is a norepinephrine dopamine reuptake inhibitor (NDRI). Bupropion belongs chemically to the aminoketones and has a chemical structure similar to that of stimulants like amfepramone and cathinone. Bupropion is a unicyclic, aminoketone antidepressant medicine, which has an acetophenone chemical structure. The IUPAC name for bupropion is 2-(tert-butylamino)-1-(3-chlorophenyl)propan-1-one. The American Academy of Pediatrics recommends a once- to thrice-a-day daily dosage of Wellbutrin and a twice-a-day dosage for Wellbutrin SR (Sustained Release); their recommended prescribing schedule is 50 mg to 100 mg thrice a day for Wellbutrin and 100 mg to 150 mg twice a day for Wellbutrin SR. Bupropion is usually not sedating, nor does it have any anticholinergic or antihistamine properties.

Atomoxetine. Atomoxetine (Strattera) is the first nonstimulant medicine that was approved for treating ADHD. Atomoxetine hydrochloride belongs to the phenylpropylamine class of organic compounds, which means that it consists of a phenyl group that has a propan-1-amine substituted at the third carbon. The IUPAC name for atomoxetine is (3R)-N-methyl-3-(2-methylphenoxy)-3-phenylpropan-1-amine. Atomoxetine functions primarily as a selective norepinephrine reuptake inhibitor; this means that it effectively inhibits the norepinephrine transporter. This particular class of medications is usually prescribed for individuals with concerns about addiction to stimulant medications or with some of the other side effects typically associated with stimulants. It has been demonstrated to be effective in treating both adults and children with ADHD, for which it has been granted approval to be prescribed for by the FDA. A major advantage to the use of atomoxetine over some other ADHD medications, particularly the stimulants, is that it is highly unlikely to be an abused drug; this is because it does not bind to any of the receptor sites typically associated with substance abuse, principally including the dopaminergic receptors. The American Academy of Pediatrics recommends a once-to twice-a-day daily dosage; with a recommended prescribing schedule of 1.2 mg/kg per day to 1.4 mg/kg per day for atomoxetine (Strattera).

Antihypertensives.   The antihypertensive ADHD medications are mainly alpha 2 agonists, such as clonidine (Kapvay) and guanfacine (Intuniv). The alpha 2 adrenergic receptor is a protein coupled receptor site that is associated with the heterotrimeric G-protein. The successful use of alpha 2 agents for treating Tourette's syndrome led to their being tried for treating individuals with ADHD, for which it is now used off label for treating.

Alpha 2 agonists, like the hypotensive medications clonidine (Kapvay) and guanfacine (Intuniv), stimulate alpha 2 receptors in the central nervous system, that is, the brain and spinal cord. If alpha 2 receptors are stimulated, then sympathetic nervous system activity decreases. The sympathetic nervous system is the main excitatory system in the human body. Thus, increased sympathetic activity results in increased awareness, while a decrease results in less awareness as well as decreases in heart rate and blood pressure.

Clonidine hydrochloride (Kapvay) is an imidazoline derived antihypertensive medicine that is a centrally acting alpha 2 adrenergic agent. In addition to use as an antihypertensive medicine and to treat ADHD, clonidine is used to treat vascular migraine headaches, treat severe dysmenorrhea, manage vasomotor effects of menopause, topically to reduce intraocular pressure associated with glaucoma, and for several variants of substance abuse treatment, including treating alcohol withdrawal along with coadministration of benzodiazepines, rapid opioid detoxification, and management of nicotine dependence. Clonidine belongs to the dichlorobenzene class of organic compounds, which means that it contains a benzene with two chlorine atoms attached to it. The IUPAC name for clonidine is N-(2,6-dichlorophenyl)-4,5-dihydro-1H-imidazol-2-amine.

Guanfacine hydrochloride causes reduced sympathetic outflow, which produces reduced vascular tone resulting in lowered diastolic and systolic blood pressure by means of activation of the central nervous system alpha 2 adrenoreceptors. Guanfacine belongs to the phenylacetamide class of organic compounds, which means that it is an amide derivative of phenylacetic acid. The

IUPAC name for guanfacine is N-diaminomethylidene-2-(2,6-dichlorophenyl) acetamide. In addition to clonidine (Kapvay) and guanfacine (Intuniv), which are the most commonly used antihypertensive medications for treating ADHD, there are other alpha 2 agonists, such as methyldopa (Aldomet) and tizanidine (Zanaflex). There are also some combination formulation products that contain an alpha 2 agonist along with other active ingredients, such as Clorpres, which contains both clonidine and chlorthalidone.

The antihypertensive ADHD medications appear to be particularly effective in treating individuals with ADHD who exhibit symptoms of aggressiveness, extreme hyperactivity, and frustration. These antihypertensive medications are frequently prescribed to be used in combination with prescribed central nervous system stimulant medications.

Beta Blockers. Beta blockers, also referred to as beta adrenergic blocking agents, are a class of medications that prevent the functioning of part of the sympathetic half of the autonomic nervous system. The beta blockers, such as atenolol (Tenorim), nadolol (Corgard), and propranolol (Dociton, Inderal), are drugs that, as their name implies, block the effects of beta noradrenergic receptors, but that generally have little to no effect upon the alpha receptors. Accordingly, the beta blockers compete with epinephrine at the beta receptors sites and also interfere with the action of epinephrine. The beta blockers, as a group, tend to lower blood pressure, decrease blood circulation, slow the pulse, and partially constrict the airways in the lungs. They are thus often used to treat hypertension, atrial fibrillation, migraine headaches, and congestive heart failure, but due to their ability to reduce symptoms of anxiety and tremor, they are sometimes a viable choice for treating ADHD; in particular, these antihypertensive medications are helpful for settling down symptoms of aggressiveness and/or hyperactivity. For example, atenolol is most typically used for treating abnormally fast heart rhythms; the IUPAC name for atenolol is 2-[4-[2-hydroxy-3-(propan-2-ylamino)propoxy]phenyl]acetamide. Nadolol is generally used for treating hypertension, angina pectoris, and arrhythmias; the IUPAC name for nadolol is (2R,3S)-5-[3-(tert-butylamino)-2-hydroxy-propoxy]-1,2,3,4-tetrahydronaphthalene-2,3-diol. Propranolol hydrochloride is used for treating hypertension, angina pectoris, arrhythmias, and myocardial infarction; the IUPAC name for propranolol is 1-naphthalen-1-yloxy-3-(propan-2-ylamino) propan-2-ol. Other examples of beta blockers include acebutolol (Sectral), betaxolol (Kerlone), bisoprolol (Zebeta), carteolol (Cartrol), carvedilol (Coreg), esmolol (Brevibloc), labetalol (Normodyne, Trandate), levobunolol (Betagan, Liquifilm), metipranolol (Optipranolol), metoprolol (Lopressor, Toprol), penbutolol (Levatol), pindolol (Visken), sotalol (Betapace), and timolol

(Blocadren). Beta blockers, such as atenolol, nadolol, and propranol, can all be used clinically for treating angina, arrhythmias, hypertension, and myocardial infarctions, while metoprolol, for instance, can be used for all of these clinical conditions as well as for congestive heart failure. The IUPAC name for metoprolol is 1-[4-(2-methoxyethyl) phenoxy]-3-(propan-2-ylamino)propan-2-ol.

Antiobsessives.   The SSRIs, such as fluoxetine (Prozac), are a class of drugs often regarded as antiobsessive medications. Fluoxetine, better known by its trade name Prozac, despite considerable negative attention in the media, is generally considered to be a relatively safe medicine with relatively few adverse side effects. It is true that a somewhat small percentage of individuals who are administered fluoxetine may become a bit more depressed or more irritable, but this is generally true of all antidepressant medications. Fluoxetine hydrochloride is the prototypical SSRI and in addition to treating major depressive disorder and ADHD fluoxetine is used to treat OCD, premenstrual dysphoric disorder, moderate to severe bulimia nervosa, panic disorder with or without agoraphobia, and along with coadministration of olanzapine for treatment resistant bipolar depression. Fluoxetine belongs to the phenylpropylamine class of organic compounds, which means that it contains a phenyl group that is substituted by a propan-1-amine at the third carbon. The IUPAC name for fluoxetine is N-methyl-3-phenyl-3-[4-(trifluoromethyl)phenoxy]propan-1-amine.

Some of the other SSRI antiobsessive medications often used to treat ADHD, in addition to fluoxetine, include fluvoxamine (Luvox), nefazodone (Serzone), paroxetine (Paxil), and sertraline (Zoloft). Fluvoxamine belongs to the benzene class of organic compounds, which means that it contains one monocyclic ring system that consists of a benzene; the IUPAC name for fluvoxamine is 2-[(E)[5-methoxy-1-[4(trifluoromethyl)phenyl]pentylidene]amino] oxyethanamine. Nefazodone hydrochloride (Serzone) belongs to the phenylpipeazine class of organic compounds, which means that it consists of a piperazine bound to a phenyl group. The IUPAC name for nefazodone is 2-[3-[4-(chlorophenyl)piperazin-1-yl]propyl]-5-ethyl-4-(2-phenoxyethyl)-1,2,4-triazol-3-one. On May 20, 2004, Bristol-Myers Squibb discontinued, due to concerns over the small possibility of liver damage, sale of Serzone in the United States. Paroxetine belongs to the phenylpiperdine class of organic compounds, which means that it consists of a phenyl group with a piperdine bound to it, which is also known as a phenylpiperdine skeleton; paroxetine is available formulated in two forms, a phenyl or as a phenylmesylate. Paroxetine has more evidence indicating its use for anxiety-related disorders than any of the other SSRIs; it is used to treat generalized anxiety disorder, major depressive disorder, OCD, panic disorder with or without agoraphobia, PTSD, premenstrual dysphoric disorder, and social anxiety disorder as well as off-label use for ADHD. Sertaline hydrochloride (Zoloft) belongs to the tametraline class of organic compounds, which means that it consists of a tetrahydronaphthalene linked to a phenyl group. The IUPAC name for sertraline is (1S,4S)-4-(3,4-dichlorophenyl)-N-methy-1,2,3,4-tetrahydronapthalen-1-amine.

Other antiobsessive medications, in addition to fluoxetine, fluvoxamine, nefazodone, paroxetine, and sertraline, include citalopram (Celexa), escitalopram (Lexapro), and venlafaxine (Effexor); another, clomipramine (Anafranil), interestingly, can be classified both as an antiobsessive medicine and as a TCA. Citalopram belongs to the phenylbutylamine class of organic compounds, which means that it contains a phenyl group with a butan-1-amine substituted at the fourth carbon; the IUPAC name for citalopram hydrobromide is 1-[3-dimethylamino)propyl]-1-(4-fluorophenyl)-3-H-2-benzofuran-5-carbonitrile;hydrobromide. Escitalopram is used to treat major depressive disorder and generalized anxiety disorder as well as for off-label use to treat ADHD; the IUPAC name for escitalopram is (1S)-1-[3 (dimethylamino)propyl]-1-(4-fluorophenyl)-3H-2-benzofuran-5-carbonitrile. Venlafaxine hydrochloride (Effexor) is an antiobsessive medicine, which is a serotonin norepinephrine reuptake inhibitor (SNRI) that is mainly prescribed for treating depression and anxiety disorders, but which is often useful for treating depression that does not respond to the SSRIs. Venlafaxine belongs to the phenylpropylamine class of organic compounds, which means that it consists of a phenyl group substituted at the third carbon by a propan-1-amine. The IUPAC name for venlafaxine is 1-[2-(dimethylamino)-1-(4-methoxyphenyl)ethyl]cyclohexan-1-ol. Clomipramine (Anafranil) is a 3-chloro analog of imipramine and is a dibenzazepine derivative TCA that is primarily prescribed for treating OCD and related conditions, like depression, schizophrenia, and Tourette's syndrome as well as off-label use for conditions such as autism, chronic pain, panic disorders, and, of course, ADHD. Clomipramine belongs to the dibenzazepine class of organic compounds, which means that it consists of two benzene rings connected by a azepine ring; the latter being an unsaturated seven member heterocycle with a carbon atom replaced by a nitrogen atom. The IUPAC name for clomipramine is (3-(2-chloro-5,6-dihydrobenzo[b][1]benzazepin-11-yl)-N,N-dimethylpropan-1-amine.

The antiobsessive medications are sometimes referred to as "antistuck" medications. All of the SSRIs and the other antiobsessive medications noted earlier are approved by the FDA for treating unipolar depression; many are also used off-label for treating ADHD.

Anticonvulsants. The anticonvulsant medications, such as carbamazepine (Tegretol) and valporic acid (Depakote), generally work by reducing abnormal electrical activity in the brain. Anticonvulsant medications are commonly used as sedating agents for anxiety and as mood stabilizers for bipolar depressive disorder, also to control agitation in dementia, as well as for ADHD. Carbamazepine is one of the major medications traditionally used for treating partial seizures and for generalized tonic clonic seizures. Carbamazepine is a tricyclic compound structurally similar to imipramine and related antidepressant medications. Carbamazepine is used as a commonly prescribed anticonvulsant medicine not only to treat certain types of seizures in individuals with epilepsy but also to treat diabetic neuropathy and trigeminal neuralgia, for which it was originally marketed, as well as for episodes of mania and bipolar depression, in addition, of course, to its off-label use for treating ADHD. Carbamazepine is sometimes also used to treat PTSD, restless legs syndrome, alcohol and drug withdrawal, diabetes insipidus, and chorea. Carbamazepine belongs to the dibenzazepine class of organic compounds, which means that it has two benzene rings that are connected by an azepine ring. The IUPAC name for carbamazepine is benzo[b][1]benzazepine11-carboxamide.

Valporic acid is a potent anticonvulsant medicine typically used for treating generalized seizures and also an effective mood stabilizer, and it is a known teratogen. Valporic acid is one of several fatty carboxylic acids that have anti-seizure effects; this includes the amides and esters of valporic acid. Valporic acid is a free acid; in addition, salts of the acid, particularly sodium valproate, are sometimes also used. However, at normal body pH, valporic acid is fully ionized, thus whether the free acid or one of its salts is used, the active drug with therapeutic efficacy is in either case the valproate ion. Valporic acid belongs to the methyl branched fatty acids, which means that it consists of an acyl chain that has a methyl branch. The IUPAC name for valporic acid is 2-propylpentanoic acid.

It is important that individuals taking these anticonvulsant medications, also known as anti-seizure medications, have their white blood cell counts and their liver functions monitored regularly. The anticonvulsant medications are particularly helpful in treating individuals with ADHD who have explosive, violent outbursts and for those who may have had some head trauma.

Monoamine Oxidase Inhibitors. The MAOIs, such as moclobemide (Amira), phenelzine (Nardil), and tranylcypromine (Parnate), are particularly effective for treating atypical depression; they are also used for treating Parkinson's disease and several other conditions, including, of course, ADHD. Several MAOIs, like isocarboxazid, phenelzine, selegeline, and tranylcypromine, are approved by the FDA for treating unipolar depression. The MAOIs are regularly used as antidepressant medications, but since they inhibit the metabolic degradation of norepinephrine and serotonin by the monoamine oxidase enzyme they can also be helpful in treating some individuals with ADHD. The MAOIs were the first class of antidepressant medications developed, and although effective antidepressants, there are newer classes of antidepressant medications that are safer, cause fewer adverse side effects, and have generally replaced there use as antidepressants, but they can still be useful in treating individuals with ADHD.

There are both selective and nonselective MAOIs, as well as both reversible and irreversible MAOIs. The selective MAOIs affect a specific isomer of the monoamine oxidase enzyme, while the nonselective ones affect both subtypes. The irreversible MAOIs are generally rapidly absorbed and quickly eliminated. Use of the irreversible MAOIs, however, depletes the monoamine oxidase enzymes, which must then be regenerated in the body before normal levels of enzymatic activity can resume. This regeneration typically takes two to three weeks, thus the effects of the irreversible MAOIs can persist for a considerably longer period of time after the medicine itself has been cleared from the body. Accordingly, there is no direct correlation between blood plasma levels of these irreversible MAOIs and the degree of monoamine oxidase enzyme inhibition. This problem does not exist for the use of the reversible MAOIs since they can detach from the enzymes which permits them to perform their normal functions.

Moclobemide (Amira) is a reversible and selective inhibitor of the monoamine oxidase type A enzyme. Moclobemide belongs to the 4-halobenzoic acids and derivative class of organic compounds, which means that it has a halogen atom located at the four position of the benzene ring. The IUPAC name for moclobemide is 4-chloro-N-(2-(morpholin-4-yl) ethyl)benzamide. Phenelzine sulfate (Nardil) is an irreversible and nonselective MAOI used mainly to treat major depressive disorder. Phenelzine belongs to the phenethylamine class of organic compounds, which means that it consists of a phenyl group substituted by an ethan-1-amine at the second position. The IUPAC name for phenelzine is (2-phenyl)hydrazine. Tranylcypromine sulfate (Parnate) is a propylamine irreversible and nonselective MAOI prescribed mainly for treating major depressive disorder, dysthymic disorder, and atypical depression, as well as panic and phobic disorders and, of course, off-label use for ADHD. Tranylcypromine is formed by cyclization of an amphetamine side chain and belongs to the aralkglamine class of organic compounds, which means that it consists of an alkyl group with an aromatic hydrocarbyl group substituted at one carbon. The IUPAC name for tranylcypromine is

(1R)-2-phenylclooropan-1-amine. Selegiline hydrochloride (Eldepryl, Emsam) is a selective, irreversible inhibitor of the monoamine oxidase type B enzyme. Selegiline is used mainly for treating individuals with newly diagnosed Parkinson's disease. Selegiline belongs to the amphetamines and derivatives class of organic compounds. The IUPAC name for selegiline is (R)-N-methyl-N-(1-phenylpropan-2-yl)(prop-1-yn-1-3-amine.

Eugeroics.   Modafinil (Provigil), adrafinil (Olmifons), and armodafinil (Nuvigil) are eugeroics of wakefulness-promoting agents generally prescribed for treating conditions like narcolepsy, excessive daytime sleepiness associated with obstructive sleep apnea, and shift work–related sleep disorders, and they are also commonly used off label for helping to treat individuals with fatigue associated with many other conditions including that for chronic fatigue syndrome, depression, fibromyalgia, myotonic dystrophy, neurological fatigue as associated with multiple sclerosis, opioid induced sleepiness, Parkinson's disease, SAD, spastic cerebral palsy, and, of course, also for ADHD. Modafinil functions essentially as an atypical dopamine transporter inhibitor and, interestingly, appears to promote wakefulness without the apparent need for compensatory sleep. It has therefore also been used off label by astronauts and by the militaries of many countries while engaged in situations of sleep deprivation. Fortunately, it demonstrates a relatively low, if even any, potential for substance abuse. Modafinil is the active metabolite of adrafinil, which was developed and prescribed for treating narcoplepsy; but since the introduction of modafinil, adrafinil has essentially been discontinued. Modafinil is a central nervous system stimulant medicine that belongs to the diphenylmethane class of organic compounds, which means that it consists of a methane that has two phenyl groups that replaced two hydrogen atoms. The IUPAC name for modafinil is 2-benzhydrylsulfinylacetamide.

Adrafinil is a mild central nervous stimulant medicine that was used to relieve excessive inattention and sleepiness, and also off label for ADHD as well as by those trying to avoid fatigue, such as shift workers. Adrafinil does not currently have approval for use from the FDA, thus its use is unregulated. It was used in France where it was marketed under the trade name of Olmifons until September 2011 when marketing permission was withdrawn.

Armodafinil is prescribed for treating narcolepsy, obstructive sleep apnea, and shift work sleep disorder; common off-label uses of armodafinil include Parkinson's disease, mytonic muscular dystrophy, excessive daytime sleepiness, and, of course, ADHD. Armodafinil, like modafinil, belongs to the diphenylmethane class of organic compounds. The IUPAC name for armodafinil is 2-[(R)-benzhydrylmethanesulfinyl]acetamide.

Antipsychotics.   Some antipsychotic medications, like haloperidol (Haldol), pimozide (Orap), and thioridazine, and many of the atypical antipsychotic medications, like clozapine (Clozaril), olanzapine (Zyprexa), quetiapine fumarate (Seroquel), and risperidone (Risperdal), are sometimes used off label to treat individuals with ADHD. The antipsychotics are generally used for treating schizophrenia and related disorders, but they have been increasingly being used by psychiatrists to treat ADHD and disruptive behaviors in children and adolescents, such as attacking other youth, authority defiance, and temper tantrums. The FDA, for example, has approved use of quetiapine fumarate (Seroquel) for children with bipolar disorder with manic episodes and for adolescents with schizophrenia; olanzapine (Zyprexa) has been approved for use with adolescents with schizophrenia or with bipolar disorder with mixed or manic episodes; and risperidone (Risperdal) has been approved for use with adolescents with schizophrenia, for treating irritability associated with autism, and for bipolar disorder with mixed or manic episodes.

Several antipsychotics are sometimes used off label for treating ADHD. The most commonly used antipsychotic medications in this regard are haloperidol (Haldol), pimozide (Orap), and thioridazine.

Haloperidol (Haldol) is a phenyl-piperidinyl-butyrophenone medicine that is used mainly to treat schizophrenia and other psychoses, as well as for treating delusions, Tourette's syndrome, and sometimes as an adjunctive therapy for cognitive impairment and, of course, ADHD. Halperidol belongs to the phenylpiperidine class of organic compounds, which means that it consists of a piperdine bound to a phenyl group. The IUPAC name for haloperidol is 4-[4-chlorophenyl)-4-hydroxypiperdine-1-yl]-1-(4-fluorophenyl)butan-1-one.

Pimozide (Orap) is an antipsychotic medicine that is used as an alternative to haloperidol and to suppress the motor and vocal tics associated with Tourette's syndrome as well as for off-label use to treat ADHD. Pimozide belongs to the diphenylmethane class of organic compounds, which means that it consists of a methane with two phenyl groups that replace two hydrogen atoms. The IUPAC name for pimozide is 3-[1-[4,4-bis(4-fluorophenyl) butyl] piperidin-4-yl]-1H-benzimidazol-2-one.

Thioridazine hydrochloride is a phenothiazine antipsychotic generic medicine that is used for treating schizophrenia and other psychoses, as well as for controlling severely agitated or disturbed behaviors, like those associated with ADHD. Thioridazine belongs to the phenylthiazine class of organic compounds, which means that it has a linear tricyclic system that consists of two benzene rings joined with a parathiazine ring. The IUPAC name for thioridazine is 10-[2-(1-methylpiperidin-2-yl)ethyl]-2-(methylsulfanyl)-1OH-phenothiazine.

Several of the atypical antipsychotics are also sometimes used off label for treating ADHD. The atypical antipsychotics used most frequently for this purpose are clozapine (Clozaril), olanzapine (Zyprexa), quetiapine fumarate (Seroquel), and risperidone (Risperdal).

Clozapine (Clozaril) is a tricyclic dibenzodiazepine atypical antipsychotic medicine that is mainly used for treating schizophrenia. Clozapine belongs to the dibenzodiazepine class of organic compounds, which means that it consists of two benzenes connected by a diazepine ring.

Olanzapine pamoate (Zyprexa) is an atypical antipsychotic medicine that is a synthetic derivative of thienobenzodiazepine that is used primarily for treating schizophrenia and bipolar disorder and that also has antinausea and antiemetic activities. Olanzapine belongs to the benzodiazepine class of organic compounds, which means that it consists of a benzene ring fused to a diazepine isomer.

Quetiapine fumarate (Seroquel) is an atypical antipsychotic medicine approved for treating schizophrenia, as well as treating acute episodes of mania associated with bipolar I disorder, and also for use along with an antidepressant medicine to treat unipolar depression. Quetiapine is sometimes also used off label for treating other conditions, such as a sleep aid, and also for treating individuals with ADHD. Quetiapine fumarate belongs to the dibenzothiazepine class of organic compounds, which means that it contains two benzenes connected by a thiazepine ring. The IUPAC name for quetiapine is 2[2-(4-benzo[b][4]benzothiazepin-6-ylpiperazin-1-yl)ethoxy]ethanol.

Risperidone (Risperdal) is an atypical antipsychotic medicine that is a benzisoxasole derivative that is prescribed mainly for treating schizophrenia and bipolar disorder and to alleviate irritability in individuals with autism. Risperidone belongs to the pyridopyrimidine class of organic compounds, which means that it consists of a pyridine fused to a pyrimidine. The IUPAC name for risperidone is 3-[2[4-(6-fluro-1, 2-benzoxazol-3-yl) pipeperidin-1-yl] ethyl]-2-methyl-6,7,8,9-tetrahydropyrido[1-2-a] pyrimidin-4-one.

Cholinergic Agents.   The cholinergic agents, such as nicotine, have also sometimes been used to treat individuals with ADHD. Nicotine is the prototypical agonist for the nicotinic cholinergic receptors. It profoundly stimulates neurons but ultimately blocks synaptic transmission; it is also a highly toxic alkaloid. Nicotine is believed to activate the dopaminergic pathway that projects from the ventral tegmental area to the cerebral cortex and limbic system. Nicotine belongs to the alkaloids and derivatives class of organic compounds, which means that it contains mostly basic nitrogen atoms. The IUPAC name for nicotine is 3-(1-methylpyrrolidin-2-yl)pyridine.

Off-Label Use.   Healthcare providers, such as a physician, can prescribe any medicine that is legally available for their patients based on their clinical judgment and professional expertise. If a particular medicine is used for a purpose other than what it was specifically approved for, as indicated on the labeling approved by the FDA, then this is regarded as off-label use of that specific pharmaceutical product. For example, if a particular drug is only approved for use with adults, but the prescriber uses his or her best clinical judgment that its use will be both safe and effective and prescribes it for a child or adolescent, that would be an instance of off-label use. In fact, it is estimated that about 50 percent to 75 percent of all pediatric prescriptions are off label and that around 20 percent of all adult prescriptions are off label. More than half of all medications approved for marketing by the FDA lack evidence of safety and efficacy for use with pediatric patients. This is particularly of concern here as the medications most commonly used off label with children are those that target the central nervous system, such as those used for treating ADHD. Healthcare providers are expected to use their professional clinical experience to determine what the best medicine might be for a particular patient with a particular set of issues.

The FDA only officially regulates the drug-approval process, not the actual prescribing of a drug. The manufacturer of a particular pharmaceutical product would have to submit a new drug application and conduct rigorous, often costly clinical trials in order to establish the safety and efficacy of a particular medicine in a specific target population. Off-label use of medications routinely leads to innovation and helps in the process of discovering new uses for respective pharmaceutical products beyond that for which they were originally tested. The manufacturers of pharmaceutical products are prohibited from marketing the off-label uses of their products to healthcare providers, and health insurance companies closely monitor off-label drug use if expensive medications are being used for untested and unproven purposes.

The anticonvulsant medications and the antipsychotic medications are the two specific pharmaceutical classes that are most commonly used off label. Anticonvulsants are generally thought to help calm hyperactive brain functioning, while antipsychotics are suspected to mediate brain dysfunction, both of which could clearly be helpful in helping alleviate symptoms in someone with ADHD. At any rate, shared decision making should be of major importance when considering off-label use of medications with children.

Other Substances

There is a vast array of substances, other than the types of FDA-approved pharmaceuticals discussed earlier, that could have potential benefits in alleviating some of the respective symptoms of ADHD. There are long-standing traditions in many cultures of the use of these types of substances for purported medicinal effects. The ancient Egyptians, for instance, developed complex pharmacopeias utilizing an array of herbs and other plants, roots, seeds, and miscellaneous other ingredients for medicinal purposes including garlic, honey, licorice, myrrh, olive oil, onions, peppermint, and specific animal body parts. These numerous substances used today include assorted dietary supplements, such as herbal remedies, homeopathic medications, and vitamin and mineral supplements, as well as myriad other products, many of which have been specifically formulated and marketed to address ADHD-related issues.

Dietary Supplements.   What we put into our bodies unequivocally impacts how our bodies, including our brains, perform. Nutritional deficiencies can certainly have a deleterious effect on many factors, including both short-term and long-term memory. Low levels of certain amino acids, which serve as precursors for neurotransmitter substances, can lead to diminished neurotransmitter levels, while elevated amino acid levels could potentially lead to excessive neurotransmitter levels. For example, consumption of the artificial sweetener aspartame has been linked to abnormally high amino acid levels which, in turn, have been associated with an increase in hyperactive behaviors. There are many substances that people have supplemented their diets with in the hope that they might be effective. These include a vast array of herbal remedies, homeopathic medications, vitamin and mineral supplements, and numerous other products. Unfortunately, there is not always a reliable body of scientific evidence to support the safety or efficacy of these substances. In fact, many are known to be toxic and the control of dosages is often problematic. Another area of concern is the real danger of self-diagnosing and prescribing, as well as the potential harm that could result from delaying the use of medicinal products with documented effectiveness.

Herbal Remedies.   Herbal remedies have been used for millennia. Herbal remedies have long been used for calming hyperactivity, including in Ayurveda from India and in traditional Chinese medicine. Some of the more commonly recommended herbal remedies for treating individuals with ADHD include those based on herbs such as *Avena sativa* (green oats), *Bacopa monnieri* (water hyssop), *Centella asiatica* (gotu kola), and *Panax ginseng* (Korean red ginseng). Herbal teas containing various herbs and flowers, such as chamomile, lemon grass, and spearmint, are also commonly recommended. Herbal remedies are regulated by the FDA, but the FDA does not evaluate the safety or efficacy of these purported remedies.

Homeopathic Medications.   Homeopaths use herbs, minerals, chemicals, and other substances in diluted formulations for purported medicinal properties. Homeopathy was developed over 200 years ago by a German physician, Dr. Samuel Christian Hahnemann. The practice of homeopathic medications is based on the premises that like cures like (*similia similibus curentur*) and that dilution increases potency. Accordingly, it is believed by homeopaths that a substance that causes disease symptoms in a normal healthy individual can be used in a diluted form as a cure. For example, a homeopathic medicine based on a dilution of *Hyoscyamus niger* (black henbane) is recommended by homeopaths for treating some individuals who experience poor impulse control.

Vitamin and Mineral Supplements.   The human body, including the brain, needs small amounts of certain substances to function normally. Vitamins are chemical substances that are necessary for normal metabolism, and there are also several minerals and trace elements that are essential to many bodily functions. Deficiencies in some of these nutrients could potentially cause symptoms similar to those of ADHD, and some reasons that supplemental consumption of these substances could remediate those symptoms. Fortunately, however, most Americans can get enough of these essential nutrients through eating a well-balanced diet. Excessive use of vitamin supplements, unfortunately, can lead to hypervitaminosis, a toxic condition resulting from an unnecessary and potentially fatal build up too much of certain vitamins; excessive intake of minerals can likewise create dangerous conditions.

Other Products.   There are many other products that have been developed and are marketed as treatments for ADHD. Some of these particular ADHD specific products are Listol, Addasil, and Synaptol, but there are many others.

Listol   Listol is a formulation of natural substances, which was developed and marketed by Progressive Health, and that is used to manage symptoms of ADHD in children and adults. The active ingredients in Listol are mostly minerals and amino acids, including calcium carbonate, copper gluconate, iron citrate, magnesium oxide, zinc oxide, and GABA powder; most of these ingredients have no proven clinical effects for treating ADHD and some can have toxic effects if taken in large doses.

Addasil   Addasil is a liquid nutritional supplement marketed as stimulating attention and concentration as well as for promoting focus in children and adults with ADHD. Addasil contains phospholipids (which helps promote the structural integrity of neurons and contribute to neurotransmitter synthesis), essential fatty acids, assorted minerals, like calcium gluconate and magnesium gluconate, and several vitamins, including thiamine (B1), riboflavin (B2), niacin (B3), pantothenic acid (B5), pyridoxine (B6), cyanocolilamin (B12), and vitamin C.

Synaptol   Synaptol, developed and marketed by Hello Life, is a liquid homeopathic formulation used to alleviate symptoms associated with ADHD. It consists of herbal extracts and other ingredients marketed as improving attention span and enhancing mental focus and concentration; these ingredients include extracts of *Aconitum ferox* (Indian aconite), *Aesculus hippocastanum* (hosre cherstnut), *Apis mellifica* (Western honey bee), *Argentum nitricum*, (silver nitrate), *Avena sativa* (green oats), *Baptisia tinctoria* (wild indigo), *Cochlearia armoracia* (hosreradish), *Scleranthus annuus* (German knotweed), *Scutellaria lateriflora* (blue skullcap), and *Viola odorata* (wood violet).

Pemoline   Magnesium pemoline, which had been marketed under the trade name of Cylert, is a product that had been available and was, previously, prescribed for treating individuals diagnosed with ADHD. Pemoline had been approved for use with individuals who were six years of age and older. Pemoline is a central nervous system stimulant drug that had severe adverse side effects associated with its use. It was a medicine that patients were advised that they would have to have regular liver function tests to monitor its usage; it was, even as it was being prescribed, recognized that about 2 percent to 3 percent of individuals taking pemoline might develop hepatitis. Pemoline belongs to the benzene class of organic compounds, which means that it is an aromatic compound that contains a monocyclic benzene ring system. The IUPAC name for pemoline is 2-amino-5-pjhenyl-4,5-dihydro-1,3-oxazol-4-one. In 2005, the FDA removed approval of magnesium pemoline and in March of 2005, Abbott Laboratories discontinued its production.

ALTERNATIVE WAYS TO HELP PEOPLE WITH ADHD

The use of alternative and complementary medicine has increased for treating ADHD and related developmental and behavioral disorders. It is, in fact, estimated that about 65 percent of parents of children diagnosed with ADHD have used alternative and complementary medicine to relieve symptoms associated with the condition.

Behavioral Therapy

Behavioral therapy consists of a broad array of therapeutic approaches to help individuals to change their self-defeating or problematic behaviors, such as many of the core symptoms associated with ADHD. Behavioral therapy is founded on the fundamental principles of operant and classical conditioning. Operant conditioning is a process that utilizes an array of techniques that helps to make a response become less or more likely to occur depending upon its consequences, such as using a demerit system to reduce the impulsive blurting out of answers by a student with ADHD in a classroom. Classical conditioning is a process that utilizes various techniques to transform a previously neutral stimulus such that it will be paired with another stimulus that already elicits a desired response; it is also referred to as Pavlovian conditioning or as respondent conditioning.

Nutrition

Nutritional therapy can also be of substantial assistance in the management of ADHD and is an approach that many parents of children with ADHD are typically very willing to try. Losing excess weight through proper nutrition, along with appropriate regular physical exercise, can be particularly helpful in the prevention of certain types of conditions which have a high association with ADHD, such as diabetes and obesity. A mostly vegetarian diet has been suggested to be helpful for those dealing with some of the symptoms associated with ADHD. Nutritional supplements, like the natural hormone melatonin, may be of some assistance in improving sleep problems for those children who take certain ADHD medications. Herbal remedies, fish oils and other nutritional approaches, like gluten free diets, have been suggested, but additional research is sorely needed before any evidence-based recommendations can legitimately be made. A balanced diet with sufficient caloric levels is clearly essential as the human brain uses about one fifth of the total energy consumed. Furthermore, a proper diet can also often decrease the amount of ADHD medications required.

Exercise

Exercise can be used to increase blood flow, strengthen weak muscles, restore proper muscular balance, stimulate immune system responses, enhance metabolic functions, and promote an overall healthier condition, all of which can assist in the managing symptoms of ADHD. For example, tai chi is a traditional Chinese practice that is based on gentle, slow movements that can help increase flexibility and concentration; similarly, there are numerous types of yoga from India that people have used for millennia to help achieve a mind-body balance and for relaxation and enhanced concentration. There are many other varieties of physical therapy and myriad corrective exercises that could possibly enhance both physical and emotional health, as well as help improve concentration.

There are many benefits demonstrated from regular physical exercise that would be helpful for managing symptoms of ADHD and promoting overall health improvement. Through the use of cardiovascular, flexibility, and strength exercises, one can possibly improve both his or her physical and psychological health and thereby possibly reduce, if not even eliminate, the use of ADHD medications. However, the wrong type of exercise or any exercise performed improperly can also lead to injury; therefore, professional guidance is recommended.

Biofeedback

Biofeedback consists of particular techniques that utilize special equipment to teach individuals how to gain conscious control over what are normally considered to be involuntary physiological functions, such as their blood pressure, heart rate, muscle tension, skin temperature, and sweating. The general idea on which biofeedback is based is the premise that by utilizing the power of one's mind to consciously control what is happening inside of their body, they can gain better control over their state of health. Electromyographic (EMG) biofeedback, for instance, uses equipment to monitor muscular tension to train individuals how to more effectively and selectively relax areas of intense tension, which can clearly help to lessen stress, like that associated with anxiety disorders, back pain, and headaches. Similarly, electroencephalographic (EEG) biofeedback, also known as neurofeedback, uses equipment to measure brain wave activity and can be particularly helpful in managing conditions such as ADHD as well as epilepsy or seizure disorders; the goal of this approach is to assist the individual with ADHD to learn how to increase his or her beta wave activity and to lessen his or her theta wave activity. In addition, galvanic skin response (GSR), also known as electrodermal activity (EDA) or skin conductance response (SCR), can be used to monitor sweating, which is often associated with some conditions like anxiety. Biofeedback devices generally provide visual or auditory feedback to help individuals learn how to voluntarily gain control over their physiological processes. Unfortunately, biofeedback takes a considerable amount of practice to sufficiently master, and it also requires some specialized pieces of equipment that can be rather expensive as well as challenging to maintain and interpret. A related technique is integrative sensory training, an approach pioneered by an occupational therapist, Jean Ayers, which utilizes various techniques intended to stimulate neuronal connections to help the brain organize itself better to deal with the overload of sensory stimuli coming into it.

Chiropractic

Chiropractic is a type of alternative medicine that employs myriad techniques that are based on the belief that subluxations, or dislocations, in the arrangement of the vertebra of the spinal column can result in nerve impingements that are claimed to produce varied health problems, including the types of symptoms that are usually associated with ADHD, like restlessness. Realignment by manipulation is the primary technique that is used by chiropractors to supposedly adjust the structural integrity of the spinal column.

Chiropractic care usually begins with the taking of a detailed personal health history and of an extensive physical examination; various laboratory tests or diagnostic imaging, such as the use of magnetic resonance imaging (MRI) or x-rays to identify any abnormalities in the patient's musculoskeletal structure, may also be conducted. Chiropractic treatment usually involves manual adjustments, known as manipulation therapy, delivered by means of respective techniques, such as high-velocity, low-amplitude spinal manipulation (HVLA-SM). Chiropractic practitioners may also freely dispense dietary advice, commonly advocating the use of specific nutritional supplements, as well as employing other varied treatment modalities, such as the application of hot or cold compresses, ultraviolet or infrared light, ultrasound, and traction. The benefits claimed for chiropractic treatment by practitioners typically include improved mobility and lessened discomfort, but such relief is routinely temporary and often requires long-term treatment. Chiropractic doctors are not legally permitted to prescribe drugs, perform surgery, or practice obstetrics.

Hypnosis

Hypnosis involves a set of specific techniques that are intended to help individuals to improve their focus and concentration, lessen the potential influence of distractions, and increase their responsiveness to suggestions set forth. Some individuals, however, respond better to hypnotic suggestions than do others; the motivations and the expectations that an individual brings to this form of treatment has a profound influence upon the potential effectiveness of the hypnotherapy. There are various hypnotherapeutic techniques that can be used for managing symptoms of ADHD, such as the varied interpersonal approaches and hypnoanalysis. Hypnotic regression is frequently employed as a technique that is generally considered the best way to get to the underlying root cause of a respective problem, recognition of which can sometimes be enough to lead to better acceptance and possibly even relief. Most hypnotic techniques are essentially designed to produce an altered state of awareness, which can usually make an individual more open to specific suggestions, such as feeling less distracted.

Massage

Massage therapy is an alternative treatment approach that is somewhat similar to chiropractic treatment as it is based primarily on the manipulation of muscles and of soft body tissues in order to alter circulatory, lymphatic, muscular, and nervous systems of the body. The kneading, pummeling, rubbing, and stroking of muscles and other tissues as typically practiced in respective massage therapy techniques have been clinically shown to effectively increase metabolism, enhance lymphatic drainage, and release substances back into circulation in order to thereby create states of both physical and mental relaxation. Clinical studies have demonstrated that massage therapy techniques can promote the release of endorphins, which can produce feelings of euphoria. Massage certainly encourages attaining a state of relaxation, and it also appears to provide opportunities for maintaining greater concentration and, overall, to promote improved daily functioning.

Respective massage therapy techniques have clearly demonstrated efficacy in providing support for strategies to improve mental concentration and focus, and these may also be useful in helping to manage other types of distractions. Reiki, for instance, is a traditional style of Japanese massage that uses light, energy healing techniques that are based on the concept of life force energy. There are actually over 100 different types of massage approaches including those like acupressure, Ayurvedic, reflexology, shiatsu, and Swedish forms.

Relaxation

Relaxation techniques, such as guided imagery, mediation, and progressive muscle relaxation, consist of a battery of techniques that can be employed to help an individual to reduce his or her level of stress. These varied relaxation techniques can not only help individuals learn how to relax specific muscle groups and to achieve a more calm mental state, but they have also been clinically shown to help reduce the levels of stress hormones in the body.

Respective meditation techniques are intended to help produce a state of mind-body inner focus and more peaceful, concentrated awareness, which can assist one in maintaining his or her focus and attention. These various relaxation approaches include the myriad schools of yoga, autogenic training, mindfulness meditation, rhythmic breathing practices, transcendental meditation, and visualization exercises. Since most relaxation and meditation techniques help an individual to achieve a state of contemplation, they generally also help to lower blood pressure, slow metabolism, and lessen anxiety, all of which are things that can help an individual with ADHD to become less distractible and, thereby, better able to appropriately maintain their attention. The fundamental purpose of relaxation techniques is to help the individual to systematically reach a homeostatic physiological state that is essentially opposite that of the stress response. Several relaxation therapies have been clinically shown to reduce feelings of anxiety. Mediating, for instance, appears to both increase one's ability to maintain focus and thereby hopefully to at least decrease the use of ADHD medications.

Electrotherapy

Various types of electrotherapy have been developed control sensations and excessive locomotor activity as sometimes exhibited by individual's with ADHD. These electrotherapy approaches generally utilize assorted technological devices that can be used to help control and manage muscle tension and related sensations. Transcutaneous electrical nerve stimulation (TENS), for instance, utilizes safe, relatively mild electrical signals that are released by small, battery powered devices which can be attached to the surface of the skin, while spinal cord stimulation (SCS), on the other hand, uses an electrode that is surgically implanted near the spinal cord of an individual to block neurotransmission signals by means of neuro-modulation. Peripheral nerve stimulation (PNS), similarly, is an approach which uses an electrode that is inserted through a small surgical incision and then placed on a nerve, while peripheral nerve field stimulation (PNFS) is a slightly less invasive approach in which an electrode is inserted under the skin by means of a needle. The most invasive electrotherapy approach that can be used, but fortunately rarely is, is deep brain stimulation (DBS) in which electrodes are placed directly into the brain, usually in either the periacueductal gray and sensory thalamus regions. Transcranial magnetic stimulation (TMS) is another and essentially noninvasive electrotherapy approach in which rapid cycling of electromagnetic induction is used to impart electrical stimulation in order to better manage excessive locomotor activity.

Acupuncture

Acupuncture is an ancient medical technique from China that involves inserting thin needles at specific anatomical points on the body along what are referred to as the meridian lines of 12 energy channels that purportedly flow below the surface of the body. Acupuncture is known to have been practiced at least as far back as 4,500 years ago in ancient China. There are at least 365 of these specific acupuncture sites along the meridians where the specialized needles can be inserted and manipulated by an acupuncturist in specific ways and for specific periods of time to produce the desired therapeutic results. Chinese medicinal specialists who perform this revered practice are said to help bring balance the life forces, known as the complementary cosmic energies of yin and yang, which are believed to flow through the human body as ch'i. These small acupuncture needles can easily produce a slight tingling feeling and can even make a selected body part feel numb, apparently, by changing the signals sent to and from the brain; it has been suggested that their mechanism of action is to selectively block the transmission of impulse signals. This medical technique has long been practiced in the East, even used as anesthesia for surgery. It has also been suggested by some that acupuncture might actually work by stimulating the release of endorphins and other neurotransmitters that, in turn, could block signals from being delivered either to the brain or, conversely, back to the extremities. Whatever the real mechanism of action may be, it is clear from numerous clinical studies that acupuncture can be a safe and effective nonpharmacological approach. Acupuncture can definitively change brain activity, particularly in the dorsomedial prefrontal cortex, which has been implicated in hyperactivity.

Aromatherapy

Aromatherapy is an approach that uses scents from the essential oils of selected plants; the essential oils are the compounds that help produce a plant's fragrance. These essential oils, usually in diluted formulations, can be applied directly to the skin, such as by facials or body wraps, inhaled, or bathed with. Essential oils of substances are sometimes recommended for relief of symptoms commonly associated with ADHD, such as the use of peppermint for feelings of depression. Essential oils appear to help provide the most relief for minor and occasional symptoms. It is another not very well understood complementary technique that has been used for thousands of years by people in many different cultures around the world to manage and control emotions and actions; at the very least, aromatherapy can probably be quite helpful in assisting some individuals with ADHD to achieve a more tranquil, calm state of mind.

Chapter 3

ADHD Medications: A Brief History

In order to understand the history of Attention Deficit Hyperactivity Disorder (ADHD) medications, it is critically necessary to have some understanding of the history of the condition of ADHD itself. A brief overview of that history lays a foundation upon which to explore some of the complex developments involved in the origins of the many varied ADHD medications, both that of the stimulants and of the non-stimulant medications.

HISTORY OF ADHD

There is a considerable history behind the condition that we currently recognize as ADHD. Our contemporary view of ADHD is at least partly shaped by these earlier notions, particularly those coming from nineteenth century ideas of children's mental health. There actually is a rather broad base of early descriptions of what we now consider to be ADHD. This historical review must also include the once widely accepted condition of hyperkinetic disorder as well as discussion of the evolution of diagnostic standards.

Children's Mental Health in the Nineteenth Century

In the early nineteenth century, the understanding of the mental health of children was extremely limited. The brains of children were generally thought to be soft and vulnerable, thus more open to external influences. Prior to that era, it was widely believed that children did not suffer from the kinds of nervous conditions sometimes inflicted upon adults.

In the nineteenth century, mental health care primarily involved the placing of individuals into institutions, particularly asylums. An asylum was then seen as a rational approach to treating madness, based upon the prevailing Enlightenment ideals of the time. In Great Britain, a series of nineteenth century legislation enabled the dramatic increase in asylums; this included the 1800 Criminal Lunatics Act, 1808 County Asylums Act, the 1828 Madhouses Act, the 1832 Madhouses Amendment Act, the 1854 Lunacy Act, and the 1898 Defective and Epileptic Children's Act. In the United States, legislation to establish asylums was generally created at the state, not the federal, level. For example, the first asylum opened in Massachusetts was the Worcester Lunatic Asylum, opened as a 120 bed hospital in 1833 after prodding from the Boston Prison Discipline Society founded in 1825 by the Rev. Louis Dwight lobbied the state legislature to establish a committee in 1827 to examine jail conditions, as most individuals with mental illness at the time were typically incarcerated. Many asylums were built in Britain and across the rest of Europe as well as in the United States throughout the nineteenth century; they were often located in rural settings away from the hustle if industrialized, urban life and were regarded as compassionate institutions of social reform. However, the early asylums were primarily custodial and physical restraints and other less enlightened measures were typical. Many social reformers in the middle of the nineteenth century, such as Dorothea Dix, a school teacher, noted that children constituted many of the inmates of America's asylums, almshouses, jails, prisons, workhouses, and similar institutions. She began advocating for better services for the mentally ill in 1841 in Massachusetts and subsequently traveled mostly down the east coast of the United States; it is believed that her efforts directly resulted in the creation of at least 32 state psychiatric hospitals. By 1880, there were 75 public psychiatric hospitals and many private ones located across the United States. By the late nineteenth century, these sorts of institutions were partly being replaced by reformatories, still largely serving as warehouses of troubled and difficult to handle children, descriptors not uncommonly applied more recently to children with ADHD. Further, by the late nineteenth century, ideas of social Darwinism predominated in Western societies, and these largely regarded insanity as basically being an incurable, degenerative disease that was inherited.

Early Descriptions of ADHD-Like Conditions

For quite some time, people have recognized that the behavior of some children is markedly different and inappropriate to the normative expectations of society. In fact, since the beginnings of humankind, individuals with mental illness have been stigmatized, ostracized, subjected to physical persecution, and even to death. At times they were thought to be possessed by demons or to be cursed or to be engaging in witchcraft.

There have been passing references in the literatures of various professions for a considerable period of descriptions for behaviors that we would now generally agree seem to be suggestive of individuals who probably had ADHD. In 1775, Melchior Adam Weikard, a prominent German physician, published in his text *Der Philosophische Artz* what is perhaps the first ever description in medical literature of behaviors we would now attribute to ADHD; he reported that they "are mostly reckless, often copious considering imprudent projects, but they are also most inconstant in execution" (Barkley & Peters, 2012, p. 628). In 1798, Sir Alexander Crichton, a well-known Scottish physician, in his 1798 work *An Inquiry into the Nature and Origin of Mental Derangement* noted that in some individuals: "attention is fo little under control, that it cannot be ftrongly directed to any fubject, except for a very fhort time ..." (Crichton, 1798, p. 5). In 1890, William James, in his *Principles of Psychology*, described what he considered to be a normal behavioral variant in which individuals tend to be "overflowing with animation" (James, 1890, p. 800) which erupts from their "mercurial" temperaments. In 1902, Sir George Frederic Still, a British pediatrician, reported to the Royal College of Physicians (subsequently published in *Lancet*) on 43 children who demonstrated serious difficulty with sustaining attention and self-regulation and who, though of normal intelligence, could not seem to learn from the negative consequences of their actions, but who were defiant, aggressive, excessively emotional, and resistant to discipline; they apparently would have met the current criteria for ADHD combined type. Still and many others at the time regarded these symptoms as stemming from a defect of moral control.

Many nineteenth century, as well as earlier and later, poets and writers explored the relationship between madness and creativity. Some, such as John Clare, were widely believed to be insane and many spent time in asylums. For quite some time, in fact, many writers have provided descriptions of children whom we would now likely say had ADHD. The bard William Shakespeare in his play *King Henry VIII* described a character with a malady of attention. In 1844, Heinrich Hoffmann, a German physician, created some illustrated children's stories, including one about *Zappelphilipp*, or Fidgety Phil, who was apparently unable to sit still at the family dinner table (Hoffmann, 2015). Hoffman's descriptions of Philips inattention and hyperactivity appear to meet contemporary diagnostic criteria of ADHD.

During the Gilded Age, there was a wave of epidemic proportions of a condition then called neurasthenia, a vague, and now essentially obsolete (at least in the United States), hereditary disease of "weak" nerves that was characterized by chronic weakness, loss of memory, lack of motivation, inattention, and so forth. The term neurasthenia was actually introduced in Boston in 1869 by a neurologist, George Miller Beard (1869). Childhood neurasthenia was a widely popular diagnosis that included then so-called "nervous children," many of whom would meet the contemporary criteria for a diagnosis of ADHD. In 1915, John Harvey Kellogg, of Kellogg's corn flake cereal fame, observed that the proportion of neurasthenic "children to the total school population is unquestionably increasing" (Kellogg, 1915, p. 49). In keeping with his views on health reform, Kellogg advocated for a vegetarian diet, open air sleeping, regular physical activity, and abstinence from "condiments, tea, coffee, pastry, and confectionery" (Kellogg, 1915, p. 50) as well as, of course, from sexual activity.

In the early 1940s, the term *Minimal Brain Dysfunction (MBD)* came into widespread use. This concept asserted that in some individuals, at least, all brain mechanisms may be present and working, but that some of their brain wiring was somehow different, such that it did not work in the normal way. These children were regarded as having a dysfunctional nervous system such that they appeared to experience difficulties with learning and also had problems with distractibility and hyperactivity, which, in turn, typically generated emotional, academic, and family problems.

"Hyperkinetic Disorder"

A concept that was in vogue for decades before ADHD is that of hyperactivity. Professionals of differing fields have attempted to explain hyperactive children from in terms of their own academic specializations. For instance, in the past, many psychoanalysts described the behaviors of children whom we would now generally recognize as having ADHD as acting out. This psychoanalytical perspective was reflected in the language employed as descriptors used in the second edition of the *Diagnostic and Statistical Manual of Mental Disorders (DSM-II)* of the American Psychiatric Association for what was then referred to as hyperkinetic reaction of childhood. From the psychoanalytical perspective, a child with what we would now recognize as ADHD would typically have been described as acting out or reacting against early experiences. In 1957, the term *Hyperkinetic Impulse Disorder* was introduced by physicians highlighting the neurological basis of the disorder asserting that "dysfunction of the diencephalon exposes the cortex to unusually intense storms of stimuli. . ." (Laufer, Denhoff, & Solomons, 1957: 38). For the rest of the 1950s and in to the 1960s, many were writing about children with hyperkinetic impulse disorder, usually attributing it to over stimulation of the cortex stemming from inadequate filtering of stimuli by the thalamus. By 1960, the term *hyperactive child syndrome* was introduced to describe a condition characterized by developmentally excessive motor activity. From the 1960s through the 1980s, there were competing camps of physicians, educators, therapists, and other professionals debating over whether the fundamental nature of the disorder was more dynamic and experiential or more brain based with metabolic abnormalities and significant genetic influences, with Hyperkinetic terminology preferred by members of the former clique (e.g., Freeman, 1976; Berger, 1981) and MBD preferred by the latter (e.g., Knights & Hinton, 1969; Edwards. *et al.*, 1971). There were advocates from both camps for stimulant medication treatment approaches (e.g., Freeman, 1976; Shaywitz *et al.*, 1978) and nonmedication therapeutic approaches (e.g., Conners & Delamater, 1980; Berger, 1981. In 1980, the release of the third edition of the *Diagnostic and Statistical Manual of Mental Disorders* (*DSM-III*) essentially replaced the Hyperkinetic versus MBD terminological debate, by adding more stress upon the inattentiveness and inability to focus characteristics of the condition with the selection of the term of Attention Deficit Disorder (ADD).

Development of Diagnostic Standards

The development of diagnostic standards for ADHD has evolved over time. When the first edition of the *Diagnostic and Statistical Manual of Mental Disorders* (*DSM-I*) of the American Psychiatric Association was released in 1952, there was no mention of any condition that would now be recognized as ADHD. The *DSM* is intended to provide a common nomenclature and standard diagnostic criteria for the classification of mental disorders. By 1968, the time of the second edition of the *Diagnostic and Statistical Manual of Mental Disorders* (*DSM-II*), the agreed upon nomenclature was, as noted earlier, Hyperkinetic Reaction of Childhood, which was "characterized by over activity, restlessness, distractibility, and short attention span" (American Psychiatric Association, 1968, p. 50). This condition was generally thought to be outgrown in most individuals during their adolescent years. In 1980, the third edition of the *Diagnostic and Statistical Manual of Mental Disorders* (*DSM-III*) listed ADD with three subtypes; these, respectively, were ADD with hyperactivity, ADD without hyperactivity, and ADD residual type. The *DSM-III* specified that the onset of symptoms had to be before the age of seven years, with a duration of at least six months; evidence was also mounting to suggest that these symptoms persisted into adulthood for many individuals. In 1987, it was felt necessary to promulgate a new nomenclature with the release of the third edition, revised of the *Diagnostic and Statistical Manual* (*DSM-III-R*), which introduced the more widely accepted term of ADHD but without subtypes. By 1994, the fourth edition of the *Diagnostic and Statistical Manual of Mental Disorders* (*DSM-IV*) was released; it specified that the symptoms of ADHD must not merely have been present but must have resulted in impairment prior to the age of seven years; the ADHD symptoms must have been present in two or more settings and cause substantial impairment in two or more areas; and, further, it included the three subtypes of inattentive, hyperactive, and combined, and added ADHD not otherwise specified, for those individuals who exhibited symptoms but did not meet all diagnostic criteria. In 2000, release of the fourth edition, text revision seemed warranted; it listed ADHD combined type, ADHD predominantly inattentive type, and ADHD predominantly hyperactive-impulsive type, as well as ADHD not otherwise specified for those individuals who did not meet the diagnostic criteria but demonstrated a behavioral pattern characterized by daydreaming, hypoactivity, and sluggishness, even if the age of onset was after the age of seven years. In 2013, the fifth, and up until this point the most current, edition of the *Diagnostic and Statistical Manual of Mental Disorders* (*DSM-5*) was published; it lists ADHD combined presentation (Code # 314.01), ADHD predominantly inattentive presentation (Code # 314.00), ADHD predominantly hyperactive/ impulsive presentation (Code # 314.01), other specified ADHD (Code # 314.01), and unspecified ADHD (Code # 314.01).

In addition to the DSM, the second most widely used alternative nomenclature is that of the International Statistical Classification of Diseases and Related Health Problems (ICD), which is produced by the World Health Organization (WHO). ICD-10-CM codes have been used for coding purposes since October 1, 2014. The DSM-5 classification of disorders is harmonized with that of the ICD. With respect to the ICD-10-CM codes for the respective variants of ADHD, they are F90.2 for the combined presentation, F90.0 for the predominantly inattentive presentation, F90.1 for the predominantly hyperactive/ impulsive presentation, F90.8 for the other specified, and F90.9 for the unspecified.

WHEN WERE ADHD MEDICATIONS DEVELOPED?

The development of ADHD medications is something of a cultural paradox. On the one hand, strong and potentially dangerous drugs provide relief for individuals with a sometimes perplexing disorder. On the other hand, many of these drugs were regularly misused or abused. Many suffer from drug addiction that can easily overwhelm their ability to think and act rationally.

Millions of individuals struggle with the symptoms of ADHD each year. Those who go untreated can suffer needlessly, and recognition of this condition is a relatively recent phenomenon. For millennia, individuals with ADHD had no organized approach to seek relief. Nevertheless, some of these individuals certainly experimented with the use of varied naturally occurring substances that had psychoactive properties, including an array of stimulant substances. No doubt, some of these proto-experimenters found that they could enhance their functional abilities when under the influence of some of these then unknown substances.

The use of medications to treat what we now identify as ADHD has a relatively shorter history. In 1937, Charles Bradley reported on the use of Benzedrine, an amphetamine, to improve the behavior of children. Bradley (1937) found that amphetamine administered to children at the Emma Pendleton Bradley Home in Providence, Rhode Island, helped to reduce their hyperactive and impulsive behaviors. In 1957, Herbert Freed and Charles Peifer reported on a study of the use of chlorpromazine (Thorazine) on what was then called hyperkinetic emotionally disturbed children. Chlorpromazine was the first recognized antidepressant medicine after depressed patients at Saint Anne Hospital in Paris showed startling improvements. By 1962, an average of 430 mg of amphetamine was being consumed per person each year in the United States. We were truly a "pepped up" nation in the 1950s to the 1960s. This was also the heyday for the marketing and consumption of two old standby nonprescription stimulants, caffeine and nicotine. In 1963, C. Keith Conners reported on a study using methylphenidate (Ritalin) to help alleviate the inappropriate symptoms of emotionally disturbed children and to improve their learning.

The youth of this highly stimulated era would, coincidently, grow up to become the vanguard of the generation of sex, drugs, and rock 'n' roll. This conjunction of factors certainly warrants deeper logical consideration, but that is a discussion for a different venue.

More recently, there has been an explosion in the types and varieties of medications available for treating individuals with ADHD. The number of prescriptions in the United States for ADHD medications for individuals aged 10 years to 19 years increased by 26 percent from 2007 to 2012; this total nearly reached 21 million annual prescriptions by 2012. Increased recognition of and treatment for adults with ADHD has also fueled the continued expansion of these trends. For instance, ExpressScripts, the largest prescription processing company in the United States, reports that the number of prescriptions for adults with ADHD has doubled in the past four years; half of those prescriptions were for amphetamine based medications.

Central Nervous System Stimulants

The use of stimulant substances contained in various plants goes back at least many thousands of years. Many central nervous system stimulant drugs are naturally occurring alkaloidal substances that people probably inadvertently stumbled upon for millennia. For instance, the leaves of the tobacco plant, *Nicotianna tabacum*, which contain nicotine, appear to have been used at least 8,000 years ago in the Americas. Leaves and twigs of the khat plant, *Catha edulis*, have been chewed in Africa since the Neolithic, up through the ancient Egyptians and until today for the mild stimulant effects of cathinone. The leaves of the tea plant, *Camellia sinensis*, were used to make a mild stimulant beverage in China more than 5,000 years ago that contained theophylline. Leaves of the coca shrub, *Erythroxylon coca*, were being cultivated and chewed in South America at least 4,000 years ago. In Mesoamerica, beans of the cacao tree, *Theobroma cacao*, were being used to make a warm chocolate beverage containing theobromine at least as early as 1,900 BC. Beans of the coffee tree, *Coffea Arabica*, were being used since at least the fourth century BC to brew a caffeine drink in what is now Ethiopia, East Africa. Similarly, long before Western contact, nuts of the kola tree, *Cola acuminate*, were being chewed in Africa and kava roots, *Piper methysticum*, were being steeped to make a stimulating beverage in Polynesia. In fact, many naturally available mild stimulant substances were regularly being consumed for some time in all corners of the world.

The recognition and identification of the respective chemical substances that have psychopharmacological stimulant properties is mainly a by-product of nineteenth century scientific investigations. For instance, the chemical caffeine was not isolated and identified until 1821. In 1828, Wilhelm Heinrich Posselt and Ludwig Reimann, two German students studying at the University of Heidelberg, isolated and purified a volatile and active alkali substance from tobacco, which they named nicotine, in honor of Jean Nicot de Villemain, the sixteenth century French ambassador to Portugal who helped introduce tobacco to the French court. Interestingly, Nicot learned about the purported curative properties while in Portugal and upon his return to the French court in 1560, he promulgated its medicinal uses among the nobility. For instance, he used tobacco in an attempt to alleviate the migraine headaches of Catherine de Medici, queen consort of Henry II of France; she popularized the use of snuff, which was imitated by other members of the French court. In 1855, a German chemist, Friedrich Gaedcke separated the alkaloid cocaine, which he called erythroxyline, from coca leaves. In 1859, Albert Niemann, studying at Gottingen University in Germany, developed a process to isolate and purify cocaine from coca leaves.

Amphetamines.   Amphetamines refers to a broad group of central nervous system stimulant drugs of the phenylethylamine class. Amphetamine, dextroamphetamine, lisdextroamphetamine, and methamphetamine are some of the psychostimulant medications that fall within the amphetamines.

Formulation and Original Uses.   In 1887, the racemic amphetamine was first synthesized in Berlin by Lazar Edeleanu, a Romanian chemist, who called it phenylisopropylamine. In 1893, Nagai Nagayoshi, a Japanese chemist, first synthesized methamphetamine from ephedrine. In 1919, Akira Ogata, a Japanese pharmacologist, synthesized methamphetamine hydrochloride by means of using red phosphorous and iodine to reduce ephedrine. In 1927, Gordon Alles independently synthesized amphetamine and reported on its stimulant effects; his work created the opportunity for the widespread production and use of amphetamines. Starting in 1932, amphetamine was marketed by Smith, Kline, and French, which later became GlaxoSmithKline, under the trade name of Benzedrine, which was a liquid free-base form of amphetamine for use as a bronchodilator inhaler. Fred Nabenhauer of Smith, Kline and French, a firm based in Philadelphia, developed the Benzedrine Inhaler, which was first marketed in 1933 for its rapid relief of congestion associated with colds and similar conditions. People soon discovered that they could break open the inhaler container and swallow paper strip that was coated with amphetamine to get a euphoric rush; Benzedrine tablets were soon produced to help reduce this illicit misuse. As early as 1936, college students at American universities were using amphetamine "pep" pills for all night studying or partying. In 1937, Smith, Kline and French began marketing dextroamphetamine tablets under the trade name of Dexedrine. Benzedrine Sulfate, an amphetamine tablet, was marketed since 1938 as an antidepressant medicine.

During World War II, amphetamines were widely used by troops and war industries on both sides for their performance enhancing and stimulant effects. For example, U.S. military forces, particularly bomber crews and jungle fighters, were issued around 180 million amphetamine pills and tablets during World War II; similarly British forces were supplied with about 72 million amphetamine tablets during the war. Nazi and Japanese soldiers and pilots, including the infamous Kamikaze pilots, were also routinely using amphetamine, which in wartime Japan was referred to as *Senryoka Zokyo Zai* (lit., the drug to inspire fighting). During World War II, methamphetamine was marketed under the trade name of Pervitin by Temmler, pharmaceutical company of Berlin; it was widely used by Nazi forces, particularly Luftwaffe pilots, who sometimes referred to it as *Hermann-Goring-Pillen* (lit., Herman Goring pills). The Nazi Fuhrer Adolf Hitler was administered injections daily of methamphetamine by his personal physician Theodor Gilbert Morell. Many of the other Nazi leaders during World War II were also regular users of stimulant drugs, such as General Erwin "Desert Fox" Rommel.

Amphetamine was used historically to treat many conditions, including depression, nasal congestion, and obesity. In 1945, Smith, Kline and French was producing a million amphetamine sulfate pills each day; there were also generic versions being manufactured. It is estimated that around 750 million amphetamine pills were produced by the United States in 1945; that was enough for half a million Americans to take 2 pills each day. In fact, by 1946, amphetamine was indicated for at least 39 different conditions ranging from caffeine dependence, chronic hiccups, low blood pressure, and seasickness. The original Smith, Kline and French U.S. patent for amphetamine expired in 1949 and production expanded to competing pharmaceutical companies. While 16,000 pounds of amphetamine were produced in the United States in 1949, it rose to 75,000 pounds by 1958, which is equivalent to 3.5 million tablets. U.S. pilots fighting in the Korean Conflict were administered high doses of amphetamines. Truck drivers, returning veterans, inmates, students, shift workers, celebrities, and many others were also regularly abusing amphetamines. The Food and Drug Administration (FDA) made amphetamine a prescription drug in 1959. Production rose to 8 billion tablets per year in the United States during the middle of the 1960s, and by 1971, 12 billion tablets were being produced each year. A similar epidemic had unfolded in Japan and across Europe, such as in France, Great Britain, and Sweden, as rebuilding efforts after World War II necessitated extreme hardships. In 1962, it is estimated that annual production of amphetamine pills had reached around eight billion. Amphetamine abuse was also rampant across Beatnik culture and commonly mentioned in Beat literature, like Jack Kerouac's *On the Road* and Allen Ginsberg's poem "Howl" as well as in the literature and lyrics of other popular genre. Amphetamines were widely administered to armed forces during the Vietnam War, just as they had in World War II. In fact, the U.S. military continues to routinely use amphetamines for its troops, including those stationed in Afghanistan and Iraq.

Use in Treating ADHD.   In 1937, there was an outbreak of pediatric viral encephalitis. Some of these children, as they recovered, exhibited distractible and hyperkinetic behaviors. Charles Bradley, a pediatrician, gave some of these children Benzedrine Sulfate, an amphetamine medicine, and noted that this treatment helped them to be less active and distractible. The report that this medicine helped problem children to become better behaved, quitter, and even more studious eventually led to its widespread use in treating ADHD.

The use of stimulant medications rose markedly over the next several decades. By 1970, it is estimated that in the United States, approximately 150,000 children were taking stimulant prescribed medications, while by 1980, it had risen to somewhere between 270,000 and 541,000 children, and by 1988, it is estimated that between 750,000 and 1.6 million school ages children were taking prescribed stimulant medications, mostly for ADHD. In 1996, Richwood Pharmaceuticals introduced a combination instant release amphetamine tablet formulation, which it marketed under the trade name of Adderall. By 1999, 3.4 percent of all children in the United States had been prescribed a stimulant medicine; now the proportion is closer to 10 percent. By the year 2000, it is estimated that over two million American children were taking some form of stimulant medicine. Various forms of stimulant ADHD medications have been introduced. For instance, in 2007, Vyvanse, the trade name of lisdextroamphetamine dimesylate, was introduced; in 2008, ProCentra, the trade name of a liquid dextroamphetamine formulation, was introduced by Independence Pharmaceuticals; and in 2016, Adzenys XR-ODT, the trade name of an amphetamine oral disintegrating tablet, was introduced by Neos Therapeutics. At any rate, it is clear that since the early 1970s, the main approach used to treating ADHD is by means of stimulant medications. At present, about 8 percent of those aged 4 years to 17 years have a diagnosis for ADHD and of these 4.5 percent not only have the diagnosis but also are receiving a stimulant medicine to treat the disorder, which most typically is either methylphenidate (Ritalin) or an amphetamine-based medicine, such as Adderall. There are currently myriad trade name and generic versions of the various stimulant ADHD medications available.

Restrictions on Availability Due to Addictive Liability.   Once the addictive potentiality of stimulants became recognized, many governments began enacting progressively stricter approaches to curtail abuse. In 1948, Japan initiated restrictions on methamphetamine as a dangerous drug. In 1949, Japan enacted the Pharmaceutical Affairs Law to place controls on amphetamines, such as only being available under a physician's prescription, and pharmaceutical companies were told to limit production. Unfortunately, Japanese authorities thought limiting oral preparations and increasing intravenous medication would limit use to hospitals, but an illicit market emerged and injection drug use escalated. Illicit use of stimulants also spread among young ethnic minorities in Japan, particularly Koreans and Chinese. In 1951, Japan enacted the Awakening Drug Control Law to severely restrict the manufacture, possession, and sale of stimulants; the importation of precursor substances was prohibited. Nevertheless, abuse rapidly increased across Japan, peaking by 1954 when it is estimated that there were over 2 million users of stimulant drugs in a population of 88.5 million. Many were arrested under the Awakening Drug Law's strict law enforcement measures, which were revised and amended several times. Educational campaigns were conducted and treatment for addicts was expanded, use of stimulants gradually declined, but there was an increase in other drugs of abuse in Japan. From 1957 to 1963, heroin use rose sharply in Japan; there was also a rise in the abuse of hypnotic drugs, like in methaqualone beginning around 1960. From 1964 to 1969, there was a decline in heroin use in Japan, but by 1964, the production of hypnotics, sedatives, and minor tranquilizers had increased ninefold over that of 1954; in addition, alcohol consumption and use of painkillers also increased substantially.

Sweden also experienced a similar increase in the postwar abuse of stimulants. The stimulant drug epidemic peaked in Sweden during 1966–1967 when one out of every three individuals arrested in Stockholm was for intravenous use of amphetamines. A broad societal approach including stricter controls, public campaigns, increased treatment eventually resulted in a decline in stimulant drug abuse in Sweden. The passage of the Controlled Substances Act (84 Stat. 1242) of the Comprehensive Drug Abuse Prevention and Control Act of 1970 listed the amphetamines as Schedule III drugs in the United States, but in 1971, they were moved to Schedule II drugs, such that users would have to get new prescriptions for each refill and pharmacies and physicians would have to keep detailed records of the prescriptions for these controlled substances. After these laws took effect, sales of amphetamines declined 60 percent in the United States. Similar efforts were developed around the globe. From 1971 to 1995, there was nearly a fivefold increase in the number of amphetamine-related psychostimulant drugs under international control.

Formulation of Extended Release Preparations. The pharmaceutical preparations of amphetamines evolved over time. Since these psychostimulants are relatively fast acting, they tend to have a somewhat short duration of action. Accordingly, various combination medications and extended release formulations were created. For example, a combination of dextroamphetamine and amobarbital, a barbiturate, were marketed by Smith, Kline and French under the trade name of Dexamyl. An extended release dextroamphetamine capsule, marketed as Dexedrine Spansule, was introduced in the 1950s by Smith, Kline and French. Lisdextroamphetamine was developed by New River Pharmaceuticals as a longer acting and less easily abused alternative to dextroamphetamine, of which it is a prodrug as it must be first converted into dextroamphetamine by enzymes in red blood cells. New River was bought out by Shire Pharmaceuticals, which soon released lisdextroamphetamine under the trade name of Vyvanse, after having received FDA approval on February 23, 2007. A U.S. patent was filed on June 1, 2004, with a priority date of May 29, 2003, and then was published on January 6, 2005, to Travis Mickle et al. of New River for the synthesis of lisdextroamphetamine hydrochloride as an abuse resistant amphetamine compound useful as an alternative treatment for ADHD. In October 2010, GlaxoSmithKline sold its rights to Dexedrine Spansule to Amedra Pharmaceuticals, a subsidiary of CorePharma.

Methylphenidate

The central nervous system psychostimulant drug, methylphenidate, appears to stimulate the arousal system in the brain stem and also activates regions of the cerebral cortex. However, compared to the amphetamines, like amphetamine, dextroamphetamine, lisdextroamphetamine, and methamphetamine, methylphenidate is a relatively mild ADHD stimulant medicine, although abuse and dependence are still possible. In addition, in clinical settings, at least, it appears to improve cognitive function.

Formulation and Original Uses. In 1944, Leandro Panizzon, a researcher at CIBA (*Gellellschaft fur Chemische Industrie Basel*), first synthesized methylphenidate. In 1950, Panizzon and Max Hartmann patented a process for synthesizing methylphenidate. In 1954, CIBA was granted a patent for use of methylphenidate as an antidepressant. In 1955, FDA approval was granted for the use of methylphenidate for numerous conditions, including depression, fatigue, narcolepsy, obesity, and schizophrenia. It was also used for several other purposes, such as to help patients afflicted with a drug induced coma, most commonly from an anesthesia. The initial trade name, Ritalin, was chosen as a tribute to Panizzon's wife Marguerite, whose nickname was Rita. In 1961, the FDA granted approval for use of methylphenidate in children with behavioral problems.

Use in Treating ADHD. The use of methylphenidate for treating ADHD has a relatively long history, having been used since the 1950s, with even wider use progressively increasing from the 1960s onward. In 1955, the FDA granted initial approval to CIBA, which is now the Novartis Corporation, for the use of methylphenidate in the United States for treating what was then generally referred to as hyperactivity or as MBD, but now known of as ADHD. In 2008, the FDA granted approval of methylphenidate for use in the United States in treating adults with ADHD. It is also widely used in other countries around the world for treating individuals with ADHD.

Dramatic Increase in Use.   The dramatic increase in the use of methylphenidate occurred in the 1990s. From 1991 to 1995, about 200,000 children aged two years to four years were prescribed methylphenidate (Ritalin). By the late 1990s, methylphenidate, marketed under the trade name of Ritalin, had become the ADHD medicine of choice in the United States as about 90 percent of individuals with ADHD were then being prescribed Ritalin. From 1990 to 2005, production of methylphenidate increased sixfold. In Great Britain, from 2007 to 2012, prescriptions for methylphenidate increased by 50 percent. Globally, consumption of methylphenidate reached 2.4 billion doses by 2013, which represented a 66 percent increase over that of 2012. The United States alone accounts for more than 80 percent of global methylphenidate consumption.

Formulation of Extended Release Preparations.   The need for extended release formulations of methylphenidate became readily apparent. The initial formulation of methylphenidate was as a racemic mixture of 80 percent erythro isomer and 20 percent threo isomer, the latter being more pharmacologically active. In 2000, the ALZA Corporation received approval from the FDA to market an extended release formulation of methylphenidate under the trade name of Concerta. With Concerta, about 22 percent of the methylphenidate is released immediately, while the remaining approximately 78 percent is subsequently released from 10 hours to 12 hours after ingestion. Methylin ER, the trade name for another extended release methylphenidate formulation, was also introduced in 2000. Other trade names for various extended release pill formulations of methylphenidate include Biphentin, Equasym XL, Medikinet XL, and Rubifen SR; extended release capsules are also marketed trade names like Metadate CD and Ritalin LA; there is also an extended release oral suspension drug marketed under the trade name of Quillivant XR, which was introduced in 2012, and manufactured by Pfizer, that consists of a roughly 20 percent instant release and an 80 percent extended release powder mixture to which the pharmacist adds water, all of which is shaken vigorously to result in a compounded product of 5 mg/ml, and this is then administered by means of an oral syringe. In 2016, a chewable methylphenidate formulation, marketed under the trade name of Quillichew ER, was introduced by Pfizer, which received FDA approval on December 4, 2015.

NONSTIMULANTS

There are numerous nonstimulant drugs that have been found to be helpful in treating individuals with ADHD. The nonstimulant ADHD medications include amantadine, the tricyclic antidepressants (TCAs), bupropion, atomoxetine, the antihypertensives, the beta blockers, antiobsessives, anticon-vulsants, eugeroics, monoamine oxidase inhibitors (MAOIs), and the antipsy-chotics as well as other medications, such as the cholinergic agents. Each of these drugs has its own history and associated issues.

Amantadine

Amantadine was first synthesized by W. Haaf of Studiengesellschaft Kohle mbH, Germany, who was granted a patent for same on October 6, 1964. On May 5, 1966, a U.S. patent application was filed for pharmaceutical use of amantadine and its derivatives by Paulshock Marvin and John C. Watts of E.I du Pont de Nemours and Company. Amantadine hydrochloride was approved by the FDA in October of 1966 as a prophylactic agent for preven-tion in the United States of Asian influenza; it was soon additionally approved when found to also be safe and effective against the influenza A virus. In 1969, amantadine was further accidently discovered to be helpful in reduction of symptoms of Parkinson's disease, akathisia, and drug-related extrapyramidal symptoms. Kathleen Clarence-Smith of Prestwick Pharmaceuticals filed a pat-ent application on November 8, 2005, with a priority date of November 9, 2004, for use of amantadine in treating hyperkinetic disorders. Amantadine hydrochloride is marketed under the trade name of Symmetrel manufactured by Endo Pharmaceuticals.

Tricyclic Antidepressants

In the late 1940s, Geigy pharmacologists were searching for new antihist-amines that might have sedative-hypnotic effects. They focused on the imino-dibenzyls that had a three ring chemical structure (for which the TCAs were eventually named), similar to that of the phenothiazines and developed 42 dif-ferent derivatives. At the time the prevailing belief was that clinical depression was caused by unresolved interpersonal conflicts, few thought that any drug could ever do more than alleviate depressive symptoms. In 1950, Geigy sent Roland Kuhn, a psychiatrist who was then working at the Thurgauishe Heil und Flegeanstalt in Munsterlingen, experimental samples of G22150 for test-ing in patients, but it did little to help them sleep. Several years later, Geigy sent samples of G22355, or imipramine, to Kuhn who noted that it elevated the mood of his patients. Geigy introduced imipramine to the European mar-ket in 1957, and, in 1958, began selling it under the trade name of Tofranil.

The TCAs were, accordingly, introduced for clinical use in the 1950s. As a class, they tend to inhibit, to varying degrees, the reuptake in the neurons of the brain of the neurotransmitters dopamine, norepinephrine, and serotonin.

Imipramine, as mentioned, was the first TCA introduced. In 1961, three pharmaceutical companies, Merck, Roche, and Lundbeck, simultaneously developed amitriptyline, the second TCA released. Merck eventually won the rights to amitriptyline, which it marketed under the trade name of Elavil. A U.S. patent was issued to J. H. Biel and C. I. Judd of Colgate Palmolive Company on July 8, 1969, for the synthesis of the TCA desipramine. Nortriptyline, another TCA, was being evaluated for use in the treatment of children and adolescents with ADHD since at least 1992.

Bupropion

Bupropion was first synthesized in 1969 by Nariman Mehta of Burroughs Wellcome, which later became GlaxoSmithKline. A U.S. patent was granted in 1974, and it received FDA approval for use of bupropion hydrochloride as an antidepressant on December 30, 1985, for marketing under the trade name of Wellbutrin. The FDA granted approval in 1996 for a sustained release bupropion hydrochloride formulation, which is marketed as Wellbutrin SR and can be taken twice a day, as compared to the three times a day necessary with the immediate release formulation. In 1997, the FDA approved use of bupropion hydrochloride as a smoking cessation aid, which is marketed under the trade name of Zyban, which is manufactured by GlaxoSmithKline after it received original FDA approval on May 14, 1997. The FDA approved an improved sustained release formulation in 2003, which is marketed as Wellbutrin XL and can be taken once per day; in 2006, Wellbutrin XL was also granted FDA approval for treatment of seasonal affective disorder (SAD). The FDA granted approval in April of 2008 for a bupropion hydrobromide formulation, which is manufactured by Sanofi-Aventis and marketed under the trade name of Aplenzin.

Atomoxetine

The history of atomoxetine as an ADHD medication centers around two major issues. These are, respectively, its development and subsequent failure as an antidepressant medicine and then its use as an ADHD medicine.

Development and Failure as an Antidepressant.   Jerry W. Misner of Eli Lilly and Company applied for a patent on February 27, 1985, for a racemization process to quickly and economically produce atomoxetine. Atomoxetine was originally called tomoxetine, but the FDA requested a name change, as they suggested that name was too similar to tamoxifen, a breast cancer medication.

Eli Lilly initially explored the use of atomoxetine as an antidepressant medicine, but it did not demonstrate a sufficient benefit to risk ratio, and development was then ceased for its use in treating individuals with depression.

Application to ADHD.   In response to the lack of success in treatment for depression, Eli Lilly then explored the use of atomoxetine as an ADHD medicine, since it does not have the undesired side effects associated with the use of methylphenidate and the TCAs. A U.S. patent for use of atomoxetine hydrochloride for treating individuals with ADHD was filed in July 17, 1996, and it was granted to John Harrison Heiligenstein and Gary Dennis Tollefson of Eli Lilly and Company on August 19, 1997. Atomoxetine hydrochloride is marketed under the trade name of Strattera by Eli Lilly. There may currently be no generic production of atomoxetine in the United States as it remains under patent protection until 2017.

Antihypertensives

Clonidine and guanfacine, alpha 2 agonists, are two of the major antihypertensive ADHD medications currently used. These particular medications were initially developed to treat hypertension; they were subsequently found to be helpful in treating ADHD; and, then a need for extended release preparations became evident.

Formulation and Original Use as Blood Pressure Medications.   The initial development and application of antihypertensive medications for treating high blood pressure has a long and complex history as many varied antihypertensive pharmacological agents have been found to be effective; these include, in addition to the alpha 2 agonists, diuretics, beta blockers, calcium channel blockers, angiotensin converting enzyme inhibitors, angiotensin II receptor blockers, vasodilators, and direct renin inhibitors, which act, respectively, at different receptors or sites in the body to help lower high blood pressure. The alpha 2 agonists, which are one of the main types of antihypertensive medications used as ADHD medications, stimulate the alpha 2 receptors in the brain to potently lower blood pressure, although they also can cause depression. On September 3, 1974, the FDA approved the use of a clonidine formulation for treating hypertension, which is marketed under the trade name of Catapres and manufactured by Boehringer Ingelheim. On October 27, 1986, the FDA approved the use of a guanfacine formulation for treating hypertension, which is marketed under the trade name of Tenex and manufactured by Promius Pharma.

Application to ADHD. The utility of the alpha 2 agonist antihypertensive medications for treating ADHD was examined in the late 2000s. There is evidence that suggests that the selective alpha 2 adrenergic receptor agonists act directly on the prefrontal cortex of the human brain to enhance executive functioning, which clearly could assist someone with ADHD. Consequently, there was extensive off-label use of immediate release guanfacine hydrochloride (Tenex) and also of clonidine hydrochloride (Catapres) to help treat symptoms of ADHD. Thus, these agents were reformulated for use in treating ADHD. On September 1, 2009, guanfacine hydrochloride was approved by the FDA for treating ADHD and for marketing under the trade name of Intuniv, which is manufactured by Shire.

Formulation of Extended Release Preparation. Clonidine is almost completely absorbed from the gastrointestinal tract when taken orally, but it is subjected to rapid liver metabolism, which results in a relatively short biological half-life with considerable interindividual variability. Consequently, it was recognized that it would be highly advantageous if an extended release process were available for these alpha 2 agonist antihypertensive ADHD medications. A transdermal clonidine patch for clonidine was developed to provide a more stable serum level. On October 13, 1993, H. Joseph Horacek filed a patent for an extended release clonidine formulation tablet with good bioavailability. On September 28, 2010, the FDA approved the use of an extended release clonidine hydrochloride formulation marketed under the trade name of Kapvay, initially manufactured by Shiongi Pharma, now by Concordia Pharmaceuticals, alone or in combination with stimulants for treating ADHD in individuals 6 years to 17 years of age; it was subsequently approved for use in treating adults with ADHD.

Beta Blockers

In 1958, a chemical compound, dichloroisoproterenol, was synthesized at Eli Lilly, and although it had no clinical uses, it was observed that it could block the effects of the catecholamines on stimulating the heart, on relaxing the uterus, and on dilating the bronchioles. In 1962, James Black, a Scottish pharmacologist, and associates working at Imperial Chemical Industries in the United Kingdom, altered dichloroisoproterenol to create pronethalol, the first beta blocker drug. Black was looking for a medicine to relieve the pain of angina pectoris by decreasing the heart's need for oxygen. However, in April of 1961, pronethalol was found to be too toxic, but it was still marketed with restrictions under the trade name of Alderlin beginning in November of

1963. Black soon developed an analogue, a nonselective beta blocking agent, propranolol, which began to be marketed in 1964 under the trade name of Inderal. Propranolol had higher potency and resulted in fewer side effects than proethalol, which was soon pulled from the market. In 1970, Imperial Chemical Industries introduced another beta blocker, practolol, which it marketed under the trade name of Eraldin; Eraldin was removed from the market a few years later after its severe side effects profile was confirmed. In 1998, James Black was awarded the Nobel Prize for Medicine for his work on developing beta blocker drugs. Beta blockers are widely used for treating myriad problems, such as atrial fibrillation, cardiac arrhythmia, congenital heart failure, glaucoma, migraine headaches, and myocardial infarction. They are also misused by many due to their ability to help reduce performance anxiety, such as those engaging in athletic competition, acting, dancing, public speaking, instrumental performance, and singing.

Atenolol.   The drug atenolol is a selective beta blocker, which makes it preferable to other beta blockers for use with individuals with diabetes or peripheral vascular disease. Atenolol was developed in 1976 as a novel selective beta blocker by the Stuart Company, which was a division of Imperial Chemical Industries. Initial FDA approval for use of atenolol in the United States was granted on August 19, 1981; it was marketed under the trade name of Tenormin; generic formulations have been available since 1988, such as the atenolol tablets packaged by companies like Aurobinda Pharma, Caraco Pharmaceutical Laboratories, Ingenus Pharmaceuticals, Mylan Pharmaceuticals, Pack Pharmaceuticals, Ranbaxy Pharmaceuticals, Sandoz, and Watson Laboratories.

Nadolol.   Nadolol is a nonselective beta blocker, which is noted for its extremely long duration of action. On September 25, 1990, Khashayar Karimian of Acic (Canada) Inc. filed a U.S. patent, with a September 25, 1989, priority date, for an improved process of making nadolol of exceptionally high purity. Nadolol is marketed under the trade name of Corgard, which is manufactured by Pfizer; generic formulations are also available.

Propranolol.   Propranolol is the prototypical beta blocking drug, developed as noted earlier by James Black, which has low and dose-dependent bioavailability and, consequently, has proven for many years to be a safe and effective medicine for many indications. Initial FDA approval for use of atenolol in the United States was granted on November 13, 1967, and it was marketed by Akrimax Pharms. Various formulations of propranolol have been developed, some of which, particularly the long acting variants with prolonged absorption over a 24 hour period, are more preferable for use in treating ADHD. Propranol is marketed under the trade name of Inderal; generic formulations are also available and have been since October 22, 1985, such as extended release capsule formulations packaged by companies such as Actavis Elizabeth, Breckenridge Pharmaceutiocal, Cadila Healthycare Limited, Mylan Pharmaceuticals, Nortec Development Associates, Upsher-Smith Laboratories, and Zylas Pharmaceuticals.

Antiobsessives

Pharmacological researchers at Eli Lilly, building upon the pioneering work of Julius Axelrod on neurotransmitter hormones, synthesized the first Selective Serotonin Reuptake Inhibitors (SSRIs) in the 1970s. Beginning in 1970, Bryan Molly and Robert Rathburn were investigating the antidepressant effects of the antihistamine diphenhydramine, which led them to a compound with a similar chemical structure, 3-phenoxy-3-phenylpropylamine. Eli Lilly researchers working under Ray Fuller subsequently synthesized many of its derivatives, including the one that would become fluoxetine. Pharmacologist's David Wong and John Horng of Eli Lilly discovered that fluoxetine oxalate, a compound they had labeled Lilly 82816 in their lab, very selectively inhibited the reuptake of serotonin. Fluoxetine had actually been intentionally designed because based on its three dimensional geometry, it was hoped that it would fit into the neurotransmitter receptor site, which it did for serotonin. It turns out that a related compound, Lilly 110140, fluoxetine hydrochloride was easier to work with and has similar chemical properties. In February of 1977, Dista Products Company, a division of Eli Lilly, filed an Investigational New Drug application with the FDA. Eli Lilly began marketing fluoxetine hydrochloride under the trade name of Prozac in 1988 after being granted FDA approval in December of 1987. Generic formulations of fluoxetine have been available since August of 2001 when its U.S. patent expired. It is also on the WHO List of Essential Medications.

Several other SSRIs followed fluoxetine, several of which are now recognized as ADHD medications. On December 30, 1991, the FDA granted approval for sertraline hydrochloride, which was then marketed under the trade name of Zoloft by Pfizer. On December 29, 1992, the FDA granted approval for paroxetine hydrochloride, which was then marketed under the trade name of Paxil by Apotex Technologies. On December 5, 1994, the FDA granted approval for fluvoxamine maleate, which was then marketed under the trade name of Luvox by Solvay Pharmaceuticals. A New Drug Application form was filed for Celexa, a ciotalopram hydrobromide formulation, on May 7, 1997, by Kathyrn Bishburg of Forest Labs; it was granted FDA approval for sale in the United States on July 17, 1998. On August 14, 2002, the FDA granted approval for escitalopram oxalate, which was then marketed under the trade name of Lexapro by Forest Labs.

The SSRIs are the major antiobsessive ADHD medications. The SSRIs, as just mentioned, were initially released for clinical use in the 1980s, and they quickly became one of the most popular antidepressants since they generally have less adverse side effects than the TCAs and the MAOIs. Prozac earned Eli Lily $350 million in 1989, and it became the most commonly prescribed psychiatric medicine in North America by 1990, and by 1994, it was the second most commonly prescribed medicine in the world, taken by about 10 million people around the globe and reaching $1 billion in annual sales.

Anticonvulsants

Anticonvulsant medications are a broad category of diverse drugs that are all used to help manage seizures in individuals with epilepsy. Some of the specific drug classes that fall under the anticonvulsant rubric include the benzodiazepines, the hydantoins, the succinimides, and others. These diverse pharmacological substances have several different mechanisms of action, but many control the firing of neurons in the brain, thus could potentially be of help in addressing ADHD. Carbamazepine and valporic acid are among the other category of drugs and they are the main anticonvulsant medications that are used for treating individuals with ADHD.

Formulation and Original Use as Antiseizure Medications. The initial formulations and application of these two anticonvulsant medications, carbamazepine and valporic acid, centered on their ability to help control seizures. In 1882, Beverly S. Burton synthesized valporic acid as an analogue of valeric acid, which occurs naturally in the herb valerian. Valporic acid was thought for many years to be metabolically inert and was regularly used in laboratory experiments as a solvent for organic compounds. In 1962, Pierre Eymard, a French scientist, found by accident that valporic acid prevented chemically induced seizures in lab rats. In 1967, it was approved in France as an antiepileptic medicine and is still widely used for such around the world. In 1953, Walter Schindler, a chemist working in Basel, Switzerland, at J. R. Geigy AG, which is now part of Novartis, discovered carbamazepine. Carbamazepine was first marketed in 1963 in Switzerland and marketed under the trade name of Tegretol for use as an anticonvulsant medicine as well as for treating trigeminal neuralgia; it was first used in the United Kingdom in 1965, and was approved by the FDA for use in the United States since 1968. Carbamazepine is sometimes also used for several other psychiatric disorders, such as bipolar depression, depression, posttraumatic stress disorder, alcohol dependence, cocaine dependence, and obsessive compulsive disorders. Both valporic acid and carbamazepine are on the WHO List of Essential Medications.

Application to ADHD.   Following their original formulation and use, it was suspected that these anticonvulsant medications might also be useful for treating ADHD. This was a reasonable expectation due to the fact that these medications substantially alter the firing rate of neurons in the brain, which is how they help to control seizure disorders. Some individuals with ADHD have outbursts of anger and aggressive behaviors and these anticonvulsant medications appear to have calming and maturing effects on them. These anticonvulsant ADHD medications also appear to be helpful in controlling impulsivity. By the 1990s, it was evident that these anticonvulsants were being used successfully around the world with many children and adolescents with ADHD. Certainly, some individuals with ADHD have found that use of an anticonvulsant along with a stimulant ADHD medicine can be effective.

Eugeroics

Modafinil was discovered by Michel Jouvet of Lafon Laboratories in France in the late 1970s who was working on a series of benzhydrl sufinyl compounds, including adrafinil, which was experimented with in 1986 as a treatment for narcolepsy. The primary metabolite of adrafinil is modafinil, which is more commonly used for clinical use. Modafinil was originally designed to assist fighter pilots in staying awake on long missions. In 1994, modafinil was approved for prescription use in France, and it was approved by the FDA for use in the United States on December 24, 1998, for the treating narcolepsy, and, then in 2003, for treating obstructive sleep apnea and shift work sleep disorder; it was also approved for use in the United Kingdom in December of 2002. Modafinil is marketed in the United States under the trade name of Provigil, which is manufactured by Cephalon Inc., which originally leased the rights for and then subsequently purchased Lafon Laboratories in 2001 as well as being marketed under other trade names by other companies and since 2012 has been available in several generic formulations. Modafinil clearly has stimulant effects, which help individuals to stay awake, and it does appear to increase their alertness, but for many, it does not necessarily improve their focus. In 2006, the FDA denied approval for the use of modafinil for treating ADHD in children over concerns about several cases of toxic epidermal necrolysis or Stevens-Johnson syndrome rashes, which are not fatal. Armodafinil is another eugeroic that is a closely related compound that is actually the R enantiomer of modafinil, which has been marketed in the United States since approval by the FDA on June 15, 2007; it is sold under the trade name of Nuvigil, which is also manufactured by Cephalon.

Monoamine Oxidase Inhibitors

The MAOI, and also the first one used in psychiatric treatment, was iproniazid. Iproniazid was initially developed as an antitubercular medicine, but in the 1950s, some psychiatrists observed that it helped increase energy and sociability in some previously lethargic, depressed patients. The fact is that some users of iproniazid experienced euphoria, and hyperactivity led to its application initially for treating depressive disorders and then later for individuals with what we now recognize as ADHD.

The initial success of iproniazid led to the development of several other MAOIs. The classic nonselective, irreversible MAOIs were introduced next; these included isocarboxazid, phenelzine, and tranylcypromine. Tranylcypromine was first synthesized in 1948 as an analog of amphetamine, but its MAOI effects were not discovered until 1959; it was introduced in the United Kingdom in 1960, and it was approved by the FDA for use in the United States in 1961, when it was marketed under the trade name of Parnate. On July 1, 1959, FDA approval was granted for the use of isocarboxazid in the United States, which was marketed under the trade name of Marplan and manufactured by Validus Pharms. On June 9, 1961, phenelzine sulfate was approved for use in the United States and marketed under the trade name of Nardil, which was manufactured by Parke Davis. Iproniazid was withdrawn from the U.S. market in 1961 amid concerns over reports of jaundice and of kidney and liver toxic effects. Similarly, tranylcypromine developed by Smith, Kline, and French was withdrawn from the U.S. market in 1964.

The problems experience with the classic MAOIs led to the development of newer MAOIs, particularly the selective MAOIs, some of which are reversible. Moclobemide was discovered in Switzerland in 1972; it was unsuccessfully experimented with as an antibiotic, an anticholesterol drug, an antidepressant, and an antipsychotic, and then its MAOI properties were discovered; it was first approved for use in Europe and is now approved in more than 50 countries around the world, but not in the United States. Selegine is a selective

MAOI that was discovered by Z. Ecseri in the early 1960s in Hungary; it was approved by the FDA for use in the United States on June 5, 1989. Rasagiline mesylate is a selective, irreversible MAOI that was invented in 1979 by Aspro Nicholas; it was approved in 2005 by the European Medications Agency, and it was approved by the FDA for use in the United States on May 16, 2006, and is marketed under the trade name of Azilect, which is manufactured by Teva Pharmaceuticals.

Antipsychotics

Typical and atypical antipsychotic medications used for treating schizophrenia that have a high affinity for serotonin receptors have been shown to be useful in treating ADHD. One of the first effective antipsychotic medications was lithium, which was introduced for clinical use in 1949 by an Australian psychiatrist J. F. J. Cade, but its popularity did not begin to soar until the middle of the 1960s when its effectiveness in treating bipolar disorder became evident. Chlorpromazine was first synthesized on December 11, 1950, by Paul Charpentier, a French chemist working at *Laboratoires Rhone-Poulenc* with a team of researchers looking for effective antihistamines. Chlorpromazine hydrochloride was initially marketed in France under the trade name of Largoctil, but it was first used in anesthesia, before its tranquilizing and antipsychotic effects became evident. Chlorpromazine was released for clinical testing on May 2, 1951, and its first use for a psychiatric condition was on January 19, 1952, at a Parisian military hospital, Val De Grace. By the 1960s, chlorpromazine hydrochloride and several related phenothiazine drugs were being used to treat schizophrenia and similar psychiatric disorders. Chlorpromazine was marketed in the United States under the trade name of Thorazine.

The search for other antipsychotic medications proceeded in earnest after the success of chlorpromazine. On February 11, 1958, haloperidol was first synthesized by Paul Jansesen, the Belgian pharmacologist who founded Janssen Pharmaceutica; he and his team of researchers were experimenting with pethidine in search of a more potent painkiller; by 1959, it was being recommended for treating conditions like delusional psychoses, mania, and paranoid psychoses. On April 12, 1967, the FDA granted approval for marketing in the United States of haloperidol under the trade name of Haldol, which was manufactured by Ortho McNeil. Clozapine was developed by researchers at Sandoz in 1961, and they were granted approval by the FDA on August 30, 1996, to manufacture oral tablets of clozapine, which they manufactured and sold under the trade name of Clozaril. A U.S. patent was filed on February 5,

1986, by Ludo E. J. Kennis and Jan Vandenberk of Janssen Pharmaceutica for synthesis of risperidone. In 1993, the FDA granted approval for the use of risperidone in the United States for treating schizophrenia, and it was marketed as Risperdal, which is manufactured by Janssen Pharmaceuticals. On December 29, 2003, the U.S. patent on risperidone expired and generic versions became available; then on August 22, 2007, it was approved as the first drug available for treating schizophrenia in individuals aged 13 years to 17 years old, and it was approved on the same day for treating bipolar disorder in those aged 10 years to 17 years; in 2006, risperidone was approved for treating irritability in children and adolescents with autism. Risperidone is listed on the WHO List of Essential Medications. Olanzapine pamoate was approved by the FDA in September 1996 for use in the United States for treating psychotic disorders; in March 2000, for short-term treatment of bipolar I disorder; and in November 2000, for treating schizophrenia. It is marketed in the United States under the trade name of Zyprexa, which is manufactured by Eli Lilly. Quetiapine fumarate was developed by AstraZeneca, which was granted initial approval from the FDA for treating schizophrenia in 1997 and marketing it under the trade name of Seroquel. Aripiprazole was developed by Otsuka in Japan and approved by the FDA on November 15, 2002, for treating schizophrenia and is marketed in the United States under the trade name of Abilify, which is manufactured jointly by an agreement between Otsuka and Bristol-Myers Squibb. The U.S. patent for aripiprazole expired on October 20, 2014, but due to a pediatric extension, generic versions were not available until April 20, 2015. These antipsychotic medications are frequently used off label for treating children and adults with ADHD.

Cholinergic Agents

There is increasing evidence that neuronal nicotinic acetylcholine receptors (nAChRs) may play a role in the pathophysiology of ADHD. Nicotine, in particular, has demonstrated positive effects on cognition in both human and laboratory animal subjects, including in small clinical trials on adults with ADHD. Nicotine was first isolated from tobacco in 1828 by Wilhelm H. Posselt and Karl L. Reimann; its chemical structure was discovered in 1893 by Adolf Pinner and Richard Wolffenstein; and, in 1904, it was first synthesized by Ame Pictet and A. Rotschy. However, undesired side effects associated with nicotine (Nicorette) preclude its general use as a therapeutic agent, other than, perhaps, for smoking cessation. Nevertheless, other cholinergic agents have been examined for their safety and efficacy in treating ADHD. For example, pozaniciline or ABT-089, a weak partial neuronal nicotinic receptor agonist, has been demonstrated to be both safe and effective for treating ADHD. Another cholinergic agent, ABT-418, also a nicotinic analog, demonstrated both safety and efficacy in treating ADHD in children and adults.

Other Medications

There are other assorted types of medications that may occasionally be used off label to help alleviate symptoms of ADHD. One example of this is a drug that has been around for some time, the cholinergic agent nicotine. Many herbal treatments, nutritional approaches, and other medicinal cures are also experimented with from time to time to expand our repertoire of approaches to successfully address ADHD and related conditions. It is important to remember that off-label prescribing occurs when a medicine is used outside of its scope of marketing authorization with respect to factors such as the disorder being treated, the demographics, primarily age, of the individual being administered, the dosage and route of administration being used, and the duration of the treatment. Off-label use is fundamentally use of licensed medications for an unlicensed indication; it is actually rather common, and should not be assumed to be reckless or inappropriate. Healthcare providers must use their professional judgment routinely in devising a treatment strategy for possibly assisting any particular individual with ADHD or any other condition. Old medications that had other recognized uses and new medications for which no use may yet be approved will certainly continue to be applied in efforts to personalize the best treatment for any one individual with ADHD. This has always been how medical knowledge has been advanced and clearly is how many drugs now recognized as ADHD medications were identified as such.

Chapter 4

How ADHD Medications Work

In order to gain a fuller understanding of how respective attention deficit hyperactivity disorder (ADHD) medications work, it would be useful to learn something about the process of neurotransmission, including some of the monoamine neurotransmitter substances, specifically norepinephrine, dopamine, and serotonin. This foundation would be helpful to more adequately comprehend how the varied mechanisms of action of these medications operate. More specifically to better understand how the respective psychostimulant, antidepressant, antihypertensive, antiobsessive, anticonvulsant, eugeroic, monoamine oxidase (MAO) inhibitor, antipsychotic, and cholinergic ADHD medications function to assist individuals with ADHD.

OVERVIEW OF NEUROTRANSMISSION

In order to better understand how respective ADHD medications work, it is first important to understand something about how the human brain and nervous system functions. The primary nerve cells that our brain and nervous system are composed of are called neurons, which communicate with each other by means of electrical and chemical signals. The average adult human brain weighs approximately 1,400 grams, or about 3.09 pounds, and has an average volume of 1,600 cm cube; it consists of around a billion neurons arranged in complex ways in order to transmit and receive electrochemical signals. These messages are how signals get to the brain and how they are processed as well as how the responses are sent. The brain can send out messages to the rest of the body at a speed of 268 miles per hour to direct us how to respond to these stimuli. Brain function depends on the interaction of these numerous neurons with each other and with other specialized cells.

Each individual neuron has several major components. Dendrites can be regarded as the beginning of the neuron; they extend out from the cell body in branchlike extensions, and they have specialized receptor sites where the chemical messages from neighboring neurons can be received. Small extensions spread out in all directions from our brain's dendrites. A single dendrite may have up to 30,000 small extensions that are dispersed outward in order to be able to receive signals from nearby receptor sites and from other neurons. The dendrites are involved with making new connections continuously and with severing old connections; this dynamic process is how human learning and memory takes place throughout our lifespan. However, some neurons have no dendrites at all and, accordingly, are referred to as unipolar neurons, while those with a single dendrite are referred to as a bipolar neuron, and the majority, that is those with more than one dendrite, are referred to as multipolar neurons. Ganglia that are located in the spinal dorsal root and those located in the cranial nerves generally tend to be unipolar. The cell body of the neuron is referred to as the soma; it hosts the cell nucleus and the usual cytoplasmic organelles, which, accordingly, helps it to conduct activities such as those that are related to metabolism and to other basic internal cellular functions. The region between the cell body and the axon is commonly referred to as the axon hillock. Most of the length of the neuron is supplied by the axon, which serves as the pathway along which the electrical message of the action potential is transmitted; the axon extends out from the soma and terminates at the synaptic terminals. Axons can span up to 5,000 cell diameters. Each neuron usually has a single axon that can range from 0.05 inches (0.127 cm) to over 3 feet (nearly 1 m) in length. Bundles of these axons located in the peripheral nervous system are commonly called nerves, while those in the brain and spinal cord of the central nervous system are generally referred to as tracts. The synaptic terminals, which are also referred to as terminal boutons, buttons, or as presynaptic endings, are specialized protuberances that contain the endogenously produced neurotransmitter substances, which are held in sack-like structures that are called the vesicles. The neurotransmitters are signaled for release, or exocytosis, by the action potential that converts the electrical message within the neuron into a chemical signal that can be transmitted onward to the next neuron. The synaptic vesicles are round membrane granule sacks that house the particular neurotransmitter molecules that are available and waiting to be released at or near the synaptic junction. The Golgi complex of the neuron is responsible for packaging many of the neurotransmitter substances into the respective synaptic vesicles. An electrical message normally travels down a neuron to open up calcium ion channels in the synaptic terminal, this causes the vesicle to move toward and to then fuse with the neural membrane; the particular neurotransmitter substance can then be released into the synapse, a process that is known as exocytosis. The surfaces of the receptive regions of most brain neurons can potentially be exposed to thousands of synapses. Synapses, which are also called synaptic clefts or gap junctions, are the spaces that are located between neighboring neurons. In 1897, Charles Sherrington was the first person to refer to the junction between nerve cells as a synapse. A synapse is generally only about an 18 millionth of an inch wide, or roughly 50 nanometers. It is estimated that a normal human brain contains more than a hundred trillion synapses; these junctions form a very large number of potential connections through which brain signals could possibly be transmitted. There are both excitatory and inhibitory synapses; the former typically have round vesicles, while the latter are characterized by their flatter vesicles. Different ADHD medications affect the functioning of different parts of our neurons in many varied ways.

There are specialized neurons that have very short axons or some that even have no axon at all, and these latter ones are referred to as interneurons; they work mainly by coordinating neuronal activity within a particular structure of the human brain, rather than by transmitting messages from one brain structure to another. There are perhaps about a thousand different kinds of specialized neurons. In fact, no single neuron is exactly the same as any other; they differ in shape, in the particular threshold necessary for them to fire, and with respect to other critical variables.

The release and uptake of specific neurotransmitter substances is how individual neurons are able to communicate across the synaptic space. Neurotransmitter substances are continually produced, released, broken down, and recaptured as the dynamic communication between neurons takes place. In 1921, Otto Loewi concluded that the signal transmitted across the synapse was of a chemical nature rather than electrical; he referred to the chemical substance that carried the message as a neurotransmitter and identified the particular compound involved as acetylcholine. More than 60 different types of neurotransmitters have already been identified and more no doubt will be discovered in the future; in fact, it has been estimated that there may be upward of 2,000 or more different specific neurotransmitter substances. There are two major groups of these neurotransmitter substances, respectively, the excitatory and the inhibitory ones. The excitatory neurotransmitters, like glutamate, usually stimulate adjacent neurons to fire, while the inhibitory neurotransmitters generally tend to block their firing. Most of the neurotransmitter substances employed at fast acting, directed synaptic clefts are amino acids, like aspartate, gamma-aminobutyric acid (GABA), glutamate, and glycine; as compared to the neuropeptides, like dynorphins, substance P, and the relatively small enkephalins, such as leucine and merhionine, which tend to have slower and more diffuse effects. For example, GABA is an inhibitory neurotransmitter that mediates gate control in the dorsal horn by activating synapsing neurons that release substance P; while glutamate, an excitatory neurotransmitter, produces a small conductance increase for sodium and potassium ions. Further, a specific neurotransmitter may be excitatory at one location and inhibitory at another, depending in large part on the type of receptor that it eventually binds to. Bernard Katz found that neurotransmitters are released in discrete packets of an approximately standard size, which is about 10,000 molecules of the respective substance. In addition to neurotransmitter substances, there are several other chemical messengers that can influence the type, the strength, the frequency, and the magnitude of neuronal signaling, these types of substances include neuromediators, neuromodulators, and neuroregulators.

After crossing a synaptic cleft, each respective neurotransmitter substance must attempt to bind to a specific type of synaptic receptor site located on the postsynaptic membrane. There is about a 1 millisecond delay for a signal sent by means of release of a neurotransmitter to be transmitted to the next neuron. Each receptor site consists of a respective protein that has places to which only a particular neurotransmitter substance can bind. However, it must be recognized that any particular type of neurotransmitter substance can usually bind to several potentially different subtypes of receptor sites. Any neurotransmitter substance that does not successfully bind at a receptor site must quickly be eliminated from the synaptic space. Some neurotransmitters are effectively removed through reuptake where they are drawn back into the presynaptic neuron. Other neurotransmitter substances are broken down by enzymes, the products of which are then recycled for use in the production of new neurotransmitter substances. For example, the neurotransmitter acetylcholine is degraded by the enzyme acetylcholinesterase, which was first identified by David Nachmansohn in 1938. ADHD medications can inhibit, or increase, at many different points, the synthesis, release, action, and deactivation of respective neurotransmitter substances.

Neurons continually monitor the levels of the two respective types of neurotransmitter substances. When the total amount of the excitatory neurotransmitters exceeds that of the inhibitory ones by a crucial extent, then the neuron can successfully transmit its signal onward to the next neuron along the neural pathway. When the incoming signal finally reaches the brain, neurons in respective regions of the brain must be activated for the message to be perceived. While there is an intimate relationship between the firing of respective brain neurons and the eventual perception of these signals, there are myriad cognitive factors that can impact what meanings that will eventually be attributed to that particular stimuli, as well as help the individual to formulate a suitable reaction. Furthermore, contrary to the rather widespread misunderstanding, nearly all parts of our brain are continually being accessed much of the time by the dynamic firing of many different neurons.

Neurons transmit electrical messages down their length, these are then translated into chemical messages that can be sent across the synaptic cleft, the junction between two or more adjacent neurons. The message travels down the length of the axon of the neuron as an electrical signal, which, as it gets to the terminal end, stimulates the presynaptic vesicles, those specialized secretory sacks that are situated at or near the synaptic terminal and which contain the respective neurotransmitter substances, to be released as their chemical messengers. The electrical messages travel down the length of the axon at a speed of up to 410 feet (125 m) per second.

The electrical message that is carried along the length of the axon is also referred to as a nerve impulse or as an action potential, as it will, hopefully, be able to change the electrical signal into a chemical one at the end of the dendritic branches, an area that is referred to as the synaptic terminal. This action potential only has a relatively short duration of about 1 millisecond. The axon of many, but not of all, neurons is coated with a myelin sheath that consists of a lipid bilayer embedded with specialized proteins; it essentially serves as an insulator. Myelination enables a neuron to transmit its electrical signals more efficiently. There are two major types of these membrane proteins; some function as signal proteins that transfer messages to the inside of the neuron after specific molecules from outside the neuron successfully bind to them; the other kind are known as channel proteins, since certain molecules can readily pass through them. Spaces between parts of the myelin sheath are referred to as nodes of Ranvier. Schwann cells, also known as the neurolimma, perform the myelination of axons of the peripheral nervous system outside of the brain. Neurons that are covered with a myelin sheath can transmit their signals over a hundred times faster than those without it.

Ions in solution cannot readily pass through the myelin sheath on their own as its membrane serves as an effective insulator. The solution outside of the neuron is known as extracellular fluid, while that inside the neuron is known as the intracellular fluid. Both extracellular and intracellular fluids have positive as well as negative ions dissolved in them, and they are generally unequally distributed across the cell membrane, which gives the neurons an electrical charge. Positive ions include those of calcium (Ca), potassium (K), and sodium (Na), while chloride (Cl) is a negatively charged ion. The difference between the electrical charge on the inside of the resting neuron and that on the outside, which is referred to as its resting potential, is about 70 millivolts. The neuron, at that point, is said to be polarized so that there can be a perpetuation of the electrical impulse.

Ions tend to flow naturally, on their own, from places of higher concentration to those of lower concentrations, which is otherwise referred to as moving down their concentration gradient. Ions, fundamentally, are types of salts that are distributed in varying concentrations throughout different parts of the body, including, in this case, inside and outside of the neurons. These positive and negatively charged ions pass through the membrane linings of our neurons by flowing through specialized pores that are called ion channels. This dynamic exchange of charged ions is fundamentally necessary for the normal functioning of our neurons. Since these ions are charged either positively or negatively, their relative concentration levels establish varying electrical potentials. Ion channels can be closed by either low pH or by a high concentration of calcium ions.

Protein pumps exist in order to help us to be able to maintain the crucial ionic imbalance. An important example of this is the sodium-potassium pump, which pumps out the influx of sodium ions that flowed into the neurons and pumps in potassium ions that tend to efflux, or flow out, of the neurons. Some neurotransmitter substances have been found to close or open up ion channels, which permits quick changes to the electrical states of neurons. Neurotransmitters that carry a positive charge can depolarize the membrane potential of the receptive neurons by flowing through the sodium channel, while those that carry a negative charge can increase, or hyperpolarize, the membrane potential traveling through the potassium channel. Depolarization is achieved when the postsynaptic membrane achieves a voltage of approximately 0.0005 volts. This depolarization and hyperpolarization serves to recharge the electrical potential of the neuron. This quick change of positive or negative charges is how an electrical signal is transmitted down the axon. As sodium ions enter the upper areas of the neuron, the neuron becomes excited, or depolarized, then as the potassium ions are passed to the out of the neuron, it becomes inhibited, or hyperpolarized. This electrical charge exchanging continues down along the length of the axon, when it reaches the terminal of the neuron, the vesicles there are stimulated to release their neurotransmitter chemical contents. In this manner, the electrical message is changed into a chemical message, which, in turn, can be sent across the synaptic space to the next neuron along the neural pathway. The postsynaptic depolarization is referred to as an excitatory postsynaptic potential, while postsynaptic hyperpolarization is referred to as an inhibitory postsynaptic potential; the former increases the chances that the receptive neuron will fire and the latter decreases this likelihood.

Neurotransmitter substances flow within the synaptic cleft and, hopefully, can bind successfully to receptor sites situated on the next neuron along the circuit, or neural pathway. A receptor site consists of highly specialized proteins, which can be activated by a specific neurotransmitter or closely related chemical substance, like, perhaps, an illicit drug. Receptor sites can be gated by carrier proteins, enzymes, guanine coupling, or ion channels. Furthermore, there are also myriad intracellular hormone gates; any receptor site gate can contribute to a difference in the firing rate of that particular neuron. Neurons located in the brain and those located in the rest of the central nervous system typically fire at a rate of about once every four milliseconds. The released ions crossing the synapse will, depending on their electrical charge, begin to either inhibit or stimulate an excitation in the postsynaptic neuron. Neurons can integrate, or combine, many individual signals from disparate other neurons into one overall transmission signal. They accomplish this process by means of either spatial summation or through temporal summation of the received transmissions. Each neuron must constantly integrate electrochemical signals over both space and time as they are continuously bombarded with stimuli across potentially many thousands of synapses. When enough of the neurotransmitters successfully bind to receptor sites, a new electrical signal is generated in the receiving neuron and this impulse makes it way down that axon to repeat the process all over again, and so on down along the neural pathway. At high levels of continual stimulation, each neuron can fire up to a rate of nearly a thousand times each second. In addition, some neurons can release more than one type of neurotransmitter substance. If the neurotransmitters fail to bind, hopefully, they are reabsorbed by means of reuptake mechanisms so that they can be recycled at a later time and, also, so that they do not continue to transmit the message that caused them to be released initially; or, if not reabsorbed, then they should be degraded by enzymes. The peptide neurotransmitters, including the monoamines, are the ones typically degraded as they are synthesized as precursors; while the classic neurotransmitters, like acetylcholine and the catecholamines, which are synthesized in the nerve terminals, are typically recycled. The half-life of circulating catecholamines is relatively short and estimated to range from between 10 seconds to 1.7 minutes. Metabolism of catecholamines primarily occurs in the cytoplasm of the same neurons where they were synthesized after release from secretory vesicles. At any rate, the respective neurotransmitter systems have numerous complex interactions with one another, and it is indeed possible that ADHD is caused by imbalances in any number of known, or as yet unknown, systems.

ADHD medications fundamentally work by altering the chemical balance of the brain. Interestingly, some of both the stimulant and the nonstimulant

ADHD medications, such as methylphenidate and atomoxetine, appear to share somewhat similar mechanisms of action and both seem somewhat comparable with respect to the extent to which they help to normalize the reduced activity within the critical frontal regions of the brain in individuals with ADHD. Methylphenidate, for instance, blocks both the dopamine and the norepinephrine transporters, while atomoxetine blocks just the norepinephrine transporter. Thus, both methylphenidate and atomoxetine can block the reuptake of norepinephrine, but they nevertheless do differ somewhat in the extent to which they can raise levels of cortical dopamine. Accordingly, both methylphenidate and atomoxetine can potentially improve activation of the brain when one is trying to make fine temporal distinctions, but they affect time estimation performance differentially, with methylphenidate positively improving behavior in a manner superior to that of atomoxetine.

MONOAMINES

The monoamines are any of the various biogenic amine neurotransmitters and neuromodulators that contain a single amino group, which is connected to an aromatic ring by a two carbon chain. The monoamine neurotransmitters, which include dopamine, epinephrine, norepinephrine, and serotonin, are all derived from aromatic amino acids. There are two major classes of monoamines, the catecholamines and the indolamines, respectively. The catecholamines, like dopamine and norepinephrine, are synthesized from amino acids, like phenylalanine and tyrosine, and they act mainly within the sympathetic and central nervous systems. The various central nervous system stimulant drugs function essentially as catecholamine analogues. The indolamines are represented by serotonin and function in many body tissues, not only including the brain but also the lining of the gastrointestinal tract and blood platelets. The function of the monoamine neurotransmitter substances is thought to be related to psychological processes like arousal, cognition, and emotion. The monoamines are naturally broken down by the MAO enzymes. Most ADHD medications target their actions to either augment or to reduce the effects of monoamines.

The monoamine theory of depression is a related area of concern that posits that a decrease in serotonergic and noradrenergic neurotransmission is the fundamental cause of depression. The selective serotonin reuptake inhibitors (SSRIs), a class of ADHD medications, typically have a rapid, almost instantaneous, onset of action at their molecular and cellular sites of action; this results in an increase in the availability of these neurotransmitters at the synaptic clefts. There are actually 14 different types of serotonin receptors. One of these is the 5-HT 1A receptor, when it is stimulated, it inhibits the firing of serotonergic neurons, thus serving as an autoreceptor inhibiting serotonergic activity. The serotonin transporter is a monoamine transporter protein, which is blocked by SSRIs and several other antidepressant medications. This blockage results in increased serotonin availability in the synapse. In response to this synaptic increase, the serotonergic neurons will reduce the number of 5-HT 1A receptors available. This downregulation can take a couple of weeks, which helps to explain why there is usually a delay in the observance of the therapeutic effects of SSRIs after initial administration. This serotonin reduction, once finally achieved, effectively disinhibits the neurons from releasing more serotonin into the synaptic junctions.

Norepinephrine

Norepinephrine, which is also referred to as noradrenalin and as 4-[(1R)-2-amino-1-hydroxyethyl]benzene-1,2-diol, is composed of one amine group and a catechol nucleus, which consists of a benzene ring with two hydroxyl groups. Norepinephrine is synthesized by means of hydroxylation of dopamine in noradrenergic neurons, known as phenochromocytes, in the adrenal medulla, and it, in turn, is synthesized into epinephrine. The hydroxylation of dopamine is accomplished by the enzyme dopamine beta hydroxylase, which is a membrane-bound enzyme located in synaptic vesicles and that use vitamin C as a cofactor. A major structural difference between norepinephrine and epinephrine is that the former contains a hydrogen atom, while the latter contains a methyl group; this methylation is accomplished by the enzyme phenylethanolamine N-methyltransferase, modulated by adjacent adrenal steroid production. A major functional difference is that norepinephrine affects the brain while epinephrine does not.

Norepinephrine in the brain is produced mainly in the locus coeruleus, which is situated in the pons of the brain stem, and activity in which is associated with vigilance and reaction speed, therefore helps to govern moods and our sense of satisfaction. There are six major noradrenergic tracts that project from the locus coeruleus to, respectively, the hypothalamus, thalamus, limbic system, cerebellum, neocortex, and spinal cord. Norepinephrine in the brain enhances attention, processing of sensory inputs, increases alertness, feelings of happiness, formation and retrieval of memory, and the ability to respond to stimuli by altering activity in the prefrontal cortex and elsewhere, all of which are critical in ADHD. Norepinephrine also increases heart rate, and decreases blood circulation and feelings of pain. Excessively high levels of norepinephrine have been implicated in causing manic states, while a deficiency of norepinephrine is associated with certain depressive states.

Following the synthesis of norepinephrine, much of it binds with adenosine triphosphate (ATP) and is stored in granules of nerve terminals. After release, norepinephrine attempts to bind to alpha 1, alpha 2, beta 1, or beta 2 receptor sites situated on postsynaptic cells, or to alpha 2 presynaptic receptors on noradrenergic cells. The sensitivity of these receptors is altered by various factors, including the level of and the duration of neuronal exposure to norepinephrine. Norepinephrine can hyperpolarize neurons by enhancing potassium conductance; this effect is mediated by either alpha or beta receptors.

The important role of the proper functioning of the alpha 2 receptors in the prefrontal cortex to ADHD is supported by experimental laboratory evidence. When neuroscientists directly infuse yohimbine, which is an indole alkaloidal drug and a potent alpha 2 antagonist, to the prefrontal cortex of monkeys, all of the core symptoms of ADHD are produced. These symptoms include weakened impulse control, impaired working memory to control distractions, and increased locomotor hyperactivity. These findings support the critical importance of normal endogenous norepinephrine stimulation of the alpha 2 receptor sites in the prefrontal cortex to our ability to adequately regulate our actions and attention. In the same vein, it supports the use of alpha 2 agonists, like clonidine (Kapvay) and guanfacine (Intuniv), in individuals with ADHD to control these core symptoms of the disorder.

The alpha 2 receptor is an autoreceptor that regulates norepinephrine release. After norepinephrine is released, it is either inactivated by the reuptake mechanisms or degraded by specific enzymes; one of the primary enzymes responsible for this is MAO, which is situated in the synaptic spaces, the other enzyme is catechol-o-methyl transferase (COMT), with vanillylmandelic acid being one of the main end products. Some drugs act as norepinephrine agonists, like clonidine, while others act as antagonists, like phenoxybenzamine. Several central nervous system stimulant agents, like amphetamine and cocaine, will increase norepinephrine levels, as will the tricyclic antidepressant (TCA) agent desipramine. Many ADHD medications have secondary effects upon norepinephrine, and for some, it is the target of their primary effect. Low levels of norepinephrine have been associated with loss of alertness and memory problems; these are some of the core characteristics of individuals with ADHD.

Dopamine

Dopamine, also known as 4-(2-aminoethyl)benzene-1,2-diol, is a catecholamine neurotransmitter that is synthesized from either the precursor non-essential amino acid tyrosine or the essential amino acid phenylalanine in dopaminergic neurons. Dopamine is a neuropeptide that is mainly released from the parvicellular neuron terminals located in the median eminence of the brain. Dopamine tends to be found mostly in the substantia nigra and the ventral tegmental area of the basal ganglia of the midbrain, thus can play a crucial role in regulating emotions such as arousal and pleasure; it is also released in the nucleus accumbens and the prefrontal cortex; other dopaminergic neuronal systems have been identified in the hypothalamus, the pituitary gland, the olfactory system, and the retinal system. About 80 percent of the brain's dopamine is contained in the nigrostriatal system, which projects from the pars compacta of the substantia nigra to terminals that innervate the striatum, both the caudate and the putamen, which are both involved in motor pathways. The ventral tegmental area innervates many forebrain areas, the most relevant of which to ADHD is by means of dopaminergic neurons to the nucleus accumbens. This mesolimbic pathway plays a crucial role in emotions, motivation, and reward. Dopamine functions as a neuromodulator in the brain's reward system. However, abnormally high levels of dopamine released for an extended period of time can lead to down regulation of the dopaminergic receptor sites in the mesolimbic neural pathway; this can lead to diminished sensitivity to both natural reinforcers, like eating and sex, as well as to that often associated with abusive use of psychoactive substances, which, in turn, can progress to addiction with the user likely to be both dissatisfied with the substance use and somewhat depressed. Another dopaminergic neural pathway projects from the ventral tegmental area to the prefrontal cortex; this mesocortical pathway in the dorsolateral prefrontal cortex appears to be related to cognition and to executive functioning, and in the ventromedial prefrontal cortex to affect and to emotions.

The functioning of dopamine in the forebrain structures that is of most concern in ADHD is that it pertains to the regulation of arousal and of attention. Dopamine is important in this regard as it both lowers the threshold needed to evoke a behavior and creates a reward for an action making it easier to evoke again; it accomplishes this feat primarily by increasing the feelings of happiness. Dopamine also decreases feelings of hunger. A deficiency in dopamine is thought to be responsible for some of the core symptoms that are associated with ADHD such as difficulties in inhibiting behaviors, problems regulating attention, and in remembering things. Excess synaptic dopamine is removed by a dopamine transporter; that dopamine is then either repackaged into synaptic vesicles for later release or else it is degraded by the MAO enzyme.

Several psychotropic drugs are chemically similar enough to dopamine to masquerade in its place. Amphetamine, methylphenidate, and cocaine, three examples, use the dopamine transporter as a critical site of action, such that by binding to the transporter they can significantly alter dopamine levels in the neural synapses. Some drugs act as dopamine agonists, like apomorphine, while others act as antagonists, like haloperidol. In this vein, the hallucinogenic drug mescaline, as found in peyote, is sufficiently structurally similar to dopamine to mimic its effects, while antipsychotic agents, like chlorpromazine and reserpine, decrease dopamine levels.

Dopamine has other effects in other parts of the body; in blood vessels, for example, it inhibits norepinephrine and serves as a vasodilator at normal levels, while in the pancreas, it reduces insulin production, and in the kidneys, it increases the excretion of sodium and enhances urine production. Dopamine is broken down by enzymatic degradation accomplished by MAO, COMT, and aldehyde dehydrogenase, with the main final end product being homovanillic acid. Low levels of dopamine have been associated with cognitive impairment and the inability to focus; these are, of course, some of the core hallmarks of ADHD.

Serotonin

Serotonin, also known as 5-hydrooxytryptamine (5-HT) or 3-(2-Aminoethyl)-1H-indol-5-ol, is biochemically derived from tryptophan, and it is synthesized in the brain mainly in, thus found in high concentrations in, the Raphe nuclei, which are situated along the midline of the pons and the upper brain stem and centered around the reticular formation. Serotonin, accordingly, serves to control basal life functions like appetite, sensory perception, pain, body temperature, and the onset of sleep; it is also involved in cognitive functions like memory and learning, which are more directly associated with ADHD as well as with feelings of happiness and fullness. Several ADHD medications modulate the synaptic activity of serotonin; these include many of the TCAs, the SSRIs, and the monoamine oxidase inhibitors (MAOIs). The hallucinogenic drug lysergic acid diethylamide (LSD) is sufficiently structurally similar serotonin, as both have a two ring indole shape, to be able to mimic its effects and to act as an agonist, as do several other hallucinogenic drugs, like DMT and psilocybin, and the TCA agent imipramine. In the brain, serotonin is not typically degraded but is removed by means of reuptake accomplished by serotonin transporters located on the surfaces of serotonergic neurons; outside of the brain enzymatic degradation is initiated by MAO, which is followed by that of aldehyde dehydrogenase, with the main final end product being the indole acetic acid derivative 5-HIAA produced primarily by the liver and then excreted by the kidneys.

MECHANISMS OF ACTION

Mechanism of action refers to the specific biochemical processes by means of which a drug produces its pharmacological effects. The mechanism of action, more specifically, refers to how a specific drug interacts with a specific molecular target, such as with receptors, enzymes, and other physiological sites, as well as implying a causative chain of the results of this biochemical action, such as causing activation, agonism, antagonism, inhibition, and so forth. Many substances can, in fact, produce pharmacological effects and simply put the neuropharmacological mechanism of action is how a specific substance, like an ADHD medicine, creates its effects.

General Concepts

The mechanism of action of respective medications, or drugs, targets variable physiological processes, particularly those at the neuronal synaptic level. The first drug identified to do this was curare, an arrow poison, which was found to block nicotinic neuromuscular transmission by its ability to bind to receptor sites for acetylcholine. Antipsychotic medications, for instance, generally seem to block dopamine transmission, while minor tranquilizers, like the benzodiazepine antianxiety medications, typically block GABA receptors.

A mode of action is a narrower, more constrained term that describes the anatomical or functional changes, generally at the cellular level, that typically results from exposure to a specific drug. Many stimulant substances, such as those containing caffeine or nicotine, will trigger a release of dopamine and thereby reinforce its reward effects. Caffeine has a chemical structure that is very similar to that of adenosine, a natural brain neurotransmitter substance. Caffeine binds to the adenosine receptor sites in the brain, which blocks access to adenosine. Adenosine makes us drowsy and depresses brain activity. Thus, as the presence of caffeine blocks adenosine from binding to its receptors, brain activity is accelerated when caffeine is present. Accordingly, it is primarily the mechanism of action, and, to a somewhat lesser extent generally, the mode of action of a particular drug that helps to determine how it will work when administered to individuals.

There appear to be some general commonalities in the mechanism of action for most ADHD medications, both for the stimulant and the nonstimulant medications, which primarily involves either the direct or indirect attenuation of dopamine and/or norepinephrine neurotransmission. However, there are important distinctions both between and within the varied classes of ADHD medications. A better understanding of the myriad mechanisms of action of respective ADHD medications could help in tailoring their likely pharmacological response to individualized profiles. Some ADHD medications are more targeted toward the release of respective neurotransmitter substances, while others are more involved with altering the reuptake of these substances.

Psychostimulants

The central nervous system stimulant drugs are among the most widely used type of pharmacological agents. The neuropharmacological mechanism of action of central nervous system stimulant medications, like amphetamine (Dyanavel XR) and methylphenidate (Ritalin), appears primarily to stimulate presynaptic inhibitory autoreceptors resulting in reduced activity in dopaminergic and noradrenergic pathways, particularly in those running from the locus coeruleus to the prefrontal cortex. Amphetamine, for example, promotes the release of the catecholamine neurotransmitter substances, particularly by focusing on the adrenergic nerve terminals; it binds to the transporters of the biogenic amines, respectively, the dopamine transporter, the norepinephrine transporter, the serotonin transporter, and the vesicular monoamine transporter. More generally, amphetamines have a similar chemical structure to dopamine and the other internally produced catecholamines, therefore tend to cause similar effects. More specifically put, use of psychostimulants, as a class, tends to increase the release and inhibit the reuptake of dopamine, norepinephrine, and serotonin; this is essentially due to the fact that amphetamines closely mimic the effects of these three natural neurotransmitter substances. The use of these stimulant ADHD medications exerts a rate-dependent effect on activity levels, mainly by enhancing locomotor output, reinforcement processes, and rate dependency; this, in turn, enhances attention and stimulus control of behavior.

Psychostimulants generally tend to increase blood flow to the areas of the frontal cortex in the brain that are critical to attention. Central nervous system stimulant medications are usually the first line of therapy for treating individuals diagnosed with ADHD; however, if these medications are not effective or sufficiently effective without undue adverse side effects, then the second line of pharmacological agents drawn upon are typically the antidepressant medications, such as desipramine (Norpramin), nortriptyline (Pamelor), imipramine (Tofranil), bupropion (Wellbutrin), or venlafaxine (Effexor). If the antidepressant medications do not work sufficiently, then the antihypertensive alpha 2 agonist medications, like clonidine (Catapres) and guanfacine (Tenex), are generally tried next. Other nonstimulant ADHD medications, like the antiobsessive SSRIs, the anticonvulsants, the MAOIs, the eugeroics, and the antipsychotics, are then tried if the first three groups have not been successful in resolving symptoms. If no single ADHD medicine is sufficient to fully accomplish this, which is not that uncommon, then multiple medications are combined for use in the same individual, usually by administering different medications at different times of the day.

Many central nervous system stimulant medications, like dextroamphetamine (Dexedrine) and methamphetamine (Desoxyn), prevent the direct reuptake of dopamine and of related neurotransmitters by brain neurons, others may block the enzymes that degrade the neurotransmitters. Amphetamine, and related psychostimulant drugs like dextroamphetamine (Desoxyn) and lisdextroamphetamine (Vyvanse), stimulates the release of norepinephrine from the vesicles in nerve terminals and from the central adrenergic receptors. At higher doses, however, amphetamine, as well as dextroamphetamine and lisdextroamphetamine, causes the release of dopamine from the mesocorticolimbic system and also from the nigrostriatal dopamine systems. The amphetamines may also act as direct agonists of the central serotonin receptors and, further, may inhibit the enzyme MAO, which would block reuptake of these respective neurotransmitter substances. Once methamphetamine enters the brain, it initiates a cascade of release of norepinephrine, dopamine, and serotonin. Methamphetamine also then somewhat inhibits dopaminergic and adrenergic reuptake and, at high doses, also inhibits MAO.

Methylphenidate's (Ritalin) mechanism of action is primarily to block the reuptake of norepinephrine and of dopamine. Methylphenidate hydrochloride (Ritalin) acts on the transporter proteins for norepinephrine, and to a lesser degree, at least at therapeutic doses, on those for dopamine. As the dopamine reward system is more closely associated with the potential for abuse, this may help to explain why methylphenidate is less widely abused than other stimulant drugs, like amphetamines and cocaine. At therapeutic levels, methylphenidate is also less likely than many other central nervous system stimulant drugs to have adverse side effects and to produce tolerance. Methylphenidate has been shown to significantly enhance activation in the bilateral inferior frontal cortex, which is a key area of cognitive control. Methylphenidate, at least at therapeutic doses, generally blocks from about 60 percent to 70 percent of the available striatal dopamine transporters, which tends to be abnormally low in individuals with ADHD who are not on ADHD medications. However, in other brain regions, such as the frontal lobes, methylphenidate blocks about 70 percent to 80 percent of the norepinephrine transporters, which serve to reuptake both norepinephrine and dopamine; this leads to increased levels of extracellular norepinephrine and dopamine. Since methylphenidate inhibits the reuptake of norepinephrine and dopamine by modulating the dopamine transporters and the norepinephrine transporters, which increases their availability in synaptic junctions, this results in increased dopaminergic and noradrenergic activity in the prefrontal cortex.

A major benefit of using central nervous system stimulants is their typically rapid onset of action. The primary psychoactive effects of psychostimulant medications are to produce feelings of being more energetic, euphoric, and calm. The fact that many central nervous system stimulants, like amphetamine, cocaine, and methamphetamine, produce a profound state of euphoria, unfortunately, increases their dependency potential. Because stimulants also activate brain inhibitory and self-organizing mechanisms, they fortunately also help us to better manage impulses and to focus attention.

Low oral doses of central nervous system stimulant medications, like methylphenidate, have been shown to improve prefrontal cortical cognitive functioning in both individuals with ADHD and normal control subjects in a similar manner, rather than as was earlier assumed that these medications produced paradoxical effects in individuals with ADHD. Many earlier studies utilized higher doses of stimulant drugs, which actually masked the therapeutic effects produced at lower doses comparable to those used in treating individuals diagnosed with ADHD. More recently conducted laboratory studies of rats confirmed that very low, oral doses of stimulants, like methylphenidate, exerted both noradrenergic and dopaminergic effects. Unfortunately, the presently used imaging techniques are not generally sensitive enough to detect the more delicate noradrenergic or dopaminergic innervation of the prefrontal cortex, but they can readily detect the more robust dopaminergic activity in the striatum. In fact, higher doses of stimulant medications have been shown to impair prefrontal cortical cognitive functioning and to produce mental inflexibility, as is customarily observed in individuals who abuse high doses of central nervous system stimulant drugs, like cocaine and methamphetamine.

Amantadine

Amantadine hydrochloride (Symmetrel) is tricyclic amine that is well absorbed and eliminated in the urine essentially unchanged. Amantadine hydrochloride acts on the presynaptic membranes of neurons enhancing the release of the neurotransmitter dopamine and, in high doses at least, also seems to inhibit dopamine reuptake. Amantadine may also induce hypersensitivity of the postsynaptic dopamine receptors, but this appears to be a somewhat transient effect. Accordingly, amantadine seems to effectively potentiate the effects of dopamine.

Antidepressants

The antidepressant ADHD medications are primarily the TCAs, which, like amitriptyline (Elavil), desipramine (Norpramin), imipramine (Tofranil), and nortriptyline (Pamelor), enhance serotonergic mechanisms, but they also tend to block histamines, alpha 1 adrenergic, and cholinergic receptor sites. Other TCAs include amoxapine (Asendin), clomipramine (Anafranil), maprotiline (Ludiomil), protriptyline (Vivactil), and trimipramine (Surmontil). TCAs are so called because they all have a characteristic three-ring nucleus structure and some essentially mimic norepinephrine, but others have very different mechanisms of action depending on which receptors a respective TCA either stimulates or inhibits. This means that an individual with ADHD might have to try out different TCAs to find which one works better for them. Nevertheless, the TCAs have generally been found to effectively decrease hyperactivity and to also enhance mood and self-esteem; they also tend to have a longer lasting therapeutic effect than the stimulant ADHD medications discussed earlier, as well as less of the rebound effects frequently reported with psychostimulant medications. The TCAs, as a class, tend generally to down regulate beta adrenergic receptor sites in the cerebral cortex of the brain and also generally sensitize postsynaptic neurotransmission of serotonin; in fact, by blocking the ability of serotonin to bind to receptors, some TCAs actually enhance the action of norepinephrine. They also tend to block some of the histamine receptor sites, which largely accounts for their sedative effects; they likewise typically block alpha adrenergic receptor sites, which accounts for their hypotensive effects; and, they also block muscarinic acetylcholine receptor sites, which specifically accounts for their anticholinergic effects, such as dry mouth, constipation, and urinary retention. These TCA antidepressant medications, accordingly, tend to cause undesired dizziness, drowsiness, constipation, dry mouth, and weight gain.

Research studies have supported the efficacy of TCAs in treating ADHD symptoms, but their wider use is severely limited due to the likely occurrence of adverse side effects. Amitriptyline hydrochloride (Elavil) is a tertiary amine TCA with sedative effects; amitriptyline decreases membrane pump reuptake by inhibiting primarily the sodium dependent serotonin transporter and, to a lesser degree, the sodium dependent norepinephrine transporter. Desipramine hydrochloride (Norpramin) is a secondary amine TCA. Nortriptyline hydrochloride (Pamelor) is a secondary amine TCA; it actually is the N-demethylated active metabolite of amitriptyline. Accordingly, nortriptyline is a more potent inhibitor of norepinephrine reuptake than amitriptyline or doxepine; it is also a potent inhibitor of the reuptake of serotonin at the neuronal membrane, as is amitriptyline.

Bupropion hydrochloride (Wellbutrin) is an atypical non-TCA medicine and smoking cessation aid that is sometimes used off label to treat individuals diagnosed with ADHD. Bupropion hydrochloride is a unicyclic compound that essentially works by mimicking norepinephrine and dopamine. Bupropion functions as both a weak norepinephrine and a dopamine reuptake inhibitor, and it is also a nicotinic acetylcholine antagonist; it may also stimulate presynaptic release of norepinephrine and dopamine. It is further speculated that bupropion may enhance noradrenergic functional activity by means of its promoting increased excretion of the hydroxyl metabolite of melatonin, while at the same time facilitating a compensatory decrease in norepinephrine turnover. Bupropion hydrochloride is approved by the Food and Drug Administration (FDA) for treating unipolar depression, but not for ADHD. Nevertheless, it has demonstrated clinical efficacy in off-label treatment of individuals with ADHD comorbid with either aggression or substance abuse.

Antihypertensives

The antihypertensive ADHD medications are primarily the alpha 2 agonists, like clonidine (Catapres, Kapvay) and guanfacine (Intuniv, Tenex), which effectively help to lower elevated blood pressure. Use of these hypotensive alpha 2 agonists appears to lead to enhanced noradrenergic input from the locus coeruleus and to direct postsynaptic stimulation of the alpha 2A receptors. The alpha 2A and 2C subtypes of receptors are found mainly on neurons located in the locus coeruleus, where they help to reduce cell firing. In fact, presynaptic alpha 2A receptors in the central nervous system inhibit the release of norepinephrine, thus serve in the negative feedback control of the noradrenergic system. The alpha 2B subtype is much less common in the brain, but what is there is concentrated primarily in the thalamus, which probably accounts for the sedating effects of the alpha 2 agonist medications.

It is now understood that the alpha 2 agonists, like clonidine and guanfacine, exert their therapeutic effects in treating ADHD by means of stimulating the postsynaptic alpha 2A receptors on the dendrites of the prefrontal cortical pyramidal cells. This results in increased functional connectivity of the prefrontal cortex neural networks, which strengthens the control of behavior and attention. Most of the alpha 2A receptors in the brain have been identified as being located postsynaptically on noradrenergic terminals.

The two main antihypertensive medications used for treating individuals with ADHD are clonidine and guanfacine, even though their use is off label. Clonidine is both a partial alpha adrenergic agonist and a partial antagonist. It acts as an agonist in the anterior hypothalamus, which results in the inhibition of excitatory cardiovascular neurons; while in the posterior hypothalamus, it acts as an antagonist, which decreases the stimulation of excitatory cardiovascular neurons, and in the medulla, it also acts as an antagonist inhibiting the stimulation of the sympathetic nervous system. The net result of these actions is decreased arterial blood pressure. The mechanism of action for clonidine hydrochloride involves the stimulation of presynaptic alpha 2 receptor sites in the brain stem, which decreases presynaptic calcium levels and thereby leads to decreased release of norepinephrine at central and peripheral terminals; this leads to peripheral vascular resistance that lowers blood pressure. It also effectively diminishes afferent pain transmission. However, the mechanism of action for clonidine that is most relevant to treating symptoms of ADHD is its binding to the postsynaptic adrenergic receptor sites, and thereby increasing adrenergic tone, in the prefrontal cortex, and it also increases noradrenergic input in the locus coeruleus. When used by itself, clonidine seems to have minimal effects upon inattention, but when used in combination with amphetamine or methylphenidate, it can be particularly effective in assisting individuals with extremely high levels of aggression, hyperactivity, and impulsivity as well as for individuals who have comorbid secondary conditions such as conduct disorders or oppositional defiant disorder.

The mechanism of action for guanfacine is restricted mainly to the activation of postsynaptic alpha 2A receptors in the prefrontal cortex of the brain, which appears to improve the delay-related firing of prefrontal cortex neurons; at the same time, guanfacine appears to selectively inhibit striatal activity, as well as decrease vasomotor tone and heart rate. Guanfacine is a more selective alpha 2A agonist, which at low doses improves prefrontal cortical cognitive functioning without many of the adverse side effects sometimes associated with nonselective alpha 2A agonists like clonidine. Unfortunately, the absorption characteristics of immediate release clonidine and guanfacine lead to rapid peak blood plasma concentrations that then decline precipitously.

Beta Blockers

The beta blockers, also known as the beta receptor antagonists, inhibit the action of the beta receptor sites by antagonizing the effects of the catecholamines and, thereby, lower heart rate, blood pressure, and contractility. Beta blocker drugs occupy the beta receptors and competitively reduce the ability of the catecholamines to occupy receptors. The major beta blocker ADHD medications are atenolol (Tenorim), nadolol (Corgard), and propranolol (Inderal). There are both nonselective and selective beta blocker medications. The nonselective beta blockers, like nadolol (Corgard) and propranolol

(Inderal), inhibit both beta 1 and beta 2 receptor sites, and are generally more effective at lowering blood pressure than the selective beta blockers, which inhibit either one or the other receptors. Other examples of selective beta 1 blockers include acebutolol (Sectral), betaxolol (Kerlone), bisoprolol (Zebeta), esmolol (Brevibloc), levobunolol (Betagan, Liquifilm), metipranolol (Optipranolol), and metoprolol (Lopressor, Toprol-XL). However, the non-selective beta blockers tend to be associated with more adverse side effects than the selective beta blockers, like atenolol (Tenorim), bisoprolol (Zebeta), and metoprolol succinate (Toprol XL). Other nonselective beta blocker medications include carteolol (Cartrol), carvedilol (Coreg), labetalol (Normodyne, Trandate), penbutolol (Levatol), pindolol (Visken), sotalol (Betapace), and timolol (Blocadren).

Atenolol (Tenorim, Tenoretic) is a selective beta 1 receptor site antagonist that competes with sympathomimetic neurotransmitters, as such it is an effective adrenergic blocking agent that inhibits responses to adrenergic stimuli by blocking beta adrenergic receptor sites within heart muscle; atenolol, accordingly, thereby decreases heart rate by about 25 percent to 35 percent slowing atrioventricular (AV) nodal conduction and it also, indirectly, reduces blood pressure, without the bronchoconstriction that is sometimes experienced by users of propranolol. Nadolol (Corgard) is a nonselective beta blocker, similar in action to timolol (Blocadren), but noted for its very long duration of action. Propranolol (Dociton, Inderal) is the prototypical beta blocker as it binds to beta receptor sites, particularly those located at adrenergic junctions, and thereby prevents activation, while also having no detectable partial agonist action at beta receptors as well as having negligible effects at alpha and muscarinic receptor sites. Simply put, propranolol essentially blocks the action of norepinephrine.

Antiobsessives

The mechanism of action of antiobsessive ADHD medications is primarily to block the reuptake of serotonin. The antiobsessive ADHD medications are primarily the SSRIs, which, like citalopram (Celexa), escitalopram (Lexapro), fluoxetine (Prozac), fluvoxamine (Luvox), paroxetine (Paxil), and sertraline (Zoloft), block the serotonin transporter from reuptaking the neurotransmitter serotonin. Fluoxetine and the other SSRIs seem to be most useful when used as supplemental medications, particularly when administered in combination with a stimulant ADHD medicine for treating those individuals with the most severe symptoms. Citalopram and escitalopram are among the most selective of the SSRIs and they have a low likelihood of inhibiting the CYP

450 enzymes, thus they have no significant drug to drug interactions; they have no significant affinity for dopaminergic, muscarinic, or norepinephrine receptors; citalopram is a mild histamine antagonist, but escitalopram does not block histamine receptors; in addition, escitalopram has an equivalent dose that is half that of citalopram. Nefazodone hydrochloride (Serzone) is another SSRI that is an atypical antidepressant ADHD medicine that inhibits the reuptake of serotonin and norepinephrine, while also serving as an agonist of selected serotonin receptors. More simply put, the SSRIs essentially mimic the effects of serotonin by making more of it available to receptors by inhibiting its reuptake. Venlafaxine hydrochloride (Effexor) is a SNRI antiobsessive ADHD medicine that blocks the reuptake of both norepinephrine and serotonin; it is associated with less adverse side effects for most individuals than the TCAs and it appears to result in improvements with both impulsivity and hyperactivity. These medications, accordingly, increase the amount of serotonin present in the neural synapses, which causes repeated activation of serotonin receptors. It appears that some symptoms associated with ADHD, in some individuals at least, are more likely related to a dysfunction of specific brain circuits, particularly those of the frontal cortex, rather than to an actual dysfunction of the serotonin system. Thus, modulation of these circuits by serotonergic neurons may underlie the specific mechanism of action of most antiobsessive medications. Although higher SSRI doses, at about 50 mg of fluoxetine or 250 mg of imipramine, appear to be more effective, this slight benefit is offset somewhat by reduced tolerability.

Anticonvulsants

The traditional anticonvulsant medications operate by blocking calcium or sodium channels or by stimulating GABA action. The standard anticonvulsant medications, by means of blocking calcium or sodium channels, inhibit the release of excitatory glutamate, which is associated with episodes of epilepsy as well as with mood episodes associated with bipolar disorder. The two major anticonvulsant medications sometimes used for treating individuals with ADHD are carbamazepine (Tegretol) and valporic acid (Depakote).

Carbamazepine (Tegretol, Carbatrol, Epitol, Equetro) increases levels of GABA. Carbamazepine stabilizes hyperexcited neuron membranes, inhibits repetitive discharges of sodium dependent action potentials, and reduces synaptic transmission of excitatory impulses. It is used for treating individuals with epilepsy, trigeminal neuralgia, and bipolar disorder, as well as, of course, ADHD.

Valporic acid (Depakote, Depakene) is a carboxylic acid derivative, which influences the activity of the GABA signaling systems, a pathway that serves to regulate the movement of chloride ions into and out of cells. More specifically, it functions as a GABA transaminase inhibitor, blocks sodium and calcium channels, is an inhibitor of the histonedeacetylase enzyme, thus indirectly increases GABA levels.

Noradrenergic Specific Reuptake Inhibitors

Atomoxetine (Strattera) is a potent and highly selective presynaptic norepinephrine transporter inhibitor, or in other words, an effective noradrenergic specific reuptake inhibitor. Atomoxetine not only exhibits specificity for the norepinephrine transporter as compared to other monoamine transporters, but also exhibits low affinity to several other receptor classes that are commonly associated with adverse side effects, including the acetylcholine receptors, the alpha and beta noradrenergic receptors, the dopaminergic receptors, the histaminergic receptors, and the serotonin receptors. In addition, it is rapidly and completely absorbed within 1 hour and it offers 24-hour coverage of ADHD symptoms in children and adults, thus can be safely and effectively administered once per day. Accordingly, atomoxetine has been found to increase the amount of the neurotransmitter norepinephrine available to receptors, while having minimal effect upon other neurotransmitter receptors and transporters. Further, atomoxetine has less abuse potential than the central nervous system stimulant ADHD medications and, accordingly, it is not scheduled as a controlled substance.

Eugeroics

Eugeroics literally means "good arousal," and this class of ADHD medications is represented by modafinil (Provigil) and armodafinil (Nuvigil). Modafinil is the active metabolite of adrafinil, which was an earlier drug developed in France by the pharmaceutical company Lafon to treat patients diagnosed with narcolepsy, but adrafinil had to be metabolized in the liver before it had its therapeutic effects. Modafinil is an analeptic drug, which means that it is a medicine that stimulates the respiratory system of the brain. Modafinil appears to function as a unique and very selective agonist of the alpha 1 adrenergic postsynaptic receptor sites, which are usually receptive to the monoamines, like dopamine and norepinephrine. Modafinil particularly affects the dopamine transporter, thus acts largely as a dopamine reuptake inhibitor. More specifically, modafinil binds competitively to the cell membrane of the dopamine transporter, which blocks the activity of the transporter, and this thereby inhibits the reuptake of dopamine resulting in elevated levels of dopamine, particularly in the nucleus accumbens and in other associated regions of the brain. Accordingly, the increase in dopamine levels increases locomotor activity and elevates extracellular levels of dopamine in the human brain, which results in improved mood, wakefulness, and enhanced cognition. Modafinil also acts as a weak, but highly selective, partial agonist at the dopamine receptor site. Modafinil, further, inhibits the release of GABA by acting on the 5-HTP serotonin receptors. In fact, modafinil has been shown to increase levels of dopamine in the striatum, particularly in the nucleus accumbens; norepinephrine in the hypothalamus and ventrolateral preoptic nucleus; serotonin in the amygdala and in the frontal cortex; and histamines in the hypothalamus. More specifically, modafinil stimulates the posterior hypothalamus, particularly the histaminergic tuberomamillary nucleus, which results in elevated histamine neurotransmitter concentrations in the central nervous system. The elevated histamine levels stimulates orexin peptides that influence regions of the cerebral cortex associated with maintaining levels of arousal and wakefulness. In addition, since modafinil has a direct agonist effect on the alpha 1 adrenergic receptor sites, it also facilitates inhibition of norepinephrine uptake, thus directly promoting wakefulness. The increased brain levels of norepinephrine also results in increased memory, learning, and attention as well as greater cerebral plasticity. Increased levels of norepinephrine also stimulate the sympathetic nervous system, thereby increasing heart rate and blood pressure and resulting in enhanced energy levels.

Armodafinil is the enantiomer or single R isomer of the racemic modafinil. Armodafinil, accordingly, has a greater delayed period of time needed to achieve peak concentration compared to modafinil. Since armodafinil, at least as compared to modafinil, takes a longer time to reach peak concentrations in the blood, it does not seem to affect the quality of nighttime sleeping patterns, which is a common complaint reported by many users of modafinil. Armodafinil appears to inhibit the reuptake of dopamine by binding to the dopamine transporter; this results in increased levels of extracellular dopamine. Armodafinil appears to be a somewhat less selective alpha 1 adrenergic drug than modafinil, thus higher doses of armodafinil are typically required to achieve comparable therapeutic results compared to those of the more potent modafinil. Further, the greater adverse side effects profile typically associated with use of armodafinil limits its widespread applicability as a eugeroic.

Monoamine Oxidase Inhibitors

The MAO enzymes oxidatively inactivates and deaminates neurotransmitter substances located in synaptic spaces. The MAOIs inhibit one or both forms of the MAO enzyme. More simply put, the MAOIs essentially mimic the effects of norepinephrine, dopamine, and serotonin. The MAO enzymes are present in the central and peripheral nervous system as well as in the gastrointestinal tract, liver, blood platelets, and mitrochondrial membranes. The MAO enzyme subtype A degrades norepinephrine and serotonin as well as epinephrine and melatonin; while the MAO enzyme subtype B degrades phenylclhylene and certain other trace amines, and both subtype A and subtype B degrade dopamine. Therefore, the MAOIs allow neurotransmitters like norepinephrine, dopamine, and serotonin to accumulate in neural synapses. It is important to recognize that there are both selective and nonselective MAOIs; the selective MAOIs only affect either subtype A or subtype B of the MAO enzyme, while the nonselective ones affect both subtypes. Since MAO subtype B inhibitors help to block the degradation of dopamine in the brain, their use makes more dopamine available and also reduces some of the excessive locomotor activity.

The MAOIs can interact with certain foods, such as those containing tyramine (like some cheeses, meats, or beans), which can create potentially fatal high blood pressure, as well as having possibly lethal interactions with other medications, including many pain or cold medications. Accordingly, individuals using MAOIs are typically placed on restricted diets. However, two of the newer MAOIs, selegiline (Emsam) and rasagiline (Azilect), have been FDA approved without dietary restrictions.

The irreversible MAOIs are generally rapidly absorbed and quickly eliminated. However, the physiological effects of an irreversible MAOI do not end when the medicine clears the system since the medicine has bound to the MAO enzymes, which must be regenerated before normal MAO activity can be resumed. Thus, the pharmacodynamic half-life of irreversible MAOIs is considerably longer than their pharmacokinetic half-life.

Nonselective MAOIs that are presently available in the United States include isocarboxazid (Marplan), phenelzine (Nardil), and tranylcypromine (Parnate); all three of these MAOIs are irreversible inhibitors of MAO enzyme activity. Individuals taking phenelzine are more likely to experience sedation and greater weight gain than those taking other MAOIs. Tranylcypromine inhibits the MAO enzyme; this enzymatic inactivation of neurotransmitter substances, particularly as focused at the adrenergic nerve terminals, results in an increased pool of stored neurotransmitter substances. Rasagiline and selegeline are selective MAOIs that only inhibit the activity of the subtype B MAO enzyme; however, rasagiline is reversible, while selegeline is irreversible. The mechanism of action of moclobemide (Amira), as opposed to that of the earlier MAOIs, is selective, in that it inhibits the activity of the subtype A MAO enzyme; and, it is reversible such that it can detach from the MAO enzyme and thereby resume facilitating the normal catabolism of the respective substrate neurotransmitter substances. Accordingly, selective and reversible MAOIs, such as moclobemide, which is not yet available in the United States, are safer and require fewer dietary restrictions than the traditional MAOIs.

Antipsychotics

The typical antipsychotic ADHD medications, such as haloperidol (Haldol), pimozide (Orap), and thioridazine hydrochloride (Mellaril), and many of the atypical antipsychotic medications, like clozapine (Clozaril), olanzapine (Zyprexa), quetiapine fumarate (Seroquel), and risperidone (Risperdal), are sometimes used to address ADHD. However, there are some differences in their respective mechanisms of action. As an oversimplification, the typical antipsychotic medications generally block receptors in the dopamine pathways of the brain, while the atypical antipsychotic medications tend to block the serotonin receptors. The action of typical antipsychotic medications is responsible not only for their antipsychotic effects, but also for causing extrapyramidal systems. Many think that psychotic symptoms can be caused by either excess of dopamine or by enhanced sensitivity of the dopamine receptors. There are, of course, considerable variations that exist within this gross generalization.

There are significant differences as to how each of the respective antipsychotic medicine functions. Haloperidol (Haldol) appears to depress the subcortical level of the brain, the midbrain, and the brain stem's reticular formation; it may also, through actions in the caudate nucleus, inhibit the brain stem's ascending reticular activating system, which would interrupt neurotransmission between the diencephalon and the cortex. Pimozide (Orap) blocks dopaminergic activity by binding to and inhibiting the dopamine 2 receptors. Thioridazine hydrochloride (Mellaril) blocks postsynaptic dopamine 1 and dopamine 2 receptors in the mesolimbic pathway of the human brain, and it also blocks alpha adrenergic effects, as well as depressing release of hypothalamic hormones, which, in turn, suppresses the reticular activating system. Clozapine (Clozaril) has lower dopamine affinity than haloperidol (Haldol) but, in addition, clozapine blocks serotonin receptors in the frontal cortex. Olanzapine (Zyprexa), similarly, acts as an antagonist on the dopamine 3 receptors in the mesolimbic pathway and also in the serotonin receptors of the frontal cortex. Quetiapine fumarate (Seroquel) is an atypical antipsychotic medicine that is sometimes used for treating individuals with ADHD. Quetiapine fumarate functions as a norepinephrine, dopamine, and serotonin antagonist, as well as a potent antihistamine with little to no anticholinergic effects. It strongly binds to serotonin receptor sites and can also act as a partial serotonin agonist. Further, since it can antagonize norepinephrine and serotonin receptor sites, which actually serve as autoreceptors, their blockage helps to stimulate the release of these neurotransmitter substances. Risperidone (Risperidal) has high affinity for dopamine 2 receptors, particularly those in the limbic system, but it acts as an antagonist with respect to serotonin 2A receptors, particularly those in the mesocortical tract, which causes an excess of available dopamine and, thereby, an increase in dopaminergic transmission.

Cholinergic Agents

Cholinergic agents, also referred to as cholinomimetic agents, consist of a large group of drugs that essentially mimic the effects of acetylcholine. There are two major types of cholinergic agents, the cholinoceptor stimulants, which act primarily on muscarinic or nicotinic receptor sites, and the cholinesterase inhibiting drugs, which act indirectly by inhibiting the hydrolysis of acetylcholine. Nicotine is the primary cholinergic agent that has been considered for use in helping individuals with ADHD, and it is a direct acting cholinoceptor stimulant drug. Nicotine, more specifically, is a selective agonist of the nicotinic acetylcholine receptor that is typically activated by the neurotransmitter acetylcholine. Nicotine is a tertiary natural cholinomimetic alkaloid that as a liquid is sufficiently lipid soluble to be absorbed directly across the skin. Nicotine binds selectively to the nicotinic receptors, particularly those receptor sites located at nicotinic cholinergic junctions, like the autonomic ganglion and neuromuscular end plates, which opens up ion channels in postsynaptic membranes. Simply put, nicotine essentially mimics acetylcholine and, of course, has a high propensity to be an abused substance.

Prolonged nicotine exposure, or agonist occupancy, of the nicotinic receptor abolishes the effector response, which causes the postganglionic neurons to stop firing and the skeletal muscle cells to relax; it also prevents the electrical recovery of the postsynaptic membrane resulting in a depolarizing blockade. At low dosages, nicotine creates a mild alerting action by stimulating the brain stem and cortex, which could be advantageous in treating individuals with ADHD; however, at higher dosages, nicotine causes tremor, emesis, and respiratory stimulation; and, at even higher dosages, nicotine causes convulsions, which can be lethal.

RATE DEPENDENCY THEORY

One explanation that has been offered for how some ADHD medications work is that of rate dependency theory. This theoretical construct posits that the effects of a drug are not only dose dependent but are also rate dependent; there is actually a considerable body of clinical research that supports this construct. In this regard, it has long been known that central nervous system stimulant drugs like amphetamine and methylphenidate can alter attention and activity rates differently by being administered under different schedules of reinforcement, specifically that the effects of the same dose of such drugs is different if there are low rates of responding than if there are high rates of responding. This is due to the fact that the pharmacological effects of these types of psychoactive substances are inversely related in both magnitude and direction to whatever the baseline rate of activity and distraction was for a particular individual with ADHD. More directly put, a small dose of amphetamine and methylphenidate, as well as other psychostimulant medications, will increase very low rates of response, while the same dose can also decrease high rates of response. Thus, it makes sense that individuals with ADHD, who tend to respond naturally at a very high rate, would, under the influence of such drugs, be expected to lower their rates of responding. Accordingly, they would, under those conditions, tend to behave in more traditionally accepted ways, such as waiting to be called on by raising their hand, rather than feeling compelled to interrupt the conversation of someone else and to blurt out a response. In fact, a clear inverse relationship has been found to exist between the severity of ADHD symptoms and the degree of therapeutic response observed for these stimulant medications.

This review of how ADHD medications work, particularly with respect to the mechanisms of action, of the diverse array of ADHD medications has shown that there are, in fact, many more similarities than differences. In fact, it seems, at a fundamental level, that there are generally major similarities, but with some minor differences, between the respective ADHD medications and how they work. This background helps to provide some elucidation as to why different individuals with ADHD may respond better to one respective ADHD medicine as compared to others, especially when we are cognizant, as discussed previously in Chapter 2, of the multiple varieties of ADHD subtypes that an individual may have and of the unique, highly individualized anatomical and physiological nature of any single human being.

Chapter 5

Effects and Applications

There are many different types of medications that are presently used, as well as some that were used in the past but no longer are, to treat attention deficit hyperactivity disorder (ADHD) and its associated symptoms. There are, not surprisingly, different effects, diverse applications, and alternative routes of administration that may be available for use of some of these varied ADHD medications, which impacts the pharmacological variables, such as dosage, bioavailability, onset of action, duration of action, half-life, and elimination, required to produce the desired therapeutic results. Understanding the effects of respective medications and their dosages helps one better understand how stimulant drugs can actually help individuals calm down, particularly as they tend to stimulate attention and self-regulation in individuals with ADHD. It is the knowledge of the effects of these respective medications in the brains and bodies of individuals with ADHD that helps to determine their potential applications.

EFFECTS OF ADHD MEDICATIONS

ADHD medications have many varied and diverse effects, and while some may have minor effects, others have more profound effects. The two primary realms where the pharmacological effects of respective ADHD medications are of concern are those that take place in the brain and those that occur throughout the rest of the body. An essential area to consider with respect to understanding the effects of ADHD medications is that of the approved applications of the respective medications, particularly what ages each has been approved for use with.

In the Brain

Central nervous system stimulant ADHD medications stimulate the release of dopamine from the basal ganglia, and they also increase activity in the prefrontal cortex as well as in the temporal lobes of the brain. Stimulants generally tend to increase dopamine and norepinephrine levels in the brain; this change in brain chemistry helps both to improve concentration and to lessen fatigue. Amphetamines as a class are the prototypical central nervous system stimulant drugs used to treat ADHD. The amphetamines, including the racemic amphetamine (Dyanavel XR), the enantiomer dextroamphetamine (Dexedrine), its prodrug lisdextroamphetamine (Vyvanse), and methamphetamine hydrochloride (Desoxyn), are noncatecholamine, sympathomimetic amines that cause a release of catecholamines, mainly dopamine and norepinephrine, from the vesicles in the presynaptic terminals of neurons of the brain. The amphetamines medications also inhibit the activity of the enzyme monoamine oxidase. They may also, by means of competitive inhibition, help block the reuptake of these two particular neurotransmitters. At any rate, all of these mechanisms help to boost the levels of neurotransmitters in the brain. Further, by activating the trace amine receptors, the respective amphetamine drugs increase biogenic amine and excitatory neurotransmitter activity levels in the human brain and thereby improve cognitive control, generate feelings of euphoria, and promote wakefulness. Methamphetamine has more pronounced effects in the brain, but less in the rest of the body than amphetamine; thus methamphetamine causes less increase in heart rate, blood pressure, respiration, and dilation of blood vessels than amphetamine.

Methylphenidate hydrochloride (Ritalin) is a non-amphetamine central nervous system stimulant ADHD medicine. Methylphenidate is one of the most commonly prescribed ADHD medications. Methylphenidate's mechanism of action is to block the reuptake of dopamine and norepinephrine; more specifically, it causes reduced activation in the right inferior frontal gyrus, the left anterior cingulate, and the bilateral posterior cingulate cortex. Some of the combined stimulant formulations, such as the amphetamine and dextroamphetamine combination product Adderall, and their derivatives can both stimulate release and produce reuptake inhibition of both dopamine and norepinephrine, and, consequently, they can enhance cognition and related factors.

The various nonstimulant ADHD medications also impact the brain in diverse ways. In fact, nonstimulant ADHD medications are designed to affect the brains of individuals with ADHD differently than the central nervous system stimulant medications do. Amantadine hydrochloride (Symmetrel) appears to strengthen neuronal response to dopamine both by stimulating the synthesis and by release of dopamine, and perhaps also by inhibiting dop-amine reuptake; it thus helps increase central dopaminergic tone and therefore is helpful in controlling impulsive behaviors.

The tricyclic antidepressant (TCA) amitriptyline (Elavil) appears to inhibit the reuptake of mainly serotonin and somewhat less so of norepinephrine in presynaptic neuron terminals in the brain and thereby increasing concentra-tions of these neurotransmitters, thus enhancing their activity in the synaptic cleft; unfortunately, for the first few weeks of use, undesired sedation is often produced. Another TCA, desipramine (Norpramin), inhibits the reuptake of norepinephrine and to a lesser extent that of serotonin; while nortriptyline (Aventyl, Pamelor), another TCA, increases the pressor effect of norepineph-rine and also appears to interfere with the transport, release, and storage of the catecholamines, it also inhibits the activity of acetylcholine, histamine, and 5-hydroxytryptamine.

Bupropion hydrochloride (Wellbutrin), an atypical antidepressant medi-cine, is a norepinephrine and dopamine reuptake inhibitor, as well as being a nicotinic antagonist, since it has moderate anticholinergic effects. Bupropion selectively inhibits systems controlled by dopamine substantially more than the TCAs, like amitriptyline and imipramine, but it causes less blockage of the reuptake of norepinephrine and serotonin at neuronal membranes than the TCAs do.

Atomoxetine hydrochloride (Strattera), a norepinephrine transporter inhibitor, is a slow and longer acting nonstimulant ADHD medicine that appears to be a selective inhibitor of presynaptic norepinephrine reuptake principally in the prefrontal cortex; it demonstrates high affinity for the nor-epinephrine transporters, but it has little to none for respective neurotransmit-ter receptor sites. The increased levels of norepinephrine that result from atomoxetine's mechanism of action, as primarily a norepinephrine reuptake inhibitor, thereby serves to prolong the effects of norepinephrine in the brain; while, to a lesser degree, it also functions as a dopamine reuptake inhibitor, it helps increase an individual's attention span and wakefulness, and also decreases their hyperactivity and impulsive behaviors; consequently, atomoxe-tine (Strattera) can be more helpful for those individuals with the predomi-nantly inattentive variant of ADHD.

The antihypertensive ADHD medications have significant effects in our brains. There is evidence that suggests that these selective alpha 2 adrenergic receptor agonists act directly on the prefrontal cortex to improve executive function. There was extensive off-label use of immediate release guanfacine and also of clonidine, which was found to help treat symptoms of ADHD. Clonidine hydrochloride (Kapvay) stimulates the alpha adrenoreceptors in the brain stem, which creates reduced synaptic outflow in the central nervous system; it also causes excretion of the catecholamines dopamine and norepinephrine. As clonidine and guanfacine hydrochloride (Intuniv) are both centrally acting selective alpha 2 adrenergic agonists, they not only are antihypertensive medications but also stimulate receptors in the prefrontal cortex, which seems to affect the production of norepinephrine; this results in improved neurotransmission, which increases the abilities to focus, by lowering distractibility and improving attention, and it also helps to control inappropriate behaviors by improving impulse control. However, clonidine hydrochloride (Kapvay) has a general affinity for alpha 2- A, B, and C receptors, as well as imidazoline receptors, and it also elevates histamine levels in the hypothalamus; while guanfacine hydrochloride (Intuniv) preferentially binds to the alpha 2 A receptors, which increases attentiveness, causes less sedation, and improves executive functioning, including enhancing working memory.

The beta blockers, as a class, have a competitive antagonist effect blocking the binding of norepinephrine to receptor sites; however, most of these effects occur in the heart not in the brain. For instance, the beta blocker medicine nadolol (Corgard) has low lipophilicity, which is characteristic of certain nonselective beta adrenergic receptor blocking agents, which, accordingly, have difficulty crossing the blood-brain barrier and, consequently, have limited effects upon the central nervous system, including the brain.

The selective serotonin reuptake inhibitors (SSRIs), like fluoxetine, which is marketed under trade names like Prozac and Sarafem, as well as related SSRIs, such as citalopram (Celexa), escitalopram (Lexapro), fluvoxamine (Luvox), paroxetine (Paxil), and sertraline (Zoloft), act upon the brain primarily by increasing the amount of the neurotransmitter serotonin. This increase in serotonin levels is accomplished by inhibiting the reuptake of serotonin, as is implied the name of their drug class, so that the serotonin lasts longer, but it does not, nor do most of the other SSRIs, appreciably inhibit the reuptake of dopamine and norepinephrine.

The anticonvulsants control seizure activity in the brain, where they have most of their pharmacological effects. For instance, carbamazepine (Tegretol), which is subject to variable transport across the blood brain barrier, blocks sodium dependent ion channels; it also has anticholinergic properties, and, in addition, it stimulates release of serotonin as well as possibly being SSRI. Valporic acid (Depakote) inhibits the enzymatic activity of gamma-aminobutyric (GABA) transaminase, thereby increases brain levels of GABA; it may also block sodium dependent ion channels.

The eugeroic ADHD medicine modafinil (Provigil) is a selective, although relatively weak, atypical dopamine reuptake inhibitor acting particularly in the nucleus accumbens, and the striatum more generally; it also blocks methamphetamine hydrochloride (Desoxyn) induced dopamine release. Further, modafinil increases the levels of norepinephrine and serotonin, while it may also inhibit GABA transmission and activate orexin peptides in the brain. Modafinil, as well as related eugeroic medications like armodafinil (Nuvigil), thus produce wakefulness without the need for compensatory sleep; they also enhance electronic coupling, which increases the efficiency of neural communication.

The monoamine oxidase inhibitor (MAOI) ADHD medications inhibit the enzymatic breakdown, thus increase the brain levels, of the neurotransmitters. The MAOI moclobemide (Amira), accordingly, increases the levels of the neurotransmitters serotonin, norepinephrine, and dopamine.

The antipsychotic ADHD medications, as a class, primarily target the dopamine receptors in the brain. There is a major distinction, however, between the typical and the atypical antipsychotics in that the latter tend to dissociate more rapidly. For instance, the antipsychotic ADHD medicine quetiapine fumarate (Seroquel) has high affinity for serotonin and dopamine receptors, but it exhibits rapid disassociation from dopamine receptors.

These and many other effects of ADHD medications in the brain are extremely energy intensive, particularly in the prefrontal cortex, which makes up about 30 percent of the human brain. The human brain, in fact, uses about one-fifth (20%) of the total energy consumed by an individual. Stimulant medications, in particular, increase the amount of energy expended. As the brain is about 80 percent water, it is also important for optimal brain functioning to keep properly hydrated. On the other hand, being dehydrated or calorically restricted makes it much more difficult for ADHD medications to attain their full therapeutic potential.

In the Rest of the Body

ADHD medications have an array of effects in the rest of the body. These effects, of course, vary somewhat depending upon the respective medicine, but generally the stimulant ADHD medications, as a class, tend to have roughly similar effects in different parts of the body. The central nervous system stimulants are characterized as sympathomimetic drugs, which means that they stimulate the sympathetic autonomic nervous system and related functions. Consequently, these drugs generally elevate heart rate and blood pressure while causing vasoconstriction. Lisdextropamphetamine (Vyvanse), for instance, can affect the circulatory system, such as by usually increasing heart rate, but less common is an increase in blood pressure; poor circulation in the fingers or in the toes, or the skin turning blue, has also been reported. Lisdextropamphetamine can also alter the functioning of the digestive system; some users experience a substantial loss of appetite, anorexia has even been reported as well. Lisdextropamphetamine also has effects related to reproduction; it can be passed on to infants by means of breast milk. Further, frequent or prolonged erections have also been reported by some users of lisdextropamphetamine. Methamphetamine hydrochloride (Desoxyn) effectively decreases appetite and also can elevate blood pressure. The other amphetamines have similar, but less pronounced, affects in the body. Amphetamines also cause dilation of the pupils and closure of the bladder sphincter, which makes urination more difficult. They also cause the lungs to expand, which is why they were once used to treat asthma and related conditions. The non-amphetamine stimulant medicine, methylphenidate hydrochloride (Ritalin), causes respiratory stimulation and decreases appetite.

Many of the nonstimulant ADHD medications have considerable effects in many parts of the human body. The antihypertensive alpha 2 agonist ADHD medications, such as clonidine (Kapvay) and guanfacine (Intuniv), lessen peripheral resistance, heart rate, and, with respect to their primary use, also effectively lower blood pressure. The beta blocker ADHD medications, such as atenolol (Tenorim), nadolol (Corgard), and propranolol (Inderal), have manifest their primary therapeutic effects by reducing heart rate and cardiac output; they also serve to reduce systolic and diastolic blood pressure as well as inhibit tachycardia. Most SSRIs, such as fluoxetine (Prozac), paroxetine (Paxil), and sertraline (Zoloft), cause sexual dysfunction and decrease sexual arousal. The anticonvulsant ADHD medications, such as carbamazepine (Tegretol) and valporic acid (Depakote), are both GABA receptor agonists, which explains their efficacy in addressing neuropathic pain; carbamazepine also has anticholinergic, antirrhythmic, and muscle relaxant properties. The antipsychotic ADHD medications, such as clozapione (Clozaril), haloperidol (Haldol), olanzapine (Zyprexa), pimozide (Orap), and risperidone (Risperdal), tend to produce muscle stiffness, flattened facial expressions, lowered seizure threshold, sedation, and sexual dysfunction. The MAOIs, such as moclobemide (Amira) and rasagiline (Azilect), are associated with dry mouth and digestive problems, like loss of appetite, weight loss, nausea, and constipation. There is conflicting evidence as to whether the MAOIs alter cortisol levels and increase growth hormone levels. The eugeroic ADHD medications, such as modafinil (Provigil) and armodafinil (Nuvigil), produce loss of appetite and consequent weight loss. The cholinergic agent nicotine (Nicorette) elevates blood pressure and heart rate and constricts pupils.

APPROVED APPLICATIONS

Respective ADHD medications are approved for specific applications and, more importantly with respect to the not too uncommon situation of off-label use, approved for use with individuals of a certain age. These variables are, of course, quite different for individual ADHD medications, including both the stimulant and the nonstimulant medications commonly used for treating individuals with ADHD.

The central nervous system stimulant medications most typically applied for treating individuals with ADHD are amphetamine, dextroamphetamine, lisdextroamphetamine, and methamphetamine. There are some minor differences, but there are considerable similarities in their application. Lisdextroamphetamine (Vyvanse), for instance, was specifically formulated to serve as a long lasting central nervous system psychostimulant ADHD medicine. It is approved for use by individuals who are 6 years of age and older who have ADHD as well as for use by individuals with a binge eating disorder who are 18 years of age and older. It is not approved to treat obesity or to use as a weight-loss drug. Lisdextroamphetamine can often take a few weeks to attain its full therapeutic effect. For individuals with ADHD, they will commonly notice an improvement in their attention span as well as possibly better control of their hyperactivity and of their impulsiveness. Adderall, which is an amphetamine and dextroamphetamine combination formulation, has been approved in an immediate release formulation only for use by individuals who are three years of age and older who have ADHD, and in extended release formulations for those six years of age and older. Formulations of racemic amphetamine, such as that marketed under the trade name Dyanavel XR, have been approved for use by individuals who are three years of age and older who have ADHD. Likewise, formulations of dextroamphetamine, such as those marketed under trade names like Dexedrine or Dextrostat, have also been approved for use by individuals who are three years of age and older who have ADHD. On the other hand, formulations of methylphenidate, a non-amphetamine central nervous system stimulant ADHD medicine, such as those marketed under trade names like Concerta or Ritalin, have been approved for use by individuals who are six years of age and older who have ADHD.

There are also some considerable differences with respect to the application of the myriad nonstimulant ADHD medications. The synthetic cyclic primary amine amantadine hydrochloride (Symmetrel) has been approved for use by individuals who are one year of age and older. The antidepressant TCA medications, including amitriptyline (Elavil), desipramine (Norpramin), and nortriptyline (Pamelor), have been approved for use by individuals who are 18 years of age and older, as has the non-TCA and antismoking medicine bupropion, which is available in hydrobromide (Aplenzin) and hydrochloride (Wellbutrin) formulations. The norepinephrine specific reuptake inhibitor atomoxetine hydrochloride (Strattera) has been approved for use by individuals who are six years of age and older who have ADHD. The antihypertensive alpha 2 agonist ADHD medications clonidine (Kapvay) and guanfacine (Intuniv) have been approved either alone or in combination with stimulants for use by individuals who are six years of age and older who have ADHD. The beta blocker ADHD medications, such as atenolol (Tenorim), nadolol (Corgard), and propranolol (Inderal), can be prescribed to individuals of any age; however, there are some contraindications; for example, propranolol should not be administered to children who weigh less than 4.4 pounds (2 kg). Many of the antiobsessive ADHD medications (SSRIs), such as fluoxetine (Prozac), nefazodone (Serzone), and paroxetine (Paxil), have been approved for use by individuals who are 18 years of age and older; however, a couple have been approved for use with younger individuals, such as fluvoxamine (Luvox), which has been approved for use by individuals who are 8 years of age and older, and sertraline (Zoloft), which has been approved for use by individuals who are 6 years of age and older. The anticonvulsant ADHD medications, such as carbamazepine (Tegretol) and valporic acid (Depakote), have been approved for use by individuals of any age. The MAOIs ADHD medications, such as phenelzine sulfate (Nardil) and tranylcypromine sulfate (Parnate), have been approved for use by individuals who are 18 years of age and older. Likewise, the eugeroic ADHD medications, like modafinil (Amira), have been approved for use by individuals who are 18 years of age and older. The respective antipsychotic ADHD medications have been approved for use by individuals of different ages; accordingly, clozapine (Clozaril) has been approved for use by individuals who are 18 years of age and older, olanzapine (Zyprexa) has been approved for use by individuals who are 14 years of age and older, pimozide (Orap) has been approved for use by individuals who are 12 years of age and older, quetiapine fumarate (Seroquel) has been approved for use by individuals who are 10 years of age and older, risperidone (Risperdal) has been approved for use by individuals who are 5 years of age and older (but it should not be used by individuals older than 16 years who have been diagnosed with irritability with autistic disorders), haloperidol (Haldol) has been approved for use by individuals who are 3 years of age and older, and thioridazine hydrochloride (Mellaril) has been approved for use by individuals who are 2 years of age and older. The cholinergic agent nicotine (Nicorette) has been approved for use by individuals who are 18 years of age and older.

It must be remembered that the use of most of these nonstimulant medications, at least with respect to treating ADHD, is generally by means of off-label prescribing. Interestingly, many of these same ADHD medications have been used for some time off label for treating myriad other conditions. For example, several different types of ADHD medications have been considered as a pharmacotherapeutic treatment for helping individuals who experience cocaine dependence; these include the TCA desipramine hydrochloride (Norpramin), the synthetic cyclic primary amine amantadine hydrochloride (Symmetrel), the SSRI fluoxetine (Prozac), and the anticonvulsant carbamazepine (Tegretol).

HOW CAN STIMULANTS CALM PEOPLE DOWN?

The central nervous system psychostimulant medications typically stimulate physiological processes, yet they are used to help calm down individuals who experience symptoms of ADHD. This apparent contradiction, however, is understandable when one considers how ADHD is generally understood to work. This is made even clearer when we consider the different types of effects that the respective ADHD psychostimulant medications appear to have in individuals with ADHD.

Different Effects in Those with ADHD

The effects of central nervous system psychostimulant medications, as discussed earlier when exploring rate dependency theory, will generally tend to decrease very high rates of response. This typically happens the same in all individuals, whether they have ADHD or not. These stimulant medications do not function differently in individuals who have ADHD, although this was what was previously assumed. It seems, however, that individuals with ADHD are different than others, particularly with respect to their brain chemistry and functioning. For example, it is now generally believed that there is more activity in the back part of the brain in many individuals with ADHD, but less activity in the front of their brains than is typical of individuals without ADHD. In this regard, it is now generally felt that the neurotransmitter systems in the brains of individuals with ADHD are operating inefficiently; they may be producing less, or more, or respective brain chemicals that alter how they process and respond to stimuli, thus how they behave. Accordingly, it makes perfect sense that individuals with ADHD, who tend to respond naturally at a very high rate, would, under the influence of such medications, be expected to lower their rates of responding. Therefore, such individuals would, under such conditions, generally tend to behave in more normally expected ways. For example, an individual with ADHD who was taking these psychostimulant ADHD medications might be more able to wait to be called upon when he or she raises a hand to answer a question, rather than feeling uncontrollably compelled to interrupt the ongoing conversations of others and to abruptly yell out a response. In fact, many individuals with ADHD who take these medications find that they help them to improve their self-control, working memory, hyperactivity, and other associated problems. However, this absolutely does not mean that ADHD medications work differently in individuals with ADHD than in those without the disorder, as was previously thought; there is no reasonable pharmacological basis for that position. Thus, at a fundamental level, ADHD medications work in an array of specific, but standardized, fashions, but there is considerable psychological and physiological variation observed within individuals with ADHD.

Stimulating Attention

The ability of central nervous system psychostimulants generally, and of some other ADHD medications, to improve attention has become an important factor for those attempting to craft a treatment plan for those dealing with this core symptom of ADHD. Inattention, or the failure to focus or to pay attention, is a commonly reported complaint among those with ADHD. A general feature of ADHD stimulant medications is that they tend to increase blood flow to the parts of the frontal cortex that are involved with attention. Other ADHD medications, such as the cholinergic agent nicotine (at least at low dosages), also help to improve attention.

Stimulants appear to paradoxically calm individuals down. These medications clearly help people focus and pay attention, whether they have ADHD or not. However, if as many believe that the brains of an individual with ADHD is not sufficiently stimulated by his or her environment, then they might be expected to continually shift their attention, be constantly on the move, and to seek thrills to remediate their boredom. The stimulating effects of these medications consequently appear to help stimulate their brain, thus distracted individuals with ADHD are better able to calm down and stay focused, primarily by the direct or indirect altering of the levels of neurotransmitters in their brains created by these medications.

Stimulating Self-Regulation

The capacity of ADHD stimulant medications to assist with behavioral inhibition in individuals with ADHD is another crucially important effect of the use of certain ADHD medications. The phenomenon of self-regulation indicates the degree to which the subjective experiences of individuals are deeply social. Individuals must know how to experience both a sense of a core self and of others, including how to experience a pervasive sense of their self-being with others in multiple contexts. The structuring of functions and regulating practices is a lifelong developmental task, but those with poor inhibitory control, which is often typical of those with ADHD, make this maturational goal more elusive. Some ADHD medications, fortunately, enhance the ability of an individual to perform this behavioral inhibition successfully. The antihypertensive alpha 2 agonist ADHD medications, for example, stimulate the postsynaptic alpha 2A receptors in the neurons of the prefrontal cortex, which increases functional connectivity in that region, thereby improves the capacity of individuals to self-regulate their behavior. Amantadine hydrochloride (Symmetrel) is another ADHD medicine that helps to control impulsive behaviors, which it does by stimulating the synthesis and release of dopamine. Atomoxetine hydrochloride (Strattera), a norepinephrine transporter inhibitor, and the antihypertensive alpha 2 agonists clonidine hydrochloride (Kapvay) and guanfacine hydrochloride (Intuniv) also help to improve impulse control.

Importance of Dose

It is critical to establish the appropriate dose for a particular ADHD medicine, as it is of any medicine, in order for it to produce its desired therapeutic effects. The dose simply refers to the quantity of a particular medicine, in this case, an ADHD medicine, which is prescribed to be taken at one time. The dosage refers to the rate of the application of a dose; it includes the determination and regulation of the size and frequency of the dose to be administered. The effective dose refers to the amount of a particular medicine, again in this case of an ADHD medicine, which is needed to produce a therapeutic response in a specific proportion of subjects. Many ADHD medications can have a desired effect at one dose, but a different response at other, either higher or lower, doses.

The use of an appropriate dose of a particular medicine is of particular concern when treating certain special populations, particularly the very young and the elderly. Accidental medicine overdose in young children has become an increasingly common, but preventable, public health problem in recent years. In addition, the elderly metabolize medications differently than younger adults; their metabolism and liver functions are typically slower; therefore, elderly individuals frequently require lower doses of ADHD medications. The elderly are also more likely to be on multiple medications and the possibility for drug interactions is thus more of an area of concern.

EFFECTS OF SPECIFIC ADHD MEDICATIONS

There are, as repeatedly mentioned throughout this book, many different types of ADHD medications. The main two different types of medications used are the central nervous system stimulant drugs and the nonstimulant ones. The effects of these respective ADHD medications vary somewhat with respect to several important variables, which include dosage, bioavailability, onset of action, duration of action, half-life, and pharmacokinetics and elimination.

Dosage

The dosage of an ADHD medicine, as just noted, refers to the amount of the medicine administered at a rate sufficient to produce therapeutic results. The dosages for the central nervous system stimulant medications are, roughly speaking, somewhat similar. The recommended initial dosage range for amphetamine (Dyanavel XR) for ADHD is 5 mg twice per day, which can be increased by 10 mg/week until the desired therapeutic effect is reached. The recommended dosage range for the stimulant dextroamphetamine (Dexedrine) for ADHD is up to 40 mg/day administered orally. The recommended dosage range for lisdextroamphetamine (Vyvanse) is between 30 mg/day and 70 mg/day administered orally. The recommended dosage range for methamphetamine hydrochloride (Desoxyn) is up to 25 mg/day administered orally. The recommended dosage range for methylphenidate hydrochloride (Ritalin) is between 5 mg/day and 60 mg/day administered orally. Since the longer acting ADHD stimulant medicine formulations have become available, thereby eliminating the need for multiple daily dosing, there has been a dramatic reduction in many of the barriers to their use, such as non-compliance, stigma, and activity restrictions.

The dosages for the various nonstimulant ADHD medications are considerably more varied than are those of the stimulant ones. For example, the antihypertensive ADHD medications, which are primarily the alpha 2 agonists, like clonidine hydrochloride (Catapres, Kapvay) and guanfacine hydrochloride (Intuniv, Tenex), differ very markedly in their dosages; while the recommended dosage range for clonidine hydrochloride is between 100 mcg/day and 600 mcg/day administered orally, the recommended dosage range for guanfacine hydrochloride is between 1 mg/day and 3 mg/day administered orally once a day, usually at bedtime. The recommended dosage range for amantadine hydrochloride (Symmetrel) is 200 mg/day taken orally or 100 mg/day for individuals over the age of 65 years. The recommended dosage range for bupropion hydrochloride (Wellbutrin) is from

100 mg/day to 300 mg/day taken orally in divided doses; similarly, the recommended dosage range for bupropion hydrobromide (Aplenzin) is from 174 mg/day to 348 mg/day.

The TCA ADHD medications are roughly similar in their recommended dosage ranges. The recommended dosage range for amitriptyline hydrochloride (Elavil) is up to 150 mg/day orally administered in divided doses. The recommended dosage range for both desipramine hydrochloride (Norpramin) and imipramine hydrochloride (Tofranil) is from 100 mg/day to 200 mg/day. The recommended dosage range for nortriptyline hydrochloride (Aventyl, Pamelor) is 25 mg orally 3 to 4 times each day not to exceed 150 mg/day.

The major beta blocker ADHD medications are atenolol (Tenorim), nadolol (Corgard) and propranolol (Inderal). The respective dosage ranges for the beta blocker medications are, again roughly speaking, quite similar; while the recommended dosage range for atenolol is between 50 mg/day and 200 mg/day administered orally, the recommended dosage range for nadolol is between 40 mg/day and 240 mg/day, and that for propranolol is between 120 mg/day and 240 mg/day.

The respective dosage ranges for the selective SSRIs are roughly similar. The recommended dosage range for oral doses of the SSRI citalopram hydrobromide (Celexa) is from 20 mg/day to 40 mg/day; for escitalopram (Lexapro), it is from 10 mg/day to 20 mg/day; for fluoxetine hydrochloride (Prozac), it is up to 80 mg/day; for fluvoxamine maleate, it is from 50 mg/day to 300 mg/day in divided doses; for nefazodone, it is from 200 mg/day to 600 mg/day in divided doses; for paroxetine hydrochloride (Paxil), it is from 20 mg/day to 50 mg/day; for sertraline (Zoloft), it is from 50 mg/day to 200 mg/day; and for venlafaxine hydrochloride (Effexor), it is from 75 mg/day to 225 mg/day in divided doses.

The dosages for the ADHD anticonvulsant medications differ considerably. While the recommended dosage ranges for carbamazepine (Tegretol) are, for maintenance purposes, between 800 mg/day and 1,200 mg/day, administered orally in divided doses; the recommended dosage ranges for valporic acid (Depakote), on the other hand, are between 10 mg/kg/day and 60 mg/kg/day when administered orally, and if the dosage exceeds 250 mg/day, then it should be administered in divided doses.

The recommended initial dosage for atomoxetine hydrochloride (Strattera), a norepinephrine transporter inhibitor, is 40 mg/day administered orally, which may be increased up to 100 mg/day administered orally. However, the effective dose of atomoxetine hydrochloride ranges from about 5 mg/day to 100 mg/day, thus doses less than 40 mg/day might be appropriate, particularly for small children.

The MAOIs differ somewhat with respect to their dosages. While the recommended dosage range for the MAOI selegiline (Eldepryl) is 5 mg administered at breakfast and again at lunch that for the MAOI rasagiline (Azilect) is between 0.5 mg/day and 1 mg/day, that for phenelzine sulfate (Nardil) is from 45 mg/day to 90 mg/day, and that for tranylcypromine sulfate (Parnate) is from 30 mg/day to 60 mg/day in divided doses.

The respective dosages for the varied antipsychotic medications differ considerably. The recommended dosage range for haloperidol (Haldol) is between 0.05 mg/kg/day and 0.075 mg/kg/day administered orally for children, and for adults, between 0.5 mg and 5 mg administered orally two to three times per day and up to 100 mg/day administered in divided doses. The recommended initial dosage range for pimozide (Orap) is between 1 mg/day and 2 mg/day administered orally, with a maintenance dose of up to 10 mg/day administered orally. The recommended dosage range for thioridazine hydrochloride (Mellaril) is between 50 mg and 100 mg administered orally three times per day, but not to exceed 800 mg/day. The recommended initial dosage range for clozapine (Clozaril) is between 25 mg/day and 50 mg/day, and then it titrates up to 300 mg/day to 400 mg/day administered orally but not to exceed 900 mg/day. The recommended dosage range for olanzapine pamoate (Zyprexa) is between 5 mg/day and 20 mg/day. The recommended dosage range for quetiapine fumarate (Seroquel) is between 150 mg/day and 750 mg/day administered orally in divided doses; while the recommended dosage range for risperidone (Risperdal) is considerably less, between 0.5 mg and 6 mg administered orally once daily, and between 1 mg and 3 mg administered orally twice daily for adults.

It is very important to remember that each individual with ADHD is somewhat different with respect to his or her dosage needs for respective medications. Some individuals need relatively small doses of stimulant medications, such as from 2.5 mg to 5 mg, two times a day, while other individuals may need to be administered the same ADHD medicine four or even five times a day. Most individuals with ADHD, however, particularly if on extended release formulations, are only administered their ADHD medications once each day. Other individuals may need higher doses of the same stimulant medicine, such as around 15 mg to 20 mg, or perhaps even one of the nonstimulant ADHD medications. It is important to recognize here that an individual's body weight does not necessarily correlate with the size of the dose that will be therapeutically effective for them. Typically, a period of trial and error is necessary before the right dosage of the right ADHD medicine for an individual is found.

Bioavailability

Bioavailability is that part of an oral dose that is available to produce pharmacological actions as measured by the percentage of its active form that reaches the left ventricle of the heart. It is expressed, by definition, as the fraction of an oral dose of a particular drug that is absorbed but not inactivated in the gastrointestinal tract, metabolized, and/or excreted in bile during first passage through the liver. Bioavailability can result from the extent to which a respective formulated dosage of a particular medicine dissolves or disintegrates in gastrointestinal fluids, is metabolized in the gastrointestinal tract, and/or by a first pass hepatic metabolism or biliary excretion. Medications that have a high bioavailability are generally less susceptible to drug-drug interactions or to dietary influences that affect first pass liver metabolism. Plasma protein binding relates to the extent that particular medications chemically bond to albumin or other blood plasma proteins, which, in turn, influences how the medicine is distributed to various target sites and body tissues and its effectiveness, as medications bound to plasma proteins are pharmacologically inactive.

The bioavailability of the central nervous system stimulant ADHD medications is fairly high. The bioavailability of oral administration of amphetamine (Dyanavel XR) varies with respect to the pH of the gastrointestinal tract, with an acidic pH less amphetamine is absorbed, while with a basic pH more of the lipid soluble base form of the medicine is absorbed. Consequently, the bioavailability of amphetamine can range from 75 percent to 100 percent, and it exhibits 15 percent to 40 percent plasma protein binding. The bioavailability of oral administration of dextroamphetamine (Dexedrine) likewise can range from 75 percent to 100 percent. The bioavailability of lisdextroamphetamine (Vyvanse) is 96.4 percent, while that of methamphetamine hydrochloride (Desoxyn) is 70 percent. However, the bioavailability of methylphenidate (Ritalin) is considerably less than that of the other stimulant ADHD medications as it can range from 11 percent to 52 percent, with an average oral bioavailability of about 30 percent; it exhibits 10 percent to 33 percent plasma protein binding.

There is somewhat more variability with respect to the bioavailability of the nonstimulant ADHD medications than there is for the stimulants. The bioavailability of amantadine hydrochloride (Symmetrel) following oral administration can range from 86 percent to 90 percent; it exhibits about 67 percent plasma protein binding. The bioavailability of bupropion hydrochloride (Wellbutrin) following oral administration can range from 60 percent to 80 percent; it exhibits 85 percent plasma protein binding; the bioavailability and plasma protein binding for bupropion hydrobromide (Aplenzin) is comparable to that of bupropion hydrochloride (Wellbutrin). The bioavailability of atomoxetine hydrochloride (Strattera), a norepinephrine transporter inhibitor, following oral administration can range from 63 percent to 94 percent; it exhibits about 98 percent plasma protein binding, primarily to albumin. The bioavailability of the eugeroic modafinil (Provigil) is more than 80 percent, and it exhibits 62 percent plasma protein binding.

The bioavailability of the respective TCAs is quite variable following oral administration. The bioavailability of amitriptyline hydrochloride (Elavil) can range from 31 percent to 61 percent, and it exhibits 82 percent to 96 percent plasma protein binding. The bioavailability of the protypical TCA imipramine hydrochloride (Tofranil) can range from 29 percent to 77 percent, and it exhibits 76 percent to 95 percent plasma protein binding. The bioavailability of desipramine hydrochloride (Norpramin) can range from 60 percent to 70 percent, and it exhibits 73 percent to 92 percent plasma protein binding. Finally, the bioavailability of nortriptyline hydrochloride (Pamelor) can range from 32 percent to 79 percent, and it exhibits 93 percent to 95 percent plasma protein binding.

The bioavailability of the alpha 2 agonist antihypertensive ADHD medications following oral administration is relatively high. Accordingly, the bioavailability of clonidine hydrochloride (Kapvay) can range from 75 percent to 95 percent following oral administration and from 60 percent to 70 percent for transdermal administration, and it exhibits 20 percent to 40 percent plasma protein binding. Similarly, the bioavailability of guanfacine hydrochloride (Intuniv) is about 80 percent with oral administration, and it exhibits about 70 percent plasma protein binding.

The bioavailability of the beta blocker ADHD medications following oral administration is less than that of most other ADHD medications as they are well distributed in the body, but not in the brain or the rest of the central nervous system. The bioavailability of atenolol (Tenorim) is about 50 percent to 60 percent with oral administration, and it exhibits about 6 percent to 16 percent plasma protein binding. The bioavailability of nadolol (Corgard) is from about 29 percent to 39 percent, and it exhibits about 16 percent to 24 percent plasma protein binding. The bioavailability of propranolol (Inderal) is from about 26 percent to 46 percent, and it exhibits 92 percent to 94 percent plasma protein binding.

The bioavailability of the SSRI antiobsessive ADHD medications varies in a manner comparable to that of the other nonstimulant ADHD medicine classes following oral administration. The bioavailability of citalopram hydrobromide (Celexa) is about 80 percent following oral administration, and it exhibits 80 percent plasma protein binding. The bioavailability of fluoxetine hydrochloride (Prozac) is about 70 percent, and it exhibits 94 percent plasma protein binding. The bioavailability of escitalopram (Lexapro) is about 80 percent, and it exhibits about 56 percent plasma protein binding. The bioavailability of fluvoxamine maleate (Luvox) is greater than 90 percent, and it exhibits 77 percent plasma protein binding. The bioavailability of nefazodone (Serzone) ranges from only 15 percent to 23 percent, and it exhibits 98 percent plasma protein binding. The bioavailability of paroxetine hydrochloride (Paxil) is approximately 50 percent, and it exhibits 95 percent plasma protein binding. Finally, the bioavailability of sertraline hydrochloride (Zoloft) is about 44 percent, and it exhibits 98.5 percent plasma protein binding, while peak plasma concentrations occurred between 4.5 hours and 8.4 hours after oral administration.

The bioavailability of the anticonvulsant ADHD medications is extremely high following oral administration. The bioavailability of carbamazepine (Tegretol) is about 100 percent, and it exhibits from 70 percent to 80 percent plasma protein binding. Similarly, the bioavailability of valporic acid (Depakote) is from 90 percent to 100 percent, and it exhibits from 89 percent to 97 percent plasma protein binding.

The bioavailability of the MAOIs has considerable variability. The bioavailability of the MAOI moclobemide (Amira) ranges from 45 percent to 70 percent after a single oral dose, but it rises to 80 percent to 90 percent with repeated administrations; moclobemide exhibits about 50 percent plasma protein binding moderately binding to albumin; peak plasma concentrations are reached within one to two hours after oral administration of moclobemide. The bioavailability of the MAOI rasagiline mesylate (Azilect) is only about 36 percent following oral administration, and it exhibits from about 88 percent to 94 percent plasma protein binding. The bioavailability of the MAOI selegiline (Eldepryl) following oral administration is about 4.4 percent with fasting and about 20 percent after food, while it is about 18 percent with transdermal administration, and it exhibits about 90 percent plasma protein binding. The bioavailability of the MAOI tranylcypromine sulfate (Parnate) is about 50 percent following oral administration.

The bioavailability of the antipsychotic ADHD medications is somewhat variable. The bioavailability of quetiapine fumarate (Seroquel) is 100 percent, and it exhibits 83 percent plasma protein binding. The bioavailability of haloperidol (Haldol) can range from 60 percent to 70 percent with oral administration, and it exhibits about 90 percent plasma protein binding. Similarly, the bioavailability of clozapine (Clozaril) can also range from 60 percent to 70 percent. Likewise, the bioavailability of risperidone (Risperdal) is about 70 percent, and it exhibits about 88 percent plasma protein binding, and that of its pharmacologically active metabolite, 9-hydroxyrisperidone, further exhibits about 77 percent plasma protein binding. The bioavailability of olanzapine pamoate (Zyprexa) is about 80 percent as about 20 percent of the oral dose is metabolized before it reaches the blood, and olanzapine exhibits about 93 percent plasma protein binding. The bioavailability of aripiprazole (Abilify) is about 87 percent, and it exhibits about 99 percent plasma protein binding. The bioavailability of ziprasidone (Geodon, Zeldox) is about 60 percent, and it exhibits about 98 percent plasma protein binding. The bioavailability of pimozide (Orap) is from 40 percent to 50 percent, and it exhibits 99 percent plasma protein binding. On the other hand, there is considerable interindividual variability in the bioavailability of chlorpromazine hydrochloride (Thorazine) ranging from 10 percent to 80 percent, and it exhibits about 90 percent to 99 percent plasma protein binding.

Finally, the bioavailability of the cholinergic agent nicotine varies with respect to the route of administration. It has a bioavailability that can range from 20 percent to 45 percent with oral administration, about 53 percent with intranasal administration, and about 68 percent with transdermal administration, and it exhibits less than 5 percent plasma protein binding. This overview of bioavailability indicates that many, but certainly not all, of the ADHD medications are well absorbed, therefore available to treat, through their respective mechanisms of action, the varied symptoms of ADHD.

Onset of Action

The onset of action is the amount of time after administration that it takes an ADHD medicine to have effects that are therapeutically noticeable. In discussing the onset of action of any ADHD medicine, it is important to distinguish between what is generally considered as a delayed onset of action with some medications, particularly the antipsychotics, and a delay in the full realization of therapeutic improvement. Many medications clearly can take time, up to several weeks in some instances, to realize their full therapeutic benefits. However, such a delay of attaining full benefits does not in and of itself necessarily imply a delayed onset of action. Some of the effects typically manifest simultaneously with the point at which a specific medicine reaches its therapeutic levels, often within a few days or, in many cases, considerably less. Some of the differences in these two phenomena may be explained by the pharmacodynamics of respective medications in which a gradual accumulation of biological intermediaries of relevant psychoactive metabolites may underpin the realization of a full therapeutic response. In addition, in a condition such as ADHD, it is reasonable to accept that attainment of a full therapeutic response would be accomplished in a manner comparable to that of the unlearning of the negative behaviors associated with the disorder, as occurs in psychological extinction. These assumptions help to explain why most individuals demonstrate a gradual improvement over the course of their treatment, rather than an instantaneous transformation.

The onset of action of any respective ADHD medicine is, of course, heavily dependent upon the pharmacodynamics and the pharmacokinetics of that particular drug. The pharmacological effects of any medicine can only happen after the particular substance has been completely solubilized and entered into the blood stream. As most ADHD medications are administered orally, they need first to be ingested, then they must pass through the stomach into the small intestine, a process which is highly variable and sometimes can take a couple of hours.

The onset of action of the stimulant ADHD medications is relatively rapid. However, there are some differences in the onset of action for respective ADHD medications depending on the type of formulation considered. For example, the onset of action of the immediate release formulations of amphetamine, methylphenidate (Ritalin), and dexmethylphenidate (Focalin) is from 30 minutes to 60 minutes, and for the immediate release formulation of dextroamphetamine (Dexedrine), it is from 30 minutes to 75 minutes; while the onset of action for the extended release formulations of amphetamine (Dyanavel XR) and dextroamphetamine is from 1.5 hours to 2 hours, and for methylphenidate is about 1 hour. The onset of action for the combination amphetamine formulation Adderall is also from 30 minutes to 60 minutes, while for lisdextroamphetamine (Vyvanse) is about 2 hours. Since methylphenidate (Ritalin), in particular, is rapidly absorbed and exhibits relatively poor binding to plasma proteins, it not only has a rapid onset of action to attain therapeutic effects for ADHD, it also tends to achieve a higher concentration in the brain than in the blood plasma localized elsewhere throughout the body.

There is considerably more variation in the onset of action for the respective nonstimulant ADHD medications and, in general, they have a longer onset of action. For instance, the onset of action of amantadine hydrochloride (Symmetrel) is two days or about 48 hours. The TCAs also have a longer onset of action than the stimulant medications; that for amitriptyline hydrochloride (Elavil) is from two days to five days generally and from four weeks to six weeks for that of its antidepressant effects; similarly the onset of action for nortriptyline hydrochloride (Pamelor) is from one week to three weeks; and the onset of action for imipramine hydrochloride (Tofranil) is from two weeks to eight weeks, although the peak plasms concentration is typically attained in one hour to two hours following oral administration. Although some effects may be observed relatively early with atomoxetine hydrochloride (Strattera), actually in about two hours, they tend to increase progressively over several weeks; furthermore, in some individuals, at least, it may take several months for the maximum therapeutic effects to be attained. The onset of action for the antihypertensive medicine guanfacine hydrochloride (Intuniv) is within one week, although peak plasma concentration is reached within 1 hour to 4 hours, with an average of 2.6 hours. On the other hand, the onset of action for ADHD medications such as bupropion hydrochloride (Wellbutrin) is from 60 minutes to 90 minutes, and that for the eugeroic modafinil (Provigil), it is from 20 minutes to 60 minutes; these ranges are more similar to that of the psychostimulant ADHD medications. However, the antipsychotic pimozide (Orap) attains peak plasma concentration between six hours and eight hours following oral administration. The MAOI moclobemide (Amira) has a quicker onset of action than the SSRIs and it has better tolerability, while the MAOI tranylcypromine sulfate (Parnate) has an onset of action of 48 hours to three weeks.

Duration of Action

The duration of action refers to the amount of time that a particular drug persists with a measurable therapeutic effect. The duration of action of many stimulant drugs, depending on the specific drug and its formulation, as well as sometimes on the route of administration employed, can be quite variable. For instance, the duration of action of both amphetamine (Dyanavel XR) and dextroamphetamine (Dexedrine) is between 3 hours and 7 hours with immediate release oral formulations and 12 hours with extended release oral formulations, while the duration of action of lisdextroamphetamine (Vyvanse) is 12 hours and that of methamphetamine hydrochloride (Desoxyn) is between 10 hours and 20 hours. Similarly, methylphenidate (Ritalin), another stimulant medicine commonly prescribed for treating ADHD, has a duration of action between 3 hours and 6 hours with an immediate release formulation, 5 hours to 8 hours with an extended release formulation, and 12 hours with a long acting formulation. The duration of action of a combination stimulant formulation like Adderall is 8 hours to 12 hours. The duration of action is of particular importance for treating those individuals with ADHD so that they can perform without the resurfacing of ADHD symptoms if the medicine successfully treats them while at a therapeutic dosage level. Unfortunately, if a child or adolescent is in school and took their ADHD stimulant medicine before arriving at school, and they are on a medication that only has, for example, a 3 hour duration of action, then unless they are administered another dose, the symptoms are likely to emerge while they are still in school. This is a major reason that extended release formulations were developed for these pharmaceutical products. The duration of action is usually not as much of a problem for those taking the nonstimulant ADHD medications.

There is somewhat less variation with respect to the duration of action for respective nonstimulant ADHD medications. In fact, the duration of action for many of the nonstimulant ADHD medications is sufficiently long to permit once a day dosing. For example, the duration of action of the antihypertensive alpha 2 agonist guanfacine hydrochloride (Intuniv, Tenex) is 24 hours for administration of a single dose, while that of clonidine hydrochloride (Catapres, Kapvay) is from 6 hours to 24 hours. Similarly, the duration of action for the beta blocker ADHD medicine atenolol (Tenorim) is at least 24 hours following single dose oral administration and about 12 hours following intravenous administration. The duration of action of the eugeroic modafinil (Provigil) is from 5 hours to 15 hours following oral administration, with an average duration of 12 hours, while the average duration of action for armodafinil (Nuvigil) is 15 hours. Similarly, the average duration of action of the MAOI moclobemide (Amira) is 16 hours. The relatively long duration of action for most of the nonstimulant ADHD medications makes this less of an issue than it typically is for the stimulant ADHD medications.

Half-Life

The biological half-life of a drug, that is the time that it takes for half (50%) of the drug to be metabolized or eliminated from the plasma, is closely related to its duration of action. Accordingly, there is a fair degree of variability with respect to the biological half-life of respective ADHD medications, some of which, at least, is attributed to individual metabolic variation. The half-life of an ADHD medicine helps in large measure to determine if it can be safely and effectively administered at a particular dosing rate, at least in immediate release formulations.

The biological half-lives of many respective central nervous system stimulant ADHD medications have a rather wide range of variation. The half-life of racemic amphetamine (Dyanvel XR) can range from 9 hours to 14 hours. The half-life of dextroamphetamine (Dexedrine) can range from 7 hours to 8 hours with an acidic urine pH of less than 5.6, while with an alkaline urine pH, it is from 18.6 hours to 33.6 hours, with an average half-life of about 16 hours. The biological half-life of the prodrug lisdextroamfetamine (Vyvanse) molecule is less than or equal to one hour, while the remainder is that of dextroamphetamine. The half-life of methamphetamine hydrochloride

(Desoxyn) has an even wider range of from 5 hours to 30 hours. On the other hand, methylphenidate (Ritalin) has a relatively narrow half-life range of from two hours to three hours.

There is a considerable range of variation in the biological half-lives of respective nonstimulant ADHD medications. The half-life of amantadine hydrochloride (Symmetrel) can range from 10 hours to 25 hours, with an average half-life of about 17 hours. The half-life of the TCAs medications ranges from 8 hours to 20 hours for imipramine hydrochloride (Tofranil); from 9 hours to 27 hours for amitriptyline hydrochloride (Elavil); from 21 hours to 125 hours for desipramine hydrochloride (Norpramin); and from 16 hours to 90 hours for nortriptyline hydrochloride (Pamelor), although in most individuals, it is about 28 hours to 31 hours. The half-life of bupropion hydrochloride (Wellbutrin) can range from 12 hours to 30 hours, with an average half-life of about 10 hours for the immediate release formulation and about 17 hours for the slow release formulation. The plasma half-life of atomoxetine hydrochloride (Strattera) in most individuals is about 4 hours to 5 hours. The alpha 2 agonist antihypertensive medicine guanfacine hydrochloride (Intuniv) has a half-life that ranges from 10 hours to 30 hours, with an average of about 17 hours in healthy individuals with normal renal function. The half-life of the selective SSRI fluoxetine hydrochloride (Prozac) ranges from one day to three days for a single dose and from four days to six days for those administered long term.

Most of the beta blockers have a relatively short half-life. Accordingly, a therapeutic dose of the beta blocker atenolol (Tenorim, Tenoretic) has a half-life of about 6 hours to 7 hours; that of nadolol (Corgard) is about 20 hours to 24 hours, which permits once a day dosing; and that of propranolol (Inderal) is from 2.9 hours to 11 hours.

The half-lives of the anticonvulsant ADHD medications are somewhat longer. The half-life of a single dose of carbamazepine (Tegretol) can range from 25 hours to 65 hours, while that of repeated doses is from 12 hours to 17 hours. The half-life of the anticonvulsant valporic acid (Depakote) can range from 9 hours to 16 hours.

The half-life of the antipsychotic ADHD medications varies considerably; the half-life of quetiapine fumarate (Seroquel) is 7 hours, but that of its active metabolite, norquetiapine, is from 9 hours to 12 hours. Similarly, the half-life of ziprasidone (Geodon, Zeldox) is about 7 hours. The half-life of haloperidol (Haldol) varies with respect to the route of administration ranging from 14 hours to 26 hours with oral administration, and 20.7 hours with intramuscular administration. The half-life of clozapine (Clozaril) ranges from 6 hours to 26 hours with an average of 14.2 hours. The half-life of thioridazine hydrochloride (Mellaril) is from 21 hours to 25 hours. The half-life of olanzapine pamoate (Zyprexa) is from 21 hours to 54 hours. The half-life of risperidone (Risperdal) is from 20 hours to 24 hours. The half-life of chlorpromazine hydrochloride (Thorazine) is around 30 hours. The half-life of pimozide (Orap) is about 55 hours in adults and about 66 hours in children. The half-life of aripiprazole (Abilify) is from 75 hours to 146 hours. The elimination half-life of the MAOI moclobenide (Amira) is between 1 and 2 hours in normal healthy individuals, but it can be up to 4 hours in elderly individuals. Likewise, the half-life of the cholinergic agent nicotine is also between 1 and 2 hours, but that of its active metabolite is around 20 hours.

Pharmacokinetics and Elimination

Pharmacokinetics is a broad term that refers to the various activities that occur within the body after the administration of a particular drug; this includes many of the factors just discussed from absorption and distribution, which relate to bioavailability, through metabolism, which is related to half-life, to excretion, or how the drug is eliminated from the body. The biological half-life of a drug is a function of both its distribution within the body and its elimination, by means of either or both metabolic disposition and/or from excretion. The rate of absorption of a particular medicine is influenced by several factors, including the route of administration, the solubility of the specific substance, and the existence of certain bodily conditions, such as lipodystrophy and the health of the user's liver. For example, if a medicine is swallowed and absorbed through the small intestine, it travels through the liver, which causes what is called the first pass effect, where it is partially metabolize before being released to circulate through the body, which can dramatically alter the dose necessary to achieve a therapeutic effect. The amount of a particular drug eventually excreted unchanged in the urine is sometimes expressed as a percentage of the dose administered.

ADHD medications are eliminated from the body by several different methods. The kidney is one of the major organs that excretes medications and their metabolites through urine production. Various enzymes in the liver break down medications into simpler compounds so that they can be excreted. If medications are not absorbed following oral administration, then they can be eliminated in the feces, as are metabolites excreted by the liver in bile. Some medications are also secreted through breast milk, which can potentially be harmful to nursing infants. Small amounts of some medications can be eliminated by means of perspiration, and some even by means of exhalation.

The pharmacokinetic differences of respective ADHD medications helps to explain why some individuals may not respond to what is typically an effective dosage of that particular substance, while other individuals may be particularly sensitive to dose-dependent adverse side effects. A better understanding of the pharmacokinetic properties of the respective ADHD medications can be of great use in helping health care providers select the best medications and also to make adjustments in dosage to optimize individual outcomes. ADHD medicine selection must, of course, be individualized based on the pharmaco-kinetics and pharmacodynamics profiles of available medications, as well as of their effects in a particular individual with respect to variables such as previous response patterns, preferences, and comorbidities.

Amantadine hydrochloride (Symmetrel) is absorbed well orally. The time to peak concentration ranges from 1.5 hours to 8 hours, with an average of 3.3 hours. It is excreted primarily in the urine by means of glomerular filtration and tubular secretion. Atomoxetine hydrochloride (Strattera) is rapidly absorbed following oral administration; it has a water solubility of 27.8 mg/mL, is metabolized by means of hepatic CYPO2D6 and, finally, excreted in the urine. The antihypertensive medicine clonidine hydrochloride (Kapvay) is almost completely absorbed from the gastrointestinal tract when taken orally, but it is subject to rapid liver metabolism. About 50 percent of the anti-hypertensive medicine guanfacine hydrochloride (Intuniv) is eliminated through urine; in fact, approximately 40 percent is excreted unchanged in the urine. The MAOI moclobemide (Amira) is well absorbed following oral administration, with more than 95 percent absorbed in the gastrointestinal tract; the first-pass hepatic metabolism of moclobemide reduces bioavailability to 45 percent to 70 percent after administration of a single dose; metabolism is primarily hepatic, with most excretion by renal processes, less than 5 percent is eliminated through the feces. The MAOI tranylcypromine sulfate (Parnate) is eliminated within 24 hours. The antipsychotic medicine olanzapine pamoate (Zyprexa) is eliminated mostly through the urine (57%) and the feces (30%).

ADHD MEDICATIONS DON'T WORK FOR EVERYBODY

The truth, unfortunately, is that ADHD medications do not work for everyone with ADHD. Every individual responds somewhat differently to respective ADHD medications. Every individual has his or her own unique individualized chemistry. These physiological and medical differences can sub-stantially alter how a specific medicine may work in one individual but vary considerably in another.

There can also be differences between brand name and generic formulations of specific ADHD medications. It may only be a slight variation, but since each individual's body is different, one manufacturer's version of a particular medicine may not digest as well as another manufacturer's version. Finding the right medication that works best, if at all, for a particular individual is essential to good professional treatment.

ADHD MEDICATIONS USED TO TREAT OTHER CONDITIONS

The use or a particular medicine for a particular medical condition is often the result of a process of trial and error. It is very common for a specific medicine to be administered to numerous individuals for a particular purpose, and then, after the fact, for a novel therapeutic effect to be observed among a subset of that population. This pattern has been particularly common in suggesting that respective medications developed and approved for other purposes, might be of assistance for relief of symptoms related to ADHD. This, in large part, explains why there are so many diverse drug classes that are now used as ADHD medications. At any rate, many ADHD medications have been and continue to be used for purposes other than ADHD.

Past Uses

Many of the respective ADHD medications have previously been used for treating myriad medical conditions. Some of the more common conditions that many of the ADHD medications have been used for include respiratory illness, depression, and weight loss.

Respiratory Illness.   Several ADHD medications were used to treat various respiratory illnesses when they were first introduced. This goes back to at least the latter half of the sixteenth century when French royalty were using tobacco as a panacea following its introduction by Jean Nicot, in whose honor nicotine was named. French nobility were then asserting that tobacco had curative properties and was effective in treating asthma and other diseases. The use of tobacco for healing goes back much earlier among Native Americans in the New World. Nevertheless, the belief in the medicinal uses of tobacco persisted for some time. For example, Theodore Roosevelt as a child around 1869 suffered from asthma and his parents, in accordance with conventional medical wisdom of the time, ordered him to occasionally smoke cigars as therapy.

The amphetamines, as a class, cause bronchodilation and vasodilation, among other effects, which have made them frequently used, since their discovery, as pharmacotherapeutic treatments for respiratory illnesses. Since the 1930s, amphetamine was widely used, particularly after the 1932 introduction of the Benzedrine inhaler, which was then available over the counter for treating asthma, hay fever, the common cold, and other breathing problems. The other amphetamine ADHD medications, such as dextroamphetamine (Dexedrine), lisdextroamphetamine (Vyvanse), and methamphetamine (Desoxyn), have also been used in the past for treating respiratory illnesses. Methylphenidate hydrochloride (Ritalin), the non-amphetamine stimulant ADHD medicine, causes respiratory stimulation and so has also been used.

Some of the nonstimulant ADHD medications have also been used for treating various respiratory illnesses. Chronic use of beta blockers, such as nadolol (Corgard), has been demonstrated to improve airway responsiveness and also to reduce eosinophilic inflammation, mucin content, and cytokine elaboration, thus improving asthma exacerbation. Further, administration of a low-dose beta blocker, such as atenolol (Tenorim) or nadolol (Corgard), along with a corticosteroid, has been shown to be more effective at reducing both the volume density of epithelial mucin and the level of eosinophils than use of either drug alone, while also achieving fully additive therapeutic effects in treating an inflammatory condition of the lungs, such as that involved in respiratory illnesses like asthma, chronic obstructive pulmonary disease, or cystic fibrosis.

Depression.   The pharmacological treatment of depression has been the focus of considerable research and exploration. The central nervous system psychostimulant ADHD medications were once used for lifting someone who was depressed. In the 1940s, for instance, methamphetamine was sold under the trade name of Methadrine and freely recommended as an antidepressant. Bupropion hydrochloride, for example, is an atypical antidepressant medicine that is also commonly prescribed for treating depression.

Antidepressant medications do not elevate the mood of nondepressed individuals and, generally, they have low abuse potential. Many of the classes of ADHD medications are also considered to be major classes of antidepressants. In fact, for many of these medications, their primary use is in the treatment of depression, particularly for treating major depressive disorder. Although, of course, many of these medications have other well-established uses, such as in treating anxiety, eating disorders, and, of most concern here, ADHD. The major classes of antidepressant medications are the TCAs, the atypical antidepressants (which includes bupropion, nefazodone, and venlafaxine), the selective SSRIs, and the MAOIs.

The fact that so many of these respective medications are used to treat both depression and ADHD is obvious and certainly merits deeper examination than is possible here. It may be sufficient, however, to note here that our current general understanding of the efficacy of the mechanism of action of antidepressants is best explained by the monoamine hypothesis of depression, which, briefly stated, suggests that depression is the result of a dysfunction of one or more of the monoamine neurotransmitters, particularly norepinephrine, dopamine, and serotonin. We have already discussed the critical importance of these medications in treating ADHD by increasing the factors regulating monoamine-mediated neurotransmission, and this same explanatory model holds true for treating depression.

Weight Loss.   Weight loss is an area of particular concern to many individuals. It is estimated that 23.4 million children in the United States between 2 years and 19 years of age are overweight or obese; of these 23.4 million children, 11.1 million are females and 12.3 million are males. In addition, approximately 97 million adults in the United States are overweight or obese. There is even evidence that suggests that those with ADHD who do not use ADHD medications are more likely than those who do to be overweight. The amphetamines have long been used to assist individuals attempting to lose weight. In the 1940s, methamphetamine was sold under the trade name of Methadrine, which, among other things, was recommended as an appetite suppressant. In the 1950s and 1960s, amphetamines were widely prescribed for weight control, but their use is much more carefully monitored today due to concerns with misuse and dependence.

Pronounced loss of appetite, often resulting in anorexia, is a common adverse reaction of all the ADHD central nervous system stimulant medications including amphetamine (Dyanavel XR), dextroamphetamine (Dexedrine), lisdextroamphetamine (Vyvanse), methamphetamine (Desoxyn), and the combination of amphetamine and dextroamphetamine formulations (Adderall). Methylphenidate hydrochloride (Ritalin) and dexmethylphenidate (Focalin), non-amphetamine stimulant medications, also effectively decreases appetite and can likewise result in anorexia. Use of atomoxetine hydrochloride (Strattera) also can result in decreased appetite. Weight loss is also an adverse effect associated with some of the nonstimulant ADHD medications, such as bupropion hydrochloride (Wellbutrin), which has demonstrated significant efficacy for weight loss, and it is generally well tolerated. Part of the mechanism of action of bupropion includes weak inhibition of norepinephrine and dopamine uptake, which helps to maintain appetite suppression.

On the other hand, weight gain is an adverse effect associated with use of many of the other classes of ADHD medications. Although some of the SSRIs, such as fluoxetine (Prozac), are associated with weight loss during initial treatment, with long-term use weight gain is far more typical of most SSRIs. In fact, paroxetine (Paxil) appears to cause more weight gain than other SSRIs. The TCAs and the MAOIs appear to induce even greater weight gain than the SSRIs. Further, when TCAs and MAOIs are combined, even more dramatic weight increase are typically observed. Use of most of the typical antipsychotic ADHD medications, such as chlorpromazine (Thorazine) and thioridazine (Mellaril), and of the atypical antipsychotic ADHD medications, such as olanzapine (Zyprexa) and risperidone (Risperdal), also tends to induce weight gain.

Current Uses

Although many of the respective ADHD medications may have been developed for and had prior uses for other conditions, some have also been found to have other uses that may currently be rather prevalent. Narcolepsy and obesity are two of the particular conditions that some ADHD medications have come to be somewhat commonly used for; there are, of course, many other medical conditions that they are used for, as well as, no doubt, more that will likely be discovered in the future.

Narcolepsy.   Narcolepsy is a condition that results in sudden episodes of deep sleep. These outbreaks can happen frequently and at inappropriate times, such as when eating, driving, when in school, or when at work. The amphetamines, as a class, are routinely prescribed to treat narcolepsy and related sleeping disorders. The amphetamines, such as amphetamine (Dyanavel XR), dextroamphetamine (Dexedrine), and the combination amphetamine and dextroamphetamine formulations (Adderall), are effective for this purpose as they tend to both suppress the sleep centers in the brain and also help to maintain wakefulness. However, some of the other amphetamines are not approved for the treatment of narcolepsy, such as lisdextroamphetamine (Vyvanse) and methamphetamine (Desoxyn). The non-amphetamine stimulant ADHD medicine methylphenidate (Ritalin) is also approved for treating narcolepsy. The eugeroic ADHD medications, such as modafinil (Provigil) and armodafinil (Nuvigil), are another class of drugs that are characterized by their ability to promote wakefulness, thus can also be prescribed to be of assistance to someone with narcolepsy.

Obesity.   Obesity is a complex, chronic disease. The issue of obesity, or excessive body fat, is, unfortunately, a highly prevalent condition that not only can shorten one's life but can also put someone at an increased risk of developing many other health conditions, such as diabetes, hypertension, cardiovascular disease, certain cancers, dementia, and ADHD. It is estimated that 12 million children in the United States between 2 years and 19 years of age are obese; of these 12 million children, 5.6 million are females and 6.4 million are males. Further, it is recognized that children whose ADHD symptoms persist into adulthood have an increased risk of being overweight or obese compared to those who only had ADHD symptoms during childhood. Obesity treatment should be focused more on improving an individual's health by preventing or treating weight-related complications, rather than on only weight loss per se. Pharmacotherapy should only be used as an adjunct to lifestyle changes and not alone. However, there is still a valuable place for pharmacotherapy as it does, compared to lifestyle directed therapy alone, produce greater weight loss and improved weight-loss maintenance.

Some of the amphetamines, including amphetamine (Dyanavel XR), dextroamphetamine (Dexedrine), and methamphetamine (Desoxyn), have long been recognized for their utility in treating obesity as they generally tend to suppress the appetite, thereby lessen the tendency of individuals to eat excessively. However, lisdextroamphetamine, for instance, is not approved for treating obesity. Further, due to their abuse potential, those amphetamines that are approved for treating obesity are typically recommended to only be used as a temporary adjunctive therapy, while the individual can hopefully establish a more sustainable pattern of both increased regular physical activity and reduced caloric intake in order to maintain weight loss. Methylphenidate (Ritalin), a non-amphetamine stimulant ADHD medicine, is not approved for treating obesity in the United States. The nonstimulant ADHD medications are, generally speaking, not used in treating obesity.

Chapter 6

Risks, Misuse, and Overdose

There are, as there are with the use of virtually any type of medication, valid concerns of the various potential risks associated with the use and misuse of attention deficit hyperactivity disorder (ADHD) medications. These risks include the possible side effects associated with use of ADHD medications, some of which can potentially be rather serious, many others less serious. Fortunately, a good deal of these concerns are somewhat unwarranted once one gains an appropriate understanding of what is actually known about these respective ADHD medications and the results of their use.

COMMON AND OTHER SIDE EFFECTS OF ADHD MEDICATIONS

There are many common and some other relatively less common side effects that can possibly be associated with the use of the respective ADHD medications. However, it is broadly acknowledged that the use of any medication can result in undesired side effects. There are some side effects that are more commonly associated with the use of the respective stimulant ADHD medications, and there are also many side effects that are commonly associated with use of the varied nonstimulant ADHD medications.

Side Effects of Stimulants

There has been a considerable amount of concern raised over the various adverse side effects associated with the use of the psychostimulant ADHD medications; this is somewhat understandable since, of course, these stimulant medications are the most commonly prescribed drugs for individuals with

ADHD. One area of particular concern that has been that around for some time is that related to impaired growth rate in children and adolescents who take ADHD stimulant medications. Other areas of concern include the possible effects of use of ADHD stimulant medications upon numerous other issues such as appetite suppression and blood pressure, among a host of others.

Effects on Growth.   Although there has been long standing public controversy, particularly in the media, over the possible long-term consequences of the use of ADHD medications, specifically the psychostimulants and atomoxetine, there is little to no research evidence in support of this assumption. There were some concerns raised by preliminary studies conducted some time ago, which suggested that use of stimulant ADHD medications, like dextroamphetamine (Dexedrine) or methylphenidate (Ritalin), might stunt the growth of children. However, better designed clinical research studies conducted more recently have concluded that such is not generally the case. While there might be some minimal suppression of growth in some children administered high rates of these ADHD stimulant medications, this is generally eliminated as soon as the dosage is properly adjusted. Evidence, in fact, indicates that children who took such ADHD medications attain normal adult heights. Previously, it was a common practice to routinely stop the use of ADHD medications as an individual reached the beginnings of adolescence due to the misunderstanding that not to do so could cause a permanent loss of height. It is now recognized that at most a slight decrease in the dosage of the ADHD medicine might be recommended, but then again, fortunately, such an adjustment is not necessary for most individuals.

Effects on Appetite, Blood Pressure, and More.   There are many undesired side effects that are commonly experienced by individuals who use stimulant ADHD medications. Some of these side effects are due to the fact that pharmacologically stimulant drugs are sympathomimetic substances, meaning that they stimulate the sympathetic part of the autonomic nervous system, accordingly, producing physiological responses such as increased heart rate, blood pressure, and respiration. Other side effects that are commonly associated with use if stimulant drugs include dry mouth, pupillary dilation, and anorexia; blood glucose also increases, as does the rate of blood coagulation. There is an increase in skeletal muscular tension, but a relaxing of the bronchi musculature and of the intestines. Urination can sometimes become more difficult. Acute toxicity to stimulants following consumption of typically large doses can result in profound psychological changes, such as intense paranoia and other psychotic states, including what is referred to as amphetamine psychosis. Amphetamine psychosis can consist of states of extreme panic, mania, delusions, hallucinations, and schizophrenic-like behaviors.

There are, of course, somewhat different constellations of side effects associated with the use of respective ADHD stimulant medications. For instance, common side effects associated with the use of dextroamphetamine (Dexedrine) include appetite loss, constipation, diarrhea, dry mouth, headaches, sex drive or ability decline, sleep difficulties, uncontrollable shaking of body parts, unpleasant taste, and weight loss. Rarer, but serious, side effects associated with the use of dextroamphetamine include abnormal movements, aggressive or hostile behaviors, blurred vision, chest pain, believing things that are untrue, excessive tiredness, fast heart rate, frenzied mood, hallucinations, seizures, unusually suspicious of others, verbal tics, and weakness in an arm or leg. In a somewhat similar vein, common side effects associated with the use of methamphetamine hydrochloride (Desoxyn) include constipation, diarrhea, dry mouth, headaches, itching, restlessness, sex drive or ability changes, sleep difficulties, unpleasant taste, upset stomach, and weight loss. Rarer, but serious, side effects associated with the use of methamphetamine include aggressive or hostile behaviors, blurred vision, believing that that are not true, excessive tiredness, fast heart rate, hallucinations, mania, motor tics, paleness of fingers or toes, seizures, slow or difficult speech, tingling in hands or feet, uncontrolled shaking of body parts, unexplained wounds appearing on fingers and toes, unusually suspicious of others, and verbal tics. Likewise, common side effects reported by users of methylphenidate (Ritalin) can possibly include accelerated heart rate, decreased appetite, dry mouth or xerostomia, headache, insomnia, nausea, and vomiting. Rarer side effects associated with the use of methylphenidate can include anxiety, excessive sweating or hyperhidrosis, irritability, and tics.

The route of drug administration used alters the likelihood of various side effects being experienced with the use of respective psychostimulant ADHD medications, as well as for other substances. For instance, intranasal use of stimulants, or snorting, is more likely to be associated with congestion, hoarseness, loss of sense of smell, nose bleeding, and sinusitis, as well as of atrophy of the nasal septum, necrosis or perforation of the septum, and problems with swallowing. Smoking of psychostimulants, in addition to the numerous pulmonary complications, also can produce varied throat ailments and productive coughs with black sputum as well as carrying an increased susceptibility to addiction due to the enhanced euphoric experience. Intravenous, and other forms of injection drug use, is associated with greater risks for the use or sharing of unsterile equipment, which can, in turn, result in complications such as abscesses, bacterial or viral endocarditis, cellulitis, hepatitis, human immuno-deficiency virus (HIV) infection, lung infections, pneumonia, renal infarction, thrombosis, and tuberculosis. Prolonged oral administration of psychostimulant drugs has also been associated with ischemic colitis and pulmonary edema.

Side Effects of Nonstimulants

There are many varied side effects that individuals may experience when using the myriad nonstimulant ADHD medications. These respective side effects, of course, vary somewhat by the particular substances used. For example, side effects commonly associated with the use of amantadine hydrochloride (Symmetrel) include blurred vision, dizziness, faintness, light headedness, and trouble sleeping; rarer, but still potentially serious, side effects include swelling of extremities, difficulty urinating, and shortness of breath. Similarly, the side effects that are commonly associated with the use of bupropion hydrochloride (Wellbutrin) include agitation, anxiety, depression, fever, hair loss, headache, hives, insomnia, nausea, and tremor. Rarer, but potentially serious, side effects associated with the use of bupropion include anorexia, breathlessness, confusion, delusions, fainting, increased heart rate, jaundice, and memory impairments. Nevertheless, there are some generalities across respective classes of nonstimulant medications.

Tricyclic Antidepressants.   A wide variety of side effects is commonly associated with the use of the Tricyclic Antidepressants (TCAs), including the possibility of a toxic overdose, and the TCAs should be used with extreme caution in treating children and adolescents. The TCAs generally can cause dry mouth and blurred vision. The TCAs also can cause diabetes and problems with cholesterol. TCAs and other antidepressant medications increase the risk of suicidal thinking and behaviors in children, adolescents, and young adults.

There are certain other more specific constellations of side effects that are more commonly experienced by some users of respective TCAs. Desipramine hydrochloride (Norpramin), in particular, can cause changes in cardiac conduction. Common side effects associated with the use of amitriptyline hydrochloride (Elavil) can potentially include appetite changes, blurred vision, confusion, constipation, drowsiness, dry mouth, excessive sweating, headaches, sex drive or ability decline, nausea, nightmares, tingling in the hands or in the feet, unsteadiness, urinating difficulties, vomiting, and weakness or tiredness. Rarer, but still potentially serious, side effects associated with the use of amitriptyline hydrochloride include crushing chest pain, irregular heart rate, jaw and other muscle spasms, fainting, hallucinations, seizures, swelling of the face and tongue, uncontrollable shaking of body parts, unusual bleeding, and yellowing of the eyes or skin. Common side effects associated with the use of imipramine (Tofranil) can include blurred vision, breast swelling, constipation, diarrhea, dizziness, drowsiness, excessive sweating, loss of appetite, nausea, ringing in the ears, sexual dysfunction, stomach cramps, tingling feelings, vomiting, weakness, and weight gain.

SNRIs.   The serotonin norepinephrine reuptake inhibitors (SNRIs) also have their own respective side effects profiles. Some of the side effects that are commonly associated with the use of the SNRI ADHD medicine atomoxetine hydrochloride (Strattera), in particular, include drowsiness, loss of appetite, and stomach upset.

Antihypertensives.   The side effects most typically associated with the use of the alpha 2 agonist ADHD antihypertensive medications, not surprisingly, relate to altered blood pressure. Side effects associated with the use of clonidine hydrochloride (Kapvay) can, consequently, include low blood pressure, as well as irritability, bradycardia or slowed heart rate, drowsiness, constipation, stomach pain, nausea, decreased sex drive, dizziness, dry eyes, dry mouth, dry nasal mucosa, and fainting. Use of the clonidine patch can also result in additional side effects including skin reactions and possible burns when having a magnetic resonance imaging (MRI). Chronic use of clonidine hydrochloride can result in edema and fluid retention; diuretic concurrent therapy is usually needed. Side effects that are commonly associated with the use of the antihypertensive ADHD medicine guanfacine hydrochloride (Intuniv) include constipation, dizziness, drowsiness, dry mouth, headache, tiredness, and weakness; rarer, but serious, side effects to guanfacine hydrochloride include severe allergic reactions, fainting, and a slow or irregular heart rate.

Beta Blockers.   The most typical side effects associated with the use of the beta blocker ADHD medications are a reflection of their therapeutic effects; accordingly, the beta blockers tend to slow heart rate and lower blood pressure. Common side effects associated with the use of the beta blocker medications generally include diarrhea, nausea, sexual dysfunction, stomach cramps, and vomiting. Rarer, but potentially serious, side effects to the beta blockers can include blurred vision, disorientation, fatigue, hair loss, insomnia, muscle cramps, rash, and weakness. The beta blockers can alter blood glucose levels, which can potentially mask hypoglycemic symptoms in individuals with diabetes. Beta blocker medications that block the beta 2 receptors can cause shortness of breath in individuals with asthma. Severe allergic reactions to beta blocker medications are rare, but can be serious.

There are certain other more specific constellations of side effects that are more commonly reported by some users of respective beta blocker ADHD medications. The side effects commonly associated with the use of atenolol (Tenorim) can include dizziness, lightheadedness, nausea, and tiredness; the risk of dizziness and lightheadedness can be reduced by getting up slowly from sitting or lying positions. The side effects commonly associated with the use of nadolol (Corgard) can include cough, dizziness, drowsiness, and weakness; rarer, but potentially serious, side effects can include bluish color of fingers and/or toes, hair loss, mood changes, sexual dysfunction, swelling of ankles or feet, unexplained weight, vision changes, and wheezing. Interestingly, the common, as well as the rarer, side effects associated with the use of the beta blocker propranolol (Inderal) are very similar to those of nadolol.

SSRIs. The selective serotonin reuptake inhibitors (SSRIs) generally have fewer side effects than the TCAs. Accordingly, most individuals tolerate SSRIs better than they do the TCAs and other ADHD medications. The majority of side effects commonly associated with use of the SSRIs tend to be acute and typically diminish over a period of a few days or weeks. These commonly experienced side effects can include diarrhea, heartburn, muscle cramps, nausea, other signs of gastrointestinal tract distress, and sexual dysfunction. These side effects are primarily caused by the mechanism of action of the SSRIs. For instance, the nausea and vomiting are caused largely by the stimulation of serotonin 3 receptors located in the brain stem and in the hypothalamus; the gastrointestinal tract effects are mainly the result of mediated stimulation of the serotonin 3 and 4 receptors; while stimulation of the 5HT2a and 5HTC receptors can lead to feelings of anxiety, mental agitation, and panic attacks. Other more occasional side effects of use of the SSRIs can include apathy, appetite changes, headache, irritability, jitteriness, and sedation.

There are certain other more specific constellations of side effects that are more commonly reported by some users of respective SSRI ADHD medications. The side effects commonly associated with the use of citalopram hydrobromide (Celexa) can include appetite loss, blurred vision, drowsiness, dry mouth or xerostomia, nausea, and tiredness. The side effects commonly associated with the use of fluoxetine hydrochlolride (Prozac) can include anxiety, appetite loss, dizziness, drowsiness, nausea, sleep difficulties, sweating, and tiredness. The side effects commonly associated with the use of escitalopram oxalate (Lexapro) can include constipation, dry mouth, dizziness, drowsiness, excessive sweating, nausea, sleep difficulties, and tiredness. The side effects commonly associated with the use of fluvoxamine maleate (Luvox) can include appetite loss, dizziness, drowsiness, nausea, sleep difficulties, sweating, vomiting, and weakness. The side effects commonly associated with the use of paroxetine hydrochloride (Paxil) can include appetite loss, blurred vision, dizziness, drowsiness, dry mouth, sleep difficulties, sweating, vomiting, and weakness. The side effects commonly associated with the use of sertraline hydrochloride (Zoloft) can include appetite loss, diarrhea, dizziness, drowsiness, dry mouth, nausea, sleep difficulties, stomach upset, and vomiting. Rarer, but still potentially serious, side effects associated with the use of SSRIs like citalopram hydrobromide, fluoxetine hydrochloride, escitalopram oxalate, paroxetine hydrochloride, and sertraline hydrochloride can include accelerated hear rate, bloody stools, blurred vision, coordination loss, fainting, hallucinations, involuntary muscle twitching or dystonia, seizures, and vomiting.

Anticonvulsants.   Side effects that are commonly associated with the use of the anticonvulsant ADHD medicine carbamazepine (Tegretol) can include anxiety, back pain, constipation, diarrhea, dizziness, drowsiness, dry mouth, headaches, heart burn, memory problems, nausea, unsteadiness, and vomiting. Carbamazepine can also cause life threatening allergic reactions such as Stevens-Johnson syndrome or toxic epidermal necrolysis; these allergic reactions can manifest with severe damage to skin and internal organs. Some individuals of Asian ancestry have an inherited genetic risk factor for Stevens-Johnson syndrome or toxic epidermal necrolysis. Carbamazepine use may also result in decreased red blood cell production. Side effects potentially associated with the use of the anticonvulsant medicine valporic acid (Depakote) can include abdominal pain, alopecia or hair loss, anorexia, congenital abnormalities, diarrhea, dizziness, drowsiness, infection, low red blood cell production, nausea, tremor, vomiting, and weakness.

Eugeroics.   Most of the side effects that are usually associated with the use of the ADHD eugeroic medications are benign and typically only cause temporary discomfort; dizziness, headaches, and nausea are the most commonly reported side effects associated with this class of ADHD medications. Diarrhea is commonly reported by users of the eugeroic modafinil (Provigil) and, accordingly, hydration is important. If modafinil is taken late at night, then insomnia is likely. Rarer, but potentially serious, side effects associated with the use of modafinil can include chest pain, high blood pressure, fast heart rate, and pharyngitis. Since use of the eugeroic medicine armodafinil (Nuvigil) has similar therapeutic effectiveness but fewer adverse side effects than typically reported by users of modafinil, it is more commonly recommended.

Monoamine Oxidase Inhibitors.   The Monoamine oxidase inhibitors (MAOIs) also have a set of side effects commonly experienced by those who use them. The most common side effects associated with the use of the MAOIs include blurred vision, decreased urine output, dizziness, dry mouth, headaches, increased appetite, weight gain, low blood pressure, muscle twitching, and sleep problems. Rarer, but potentially serious, side effects associated with the use of MAOIs include fever, skin rashes, slurred speech, sore throat, staggering, and yellow eyes.

There are certain other more specific constellations of side effects that are more commonly reported by some users of respective MAOI ADHD medications. Commonly reported side effects associated with initial use of moclobemide (Amira) can include dizziness, headache, nausea, nervousness, and sleep difficulties. Other common side effects associated with the use of moclobemide can include anxiety, appetite loss, blurred vision, dry mouth, and sweating. Rarer, but potentially still serious, side effects that are associated with the use of moclobemide can include accelerated heart rate, chesty pain, pounding or throbbing in the head, rash, slurred speech, and stomach pain. The side effects commonly associated with the use of phenelzine sulfate (Nardil) can include chills, cold sweats, confusion, dizziness, over active reflexes, sudden jerky movements, and trembling of the hands and/or feet. Rarer side effects that are associated with the use of phenelzine sulfate can include dark urine, drowsiness, fever, irregular heart rate, pale lips or nails or skin, rapid shallow breathing, rash, shortness of breath, sweating, swelling of the feet or the lower legs, uncontrolled eye movements, vomiting of blood, yellow eyes or skin, and general weakness. The side effects that are commonly reported by users of the MAOI tranylcypromine sulfate (Parnate) can include appetite loss, blurred vision, chills, constipation, diarrhea, drowsiness, dry mouth, nausea, restlessness, ringing in the ears, sexual dysfunction, and urinary output decrease. Rarer, but potentially serious, side effects associated with the use of tranylcypromine sulfate can include accelerated heart rate, confusion, light sensitivity, muscle twitching, sweating, swelling of the ankles or the feet, tight feeling in the chest or in the throat, and tremor. Use of the MAOI venalafaxine (Effexor) can cause an increase in blood pressure in some individuals.

Antipsychotics.   There are some side effects that are often experienced by use of the antipsychotic ADHD medications, both the typical and the atypical antipsychotics. The atypical antipsychotic medications can cause weight gain in both children and adults. Akathisia, or the inability to sit still, muscle twitching, and restlessness, is sometimes a side effect of antipsychotic medications. Akinesia, or the loss or difficulties with voluntary control of movements, is another possible side effect of antipsychotic medications.

There are certain other more specific constellations of side effects that are more commonly reported by some users of respective typical antipsychotic ADHD medications. The side effects that are commonly associated with the use of typical antipsychotic medicine chlorpromazine hydrochloride (Thorazine) can include anxiety, blurred vision, breast swelling, constipation, dizziness, drowsiness, dry mouth, impotence, menstrual changes, sleep difficulties, swelling of hands and/or feet, and weight gain. Rarer, but still potentially serious, side effects that are associated with the use of chlorpromazine hydrochloride can include confusion, high fever, muscle twitching, pale skin, seizures, slow heart rate and/ breathing, tremor, urinary output decrease, and vomiting. The side effects that are commonly associated with the use of haloperidol (Haldol) can include dizziness, hyperactivity, involuntary and often jerky movements, nausea, and tiredness. Rarer, but still potentially serious, side effects that are associated with the use of haloperidol can include constipation, dry mouth, enlarged breasts or gynecomastia, erectile dysfunction, insomnia, menstrual irregularities, sedation, vomiting, and weight gain. The side effects that are commonly associated with the use of thioridazine hydrochloride (Mellaril) can include breast swelling, constipation, diarrhea, drowsiness, dry mouth, menstrual irregularities, mild itching, sexual dysfunction, vomiting, and weight gain. Rarer, but still potentially serious, side effects that are associated with the use of thioridazine hydrochloride can include chest pain, light sensitivity, muscle twitching, nausea, pale skin, restlessness, seizure, slow heart rate or breathing, tremor, urinary output decrease, and vision problems. The side effects that are commonly associated with the use of pimozide (Orap) can include involuntary control of movements, muscle twitching, restlessness, sedation, and vision problems. Rarer, but still potentially serious, side effects that are associated with the use of pimozide can include accelerated heart rate, bladder control loss, excessive sweating, fever, irregular blood pressure, seizures, and severe muscle stiffness.

There are certain other more specific constellations of side effects that are more commonly reported by some users of the respective atypical antipsychotic ADHD medications. The side effects that are commonly associated with the use of atypical antipsychotic medicine clozapine (Clozaril) can include accelerated heart rate, blurred vision, constipation, dizziness, drowsiness, headache, and hyperventilation. Rarer, but still potentially serious, side effects that are associated with the use of clozapine can include appetite changes, dark urine, decreased movement, difficulty breathing, excessive sweating increased thirst or urination, nausea, pale skin, severe muscle stiffness, vomiting, weakness, and yellow eyes or skin. The side effects that are commonly associated with the use of the atypical antipsychotic medicine risperidone (Risperdal) can include agitation, anxiety, constipation, dizziness, drowsiness, involuntary muscle twitching, nausea, and weight gain. Rarer, but still potentially serious, side effects that are associated with the use of risperidone can include accelerated heart rate, appetite loss, confusion, difficulty breathing, extreme thirst, pale skin, and poor coordination. The side effects that are commonly associated with the use of olanzapine pamoate (Zyprexa) can include dizziness, drowsiness, dry mouth, excessive abnormal muscle movement or hyperkinesia, involuntary control of movements, stomach pain or dyspepsia, and weakness. Rarer, but still potentially serious, side effects associated with the use of olanzapine pamoate can include bladder control loss, bloody or cloudy urine, breathing difficulties, chest pain, coordination problems, large purplish patches on skin, memory problems, twitching, and weakness. The side effects that are commonly associated with the use of ziprasidone (Geodon/ Zeldox) can include dizziness, drowsiness, headache, nausea, and weight gain. Rarer, but still potentially serious side effects that are associated with the use of ziprasidone can include accelerated heart rate, chest pain, fainting, pounding in the ears, seizures, and swelling of the tongue. The side effects that are commonly associated with the use of aripiprazole (Abilify) can include dizziness, drowsiness, incontinence, lethargy, salivation, and sedation. Rarer, but still potentially serious, side effects that are associated with the use of aripiprazole can include accelerated heart rate, blood pressure fluctuations, excessive sweating, high fever, pale skin, seizures, severe muscle stiffness, sudden loss of consciousness, extreme tiredness, and uncontrolled movements. Aripiprazole (Abilify) is less likely than the other antipsychotic medications to cause metabolic problems and to result in weight gain.

Cholinergic Agents.   Cholinergic agents generally produce similar effects to the neurotransmitter acetylcholine. Accordingly, the side effects most often associated with the use of cholinergic agents can possibly include breathing difficulties, convulsions, dizziness, headaches, excessive stomach acid and saliva, muscle cramps, nausea, slowed heart rate, and vomiting. Side effects commonly reported by users of the cholinergic agent nicotine (Nicorette) can include blurred vision, dizziness, drowsiness, headache, nervousness, and pounding in the ears. Rarer, but still potentially serious, side effects that are associated with the use of nicotine can include irregular heart rate, hives, itching, rash, and swelling of the skin.

Managing Side Effects

Many side effects of the ADHD medications will typically dissipate after a few weeks of commencing use of the respective medication. Nevertheless, there are a few easy to follow recommendations that can be helpful in preventing or reducing most of side effects. These recommendations include both being well informed and following a few simple precautions. Learning as much as possible about the ADHD medicine that an individual, or his or her child, is taking is, of course, a good first step. Carefully reading the package insert that by U.S. law must accompany the medicine will furnish valuable information on what to avoid and proper dosage details. Maintaining a log to monitor the effects of the medicine experienced is also highly recommended as it can be used to help determine if either the dosage or the medicine should be changed.

Most of the suggested precautions to be taken to help manage side effects of ADHD medications are essentially good common sense practices. For instance, most ADHD medications should be taken along with food to help minimize the likelihood of stomach aches. It is a good general guide to start with small recommended dosages and to progressively work up to larger doses if necessary until the therapeutic result is attained; if the medicine is noted to be effective and if there are no serious adverse reactions, then an increase in dosage is not warranted. Stimulant ADHD medications should generally be taken early in the day to help minimize any difficulties in falling asleep at the end of the day. Is the use of an extended release formulation ADHD stimulant medicine results in insomnia, then switching to a shorter acting formulation is indicated. If an individual wishes to discontinue the use of an ADHD medicine, and after talking it over with their physician or other healthcare provider, then it is usually advisable to taper off the medicine slowly; stopping some ADHD medications abruptly can result in irritability, fatigue, or depression. Maintaining proper health checkups is critical, particularly checking blood pressure regularly if dizziness is experienced. Problems with high blood pressure might mean that the dosage should be adjusted, or that a longer acting formulation be tried, or that a different medicine entirely should be prescribed. It is also important to drink plenty of fluids while taking ADHD medications; this can be particularly helpful in resolving issues with dizziness. Any mood changes experienced should be carefully noted and discussed with a healthcare provider; this can indicate that the effectiveness of the respective ADHD medicine is wearing off and that either a different formulation or perhaps even a different medicine should be tried.

ADHD MEDICATIONS' INTERACTION WITH OTHER MEDICATIONS

A medicine interaction is, most simply, when some of substance or condition adversely impacts how that medicine works. The ADHD medicine can be affected in several different ways. The pharmacological effects of the respective ADHD medicine can be, minimally to substantially, increased; the effects of the medicine can be, minimally to substantially, decreased; the side effects may, minimally to substantially, be intensified; or, new side effects can surface. These interactions not only result from mixing different medications but can also happen from mixing ADHD medications with various foods, beverages, nutritional supplements, and other substances.

The ADHD medications, as is true of any medicine, can have potentially serious interactions when combined with other medications. Use of stimulant ADHD medications and of the MAOIs, for instance can result in dangerous, if not even fatal, increases in blood pressure. Some of these other medications, such as those containing theophylline, used along with ADHD stimulant medications can result in agitation, dizziness, heart palpitations, and weakness. Methylphenidate (Ritalin, Concerta), one of the most commonly prescribed ADHD stimulant medications, should not be used with MAOIs; in fact, it is recommended that either methylphenidate or any MAOI should not be used for at least two weeks before beginning the other. Methylphenidate should also not be used along with any antihypertensive medications, any TCAs, any SSRIs, any anticonvulsants, or any blood thinners, without discussion with a healthcare provider, such as a physician, as this is known to increase the blood levels of those other medications. Combination stimulant formulations, such as Adderall, are contraindicated for any individual who has Tourette's syndrome, a mother who is breastfeeding, and anyone with an over active thyroid gland or who is having thoughts of suicide. Atomoxetine hydrochloride (Strattera) should not be used with the MAOIs; in fact, it is recommended that either atomoxetine or any MAOI should not be used for at least two weeks before beginning the other. Atomoxetine should also not be used with any asthma medicine or with SSRIs, like fluoxetine (Prozac) or paroxetine (Paxil), without discussion with a healthcare provider. Coadministration of atomoxetine and the MAOI tranylcypromine sulfate (Parnate) is also contraindicated as it may result in serious and potentially life threatening reactions. Coadministration of tranylcypromine sulfate and bupropion hydrochloride (Wellbutrin) is also contraindicated as it increases the risk of toxicity. TCAs may decrease the effects clonidine hydrochloride (Kapvay). If clonidine and a beta blocker are used together, there is the possibility of rebound hypertension if the clonidine is stopped suddenly. Coadministration of MAOIs with TCAs, such as amitriptyline hydrochloride (Elavil) and nortriptyline hydrochloride (Palelor), with bupropion hydrochloride (Wellbutrin), and with SSRIs, such as fluoxetine (Prozac) and paroxetine hydrochloride (Paxil), should be avoided as this may lead to high serotonin levels that can result in confusion, hypertension, tremor, coma, and even death.

Some of the ADHD medications are either weak or potent inhibitors of various enzymatic systems involved in the metabolism of other ADHD medications, and, accordingly, their use can result in profound interaction with these other medications. For instance, the beta blockers, like propranolol (Inderal), are recognized to be potent CYP2D6 inhibitors, thus profoundly increase, from three times to five times, the blood plasma concentrations, thus the effects, of other ADHD medications like thioridazine hydrochloride (Mellaril). Several of the SSRIs are also potent enzyme inhibitors. The SSRI fluvoxamine maleate (Luvox) is a potent CYP1A2 inhibitor, thus increases the plasma concentration of other ADHD medications like the antipsychotics clozapine (Clozaril) and olanzapine pamoate (Zyprexa). Similarly, the SSRIs fluoxetine hydrochloride (Prozac) and paroxetine hydrochloride (Paxil) are potent inhibitors of CYP2D6 and CYP3A4, thus increase blood plasma concentrations of drugs like the antipsychotic medicine clozapine (Clozaril). On the other hand, some ADHD medications are enzyme inducers, thus can decrease the pharmacokinetics of other drugs. For instance, the anticonvulsant ADHD medicine carbamazepine (Tegretol) can decrease the plasma concentrations of antipsychotics by 20 percent or more.

Avoiding Interactions

There are several easy to follow suggestions that can be of help in avoiding interactions of ADHD medications with other substances. These suggestions include being well informed as well as following some simple precautions. With respect to being well informed, it is recommended that one should carefully read drug labels and package inserts, as well as further researching and learning about the particular medications that one, or one's child, is taking, paying close attention to what each is used for, their side effects, and any special warnings.

Most of the recommended precautions to be taken in order to avoid any drug interactions are pretty much common sense. For instance, all medications should be kept in their original containers, which should be clearly marked; mixing different medications in a container is certainly a dangerous practice. Of course, one should always talk to their physician or other healthcare providers, particularly the pharmacist, as to what foods, beverages, and medications should be avoided when taking a respective ADHD medicine, including use of any over-the-counter products. The stimulants, for instance, and many other medications should not be taken with citrus juices, like orange juice, grapefruit juice, or lemonade, or with anything containing citric acid, as this tends to decrease the effects of the medications. It is also helpful to maintain a complete list of all medications, over the counter medications, and supplements that one is taking and sharing such a list with your healthcare providers. It is also advisable to only fill all prescriptions at the same pharmacy, which could help alert the consumer to any potentially dangerous drug interactions.

MISUSE OF ADHD MEDICATIONS

ADHD medications are misused by many individuals for what are mostly similar reasons. These ADHD medications most typically are misused by individuals who want to stay awake, to help them study, and to help them improve their school or work performance. Another very common reason for misusing ADHD medications is to suppress appetite to help with weight loss efforts. There are, of course, those individuals who misuse these substances for recreational purposes, primarily for the euphoric "high" feelings that can be experienced. The stimulant ADHD medications, the eugeroic ADHD medications, and the cholinergic agents are the most likely types of drugs to be misused for these typically reasons, but, naturally, others can also be misused.

The Drug Abuse Warning Network (DAWN) monitors drug-related hospital emergency department visits in the United States as part of the activities of the Substance Abuse and Mental Health Services Administration (SAMHSA), including monitoring of emergency department visits for ADHD stimulant medications. DAWN reports that emergency department visits for ADHD stimulant medications increased significantly from 13,379 in 2005 to 31,244 in 2010. While the emergency department visits for ADHD stimulant medications among males nearly doubled from 9,059 in 2005 to 17,174 in 2010, they increased even more among females rising from 4,315 in 2005 to 14,068 visits in 2010.

DAWN reported that the most statistically significant increase in hospital emergency department visits for ADHD stimulant medications was among adults 18 years of age and older. Although the number of emergency department visits associated with ADHD stimulant medications among children younger than 18 years old did not increase significantly from 2005 to 2010, there were still modest increases, for those aged 5 years to 11 years, the number of emergency department visits increased from 3,322 in 2005 to 3,791 visits in 2010; and, for those aged 12 years to 17 years, the number of emergency department visits increased from 2,702 in 2005 to 3,461 visits in 2010.

The increases in hospital emergency department visits for ADHD stimulant medications among adults from 2005 to 2010, as mentioned, were statistically significant. For those individuals aged 18 years to 25 years, the number of emergency department visits increased from 2,131 in 2005 to 8,148 visits in

2010. For those individuals aged 26 years to 34 years, the number of emergency department visits increased from 1,754 in 2005 to 6,094 visits in 2010. For those individuals aged 35 years and older, the number of emergency department visits increased from 2,519 in 2005 to 7,957 visits in 2010. Most importantly, the number of hospital emergency department visits for ADHD stimulant medications involving nonmedical misuse increased significantly from 5,212 in 2005 to 15,585 in 2010; this nonmedical misuse accounted for half (50%) of all hospital emergency department visits in the United States for ADHD stimulant medications. Further, nearly a third (29%) involved adverse reactions. In addition, of the total 31,244 hospital emergency department visits for ADHD stimulant medications in 2010, a quarter (25%) involved use of one other drug and nearly two fifths (38%) involved use of 2 or more other drugs. These drug combinations involved many of the classes of nonstimulant ADHD medications. There were 8,083 emergency department visits in 2010 involving misuse of an ADHD stimulant medicine and an antianxiety or insomnia medicine, like the eugeroics, 26 percent of the time. There were 3,199 emergency department visits in 2010 involving misuse of an ADHD stimulant medicine and an antidepressant medicine, like the TCAs or the SSRIs, 10 percent of the time. There were 2,050 emergency department visits in 2010 involving misuse of an ADHD stimulant medicine and an antipsychotic medicine, like the atypical antipsychotic risperidone (Risperdal), 26 percent of the time. There were 1,741 emergency department visits in 2010 involving misuse of an ADHD stimulant medicine and a cardiovascular agent, like the beta blockers, 6 percent of the time. There were 1,150 emergency department visits in 2010 involving misuse of an ADHD stimulant medicine and an anticonvulsant medicine, like valporic acid (Depakote), 4 percent of the time.

About one out of every five U.S. college students aged 18 years to 25 years misuses ADHD stimulant medications. The most common type of individual likely to misuse ADHD medications is a male college student with just a slightly lower grade point average than that of nonmisusers, but who is likely to have a very full schedule trying to manage not just academic responsibilities but also juggling work and a full social life. This suggests a profile of someone trying to keep up with multiple tasks and responsibilities. In a similar vein, one out of seven of every nonstudent of the same age range also misuses these ADHD stimulant medications. The most commonly misused stimulant medications by this age group of young U.S. adults are those typically prescribed for treating ADHD, such as combination amphetamine formulations (Adderall), methylphenidate (Ritalin, Concerta), and lisdextroamphetamine (Vyvanse). In several studies, about 50 percent of U.S. college students report the misuse of ADHD stimulant medications in order to improve their academic performance. About 33 percent of these young adults believe that the use of these medications would help them get better grades or to be more competitive at school, or athletics, or work. Somewhere around less than half, perhaps about 40 percent, say that they misuse these stimulant medications to help them stay awake; while about a quarter (25%) of young adults in the United States typically report that they misuse these stimulant medications to help improve their work performance. There are many anecdotal reports of high school and college students using these stimulant medications around times of academic deadlines, such as midterm examinations and final examinations. This sporadic type of misuse, particularly at times of already high stress, can lead not only to sleep deprivation but also to increased susceptibility to experience states of paranoia and even hallucinations.

There are many serious negative consequences associated with the misuse of ADHD medications. In addition to the physiologically based pharmacological side effects, individuals who misuse ADHD medications suffer myriad other adverse consequences. For one thing, these individuals may not be acquiring the normally developed coping skills, time-management skills, and study skills that are essential to living a fulfilling, healthy, and happy life. An individual who uses a prescribed medicine without a prescription, or who shares or sells an ADHD medicine that is listed as a Schedule II drug under the Controlled Substances Act, may be committing a felony crime. Some colleges and universities consider misuse of an ADHD medicine a form of cheating, which can potentially result in probation, suspension, or dismissal from the institution. Further, many higher education students also regard nonprescribed use of an ADHD medicine as cheating. There are even indications that nonmedical use of an ADHD may not result in higher grades. In this vein, college and university students who have a B or less grade-point average are nearly twice as likely to report nonmedical use of an ADHD prescription stimulant medicine as are those students who have a B+ or better grade-point average.

ABUSE POTENTIAL OF ADHD MEDICATIONS

The abuse potential of the respective ADHD medications, particularly that of the psychostimulant drugs like amphetamine, methamphetamine, and methylphenidate, is underscored by the common occurrence of the diversion of these controlled substances from legal to illicit venues as well as the propensity for their recreational, nonmedical use. There is even more compelling evidence of their abuse potential when one examines the dramatic differences in addiction rates among those with ADHD who are not properly treated.

Diversion of Psychostimulants

ADHD medications that are legitimately manufactured for medical purposes can, unfortunately, be diverted top illegal uses. This drug diversion consists of primarily the psychostimulants, but sometimes of other ADHD medications as well, consists of the use and abuse of both prescribed and nonprescribed medications, particularly among adolescents and young adults. This drug diversion and misuse of ADHD medications is done both by individuals with and those without ADHD.

Various studies have reported that the nonprescription use of stimulants within the past year ranged from 5 percent to 9 percent among public school students (Grades 8 to 12) and from 5 percent to 35 percent among college students. Further, the lifetime prevalence rates of diversion by students with prescriptions for stimulant medications who were asked to give, sell, or trade their medications ranged from 16 percent to 29 percent. Those suggested to be at the greatest risk for misusing and diverting stimulant medications have been identified as being white, fraternity or sorority members, those with lower grade-point averages, and those who used immediate release rather than extended release psychostimulant formulations. Misuse most frequently consists of taking more pills than prescribed as well as taking pills more frequently than prescribed; about half of the individuals engaged in this types of diversion say that they have deliberately missed doses of their prescribed psychostimulants to save them up for diversion. About a third of those individuals who had prescriptions for ADHD stimulant medications report that they have given away their medications to others and about a quarter report that they had sold some of their medications, usually to friends or relatives. This despite the fact that there are substantial legal penalties that can be imposed upon individuals who divert their prescribed ADHD medications to others. Further, there is evidence that suggests that those who divert their ADHD stimulant medications are more likely to be frequent victims of victimization. Some of the common reasons reported for the misuse of prescribed psychostimulant medications include to improve alertness, or to stay awake, to improve concentration, to get high, or for curiosity.

There are various criminal justice initiatives directed at reducing the diversion of psychostimulant drugs and other ADHD medications. The Drug Enforcement Administration (DEA) has a group of Diversion Investigators specifically charged with enforcing laws prohibiting the diversion of controlled substances to illegal black markets. The DEA estimates that there may be around 13,000 physicians or pharmacists who knowingly provide opportunities for the illicit diversion on dangerous and controlled substances, including the psychostimulants and their precursors. Unfortunately, these criminal diversion activities can easily be covered up, such as by falsifying reports of bogus burglaries, robberies, or by starting suspicious fires or similar acts. During President Barack Obama's two administrations, many initiatives were made to enhance law enforcement efforts against drug diversion. A partnership of many federal and local law enforcement agencies called the Organized Crime Drug Enforcement Task Force was created to identify and disrupt criminally organized drug trafficking operations. This task force has a Diversion Control Program to specifically enforce the regulations of the Controlled Substance Act against drug diversion. There are several other international, federal, and state initiatives also intended to interdict domestic and international drug trafficking that includes diversion of legally manufactured psychostimulant drugs from other countries; these include initiatives such as the Caribbean Basin Security Initiative, the Drug Low Attack Strategy, the Merida Initiative, and Plan Colombia.

Recreational Use of Psychostimulants

Since the 1930s, there has been somewhat widespread recreational, or non-medical, use of psychostimulant drugs. Methamphetamine hydrochloride (Desoxyn), unfortunately, although sometimes legally prescribed for ADHD is also a commonly abused and very addictive drug that can be made relatively easily, but dangerously, by converting pseudoephedrine, which is an ingredient available in several over the counter cold and allergy products, such as that marketed under the trade name of Sudafed. Methamphetamine and pseudoephedrine molecules only differ chemically by a single oxygen atom. There are two techniques that are most popularly used by clandestine labs to remove this oxygen atom. One method utilizes red phosphorous and hydriodic acid, the other method, variously referred to as the Birch method or the Nazi method, utilizes anhydrous ammonia and a reactive metal. The ingredients for both methods are readily obtainable from many local stores, including Walmart.

Risk of Addiction in the General Population

There are many reasons that can possibly increase an individual's risk of addiction. The factor around the initiation of drug use is a highly significant variable with respect to the likelihood of an individual becoming an addict. The initial use of substances can be caused by many possible reasons. Frequently, individuals are offered an initial exposure to drugs by peers or by older siblings, or even by parents. Sometimes, individuals are prescribed medications by physicians in order to manage various conditions. Some individuals may self-medicate in attempts to remediate or to avoid various personal problems. Others might simply have initiated their use of substances out of individual curiosity. Whatever the reason that use of a drug began, a certain fraction of those who initiate use will eventually progress on to addiction. One thing that research studies have consistently indicated is that the younger age that an individual initiates substance use, then the more likely it is that they will eventually develop drug addiction.

There are many varied reasons that some individuals become addicted to drugs, but others do not. Evidence strongly indicates that there are genetic and other familial and environmental factors that can increases one's susceptibility to becoming drug addicted. Genetics, at the most, accounts for about 50 percent of the individual variation in the susceptibility to addiction. At any rate, it is clear that individuals who have family members with substance abuse problems are far more prone to develop such a problem themselves compared to those without a positive family history. There may be fundamental differences in brain structure and brain chemistry among those who become addicted. Environmental factors including things like growing up in a stressful household or in a cultural milieu that accepts drug use are also significant risk factors.

Risk of Addiction in Those Medicated for ADHD

Many studies have concluded that children with ADHD are far more likely than other children to have serious substance abuse problems when they become adolescents and adults. However, what further research has indicated is that children who appropriately take ADHD medications, such as methylphenidate (Ritalin) and combination stimulant formulations like Adderall, are not at a greater risk for developing substance abuse problems later in life. Moreover, the evidence actually shows that those with ADHD who are not taking appropriately prescribed ADHD medications are, in fact, at a greater risk. This greater risk is underscored by the fact that individuals who demonstrate core symptoms of ADHD, such as hyperactivity or difficulties in maintaining focus, are inherently at a greater risk for subsequently developing substance abuse problems, particularly if it goes untreated. In fact, this supports the generally accepted estimate that up to 25 percent of individuals who have a lifetime history of addiction may also have ADHD. It is also recognized that ADHD is often comorbid with other psychiatric conditions, many of which are understood to be associated with an increased risk of substance abuse, such as depression or schizophrenia. Finally, since there has been a general tendency to discontinue ADHD medications in adolescents, it is thus all the more likely that those individuals with ADHD who make the transition to adulthood but discontinue their pharmacological treatment are more likely to experience substance abuse problems. It is estimated that each year in the United States, there are over 24 million individuals who abuse amphetamines; it may, accordingly, be reasonably assumed that many of these individuals do so as a result of having untreated ADHD.

SIGNS OF PSYCHOSTIMULANT ABUSE AND ADDICTION

Individuals who abuse or are addicted to psychostimulant drugs tend to exhibit an individualized constellation of an array of possible symptoms. One of the most prominent signs of psychostimulant abuse and addiction, as it is for many other types of substance abuse, is that of the very intense cravings for the particular drug of choice. Other subtle, somewhat diffuse effects include anxiety, extreme depression, excessive fatigue, and increased hunger. Some general physical symptoms of psychostimulant drug abuse and addiction, but of many other drugs as well, include dry mouth and blurred vision.

There is a set of physical symptoms that tend to reflect the specific physiological effects of the respective psychostimulant medications. These physical symptoms include the basic indicators of stimulant use, such as dilated pupils, an increased respiratory rate, hypertension, increased body temperature, muscular tension, and cardiovascular system abnormalities as well as several other symptoms that typically result from chronic psychostimulant use. These other physical symptoms of psychostimulant drug abuse and addiction include angina pectoris, cardiac arrhythmias, headaches, malnutrition, nausea, seizures, and skin disorders.

There are also several different behavioral signs of psychostimulant drug abuse and addiction that may be noted. These observed changes in behavior include some that might be considered positive, but that nevertheless can be indicative of abuse. These purported positive signs of psychostimulant drug abuse and addiction include things like improved academic or occupational performance, enhanced athletic prowess, improved recall and memory, ability to stay focused and awake for excessive periods of time, less need for sleep, and a dramatic increase in energy levels. Many of the other possible behavioral signs of psychostimulant drug abuse and addiction may not be so desirable, such as altered sexual behaviors, excessive talkativeness, decreased appetite, and a reduction of the normal, socially expected behaviors. Several of the potential behavioral signs of psychostimulant drug abuse and addiction can possibly have dangerous consequences, such as the setting of unrealistic goals to achieve, expressing unrealistic beliefs in their own personal abilities and power, and engaging in more risk-taking behaviors; all of which are often associated with states of mania. There can also be pronounced changes in mood, such as having pronounced mood swings, being overly euphoric, or appearing unusually anxious or depressed.

There are also some psychological signs that may be indicative of psychostimulant drug abuse and addiction. These psychological symptoms can often include being overly aggressive or hostile. Other psychological manifestations of psychostimulant drug abuse and addiction can include an individual who experiences feelings of paranoia, delusions, hallucinations, and even psychotic symptoms.

There are also some adverse social consequences that are commonly observed among individuals who either abuse or are addicted to psychostimulant drugs. These social consequences are, of course, shared with the abuse and addiction of many other types of substances. Interpersonal relationships are likely to be strained; divorce is not uncommon. Many individuals undergo financial ruin and job loss is also not unusual, as are problems with criminal justice system.

The physical ravages of chronic psychostimulant drug abuse and addiction frequently become apparent as well. These physical manifestations include dehydration, malnutrition, and vitamin deficiencies; emaciation is actually frequently observed. There can sometimes be an apparent lack of physical coordination, periods of incoherence, and even total physical collapse. Potentially fatal signs include seizures and respiratory depression. Other severe medical conditions associated with abuse or addiction to psychostimulant drugs include stimulant induced psychosis and toxic psychosis. Of course, unsuccessful attempts to cut down or stop use, continued use despite awareness of the associated problems, as well as the development of tolerance to psychostimulant drugs, manifested by taking progressively larger doses of the respective drug, and taking them for longer periods of time, are classic hallmarks of drug abuse and addiction. Another prominent characteristic is when the psychostimulant substance and the pursuit of it become central to the individual's life to the point of where attention to other important areas is diminished, if not even ignored, such as family, friends, work, and personal safety.

OVERDOSE ON ADHD MEDICATIONS

When an individual consumes an excessively large dose of a respective ADHD medicine, the resulting effects can vary considerably depending on several variables, such as the particular substance being used, the amount consumed, the individual's personal history of exposure to that particular and to closely related substances, and to whether other substances were being taken in combination with the ADHD medications. In considering overdoses of ADHD medications, it is important to recognize that ADHD medications come in several different dosage strengths that, of course, alter the likelihood of an overdose.

The mechanism of toxicity with respect to ADHD stimulant medications, like amphetamine (Dyanavel XR), dextroamphetamine (Dexedrine), methamphetamine hydrochloride (Desoxyn), and methylphenidate (Ritalin), is primarily related to excessive extracellular levels of the neurotransmitters dopamine, norepinephrine, and serotonin. The clinical syndrome associated with stimulant drug overdose involves mainly cardiovascular and neurological effects, but important secondary complications can potentially include gastro-intestinal, muscular, pulmonary, and renal effects. When experiencing a psy-chostimulant drug overdose, the individual may present with symptoms such as agitation, anxiety, combative behavior, confusion, delirium, excessive sweat-ing, hallucinations, hyper-reflexes, movement disorders, paranoia, and seiz-ures. Seizures can be fatal or they can also produce lifelong disabilities, such as brain damage. Sudden cardiac death is also possible with stimulant drug overdose as are heart arrhythmias, heart attacks, or heart failures. The rapid pulse rate associated with stimulant drug overdose can also produce damage to blood vessels or heart valves, as well as stroke or bleeding in the brain. Difficulties with breathing can cause low blood oxygen levels that result in blue-colored lips or fingernails. The increase in body temperature associated with stimulant use can lead to hyperthermia, or excessively high body temper-ature, which can cause dehydration as well as malfunctioning of vital organs and body systems; overdose can also result in paradoxical hypothermia, or cold body. Management of a stimulant drug overdose is primarily supportive; although benzodiazepines may be used judiciously; if unresponsive to benzo-diazepines, second-line approaches can include administration of anti-psychotic medications, such as haloperidol (Haldol) or ziprasidone, or of alpha agonists, such as dexmedetomidine or propofol. Individuals experienc-ing an overdose on methamphetamine hydrochloride (Desoxyn) typically present with an altered mental status consisting of aspects such as confusion, delusions, hallucinations, paranoia, and suicidal ideation. As tolerance to methamphetamine is developed rapidly relative to other medications, there is less likelihood of individuals experiencing cardiovascular complications. The route of administration used also alters the risk profile. For instance, oral administration of methamphetamine is less likely to result in cardiotoxicity, and, further, as the oral route of administration creates a longer time period to reach peak blood concentration, it also appears to be associated with less susceptibility to addiction, certainly as compared to smoking, but intravenous, or other injection methods, is more associated with toxicity.

There are numerous signs that are associated with an overdose of the many respective nonstimulant ADHD medications. These signs are naturally quite variable as are the pharmacological properties of the different ADHD medications. For example, an individual who experiences an overdose of amantadine hydrochloride (Symmetrel) may present with symptoms that can include agitation, aggression, confusion, convulsions, difficulty breathing, fainting, fast heart rate, fever, hallucinations, severe headaches, personality changes, problems with balance or walking, tremor, and urinary output diminished or ceased.

A TCA ADHD medicine overdose initially manifests with mild symptoms mainly those related to anticholinergic effects, which can include accelerated heart rate, agitation, confusion, drowsiness, dry mouth, headache, nausea, urinary retention, and vomiting. More serious complications from a TCA overdose can include cardiac rhythm irregularities, hallucinations, low blood pressure or hypotension, and seizures.

An overdose from the monocyclic antidepressant ADHD medicine bupropion hydrochloride (Wellbutrin) can include symptoms such as fainting, hallucinations, irregular heart rate, lethargy, muscle stiffness, shallow breathing, and slurred speech. Seizures typically occur within the first six hours of a bupropion overdose, and coma is possible. A bupropion hydrochloride overdose can potentially be fatal.

Presentation of an overdose of the SNRI ADHD medicine atomoxetine hydrochloride (Strattera) is generally mild. Clinical concerns of an atomoxetine overdose include agitation, drowsiness, gastrointestinal upset, hyperactivity, hyper-reflexes, hypertension, tachycardia, tremor, and seizure. The management of this condition is largely supportive but usually includes attention to both sedation and seizures.

An overdose of the alpha 2 agonist antihypertensive ADHD medicine clonidine hydrochloride (Kapvay) involves primarily cardiovascular and neurological effects, most typically consisting of bradycardia, depressed senses, and hypotension; however, in cases of overdose, paradoxical hypertension can occur early. An overdose of guanfacine hydrochloride (Intuniv) can include diaphoresis, drowsiness, dry mouth, and lethargy. Clinical management of either a clonidine or a guanfacine drug overdose is largely supportive but typically includes focus on blood pressure support.

An individual who is experiencing an overdose on a beta blocker ADHD medicine may present with symptoms that can include blurred vision, breathing difficulties, coma confusion, drowsiness, excessive sweating, fever, heart rhythm irregularities, lightheadedness, nervousness, seizures, and shock. Wheezing is also possible in a TCA overdose for individuals with asthma.

An SSRI ADHD medicine overdose may include symptoms such as agitation, body temperature and/or blood pressure fluctuations, confusion, diarrhea, dilated pupils, drowsiness, headaches, nausea, rapid heart rate, tremor, and vomiting. An SSRI overdose can lead to what is known of as serotonin syndrome, which can present with symptoms such as high fever, seizures, and unconsciousness; it can potentially be fatal.

An overdose of the anticonvulsant ADHD medicine carbamazepine (Tegretol) can involve coma, sleepiness, and epileptic seizures and in fatal cases can include respiratory depression and respiratory arrest. An overdose of the anticonvulsant ADHD medicine valporic acid (Depakote) can include symptoms such as an irregular heart rate, coma, and sleepiness. Management of an overdose of an anticonvulsant medicine is mainly supportive, but may also include procedures to enhance elimination and decontamination.

An overdose on the eugeroic ADHD medicine modafinil (Provigil) typically results in excessive extracellular levels of the neurotransmitters dopamine, norepinephrine, and serotonin in the neocortex of the brain. The neurological effects of a modafinil overdose include increased agitation, anxiety, dizziness, dystonia, headache, insomnia, and tremors. Management of a modafinil drug overdose is largely supportive and includes concerns with sedation and blood pressure. An overdose of the eugeroic ADHD medicine armodafinil (Nuvigil) will likely cause symptoms similar to an overdose on modafinil and can include chest pain, diarrhea, nausea, and unusual bruising or bleeding.

An overdose on an atypical antipsychotic ADHD medicine can include symptoms such as agitation, cardiovascular toxicity, coma, hypertension, sedation, and seizures. Overdose from respective antipsychotic ADHD medications can present with somewhat variable patterns. For instance, an overdose from aripiprazole (Abilify) may include symptoms such as accelerated heart rate, gastrointestinal distress, low blood pressure, and sedation. An overdose from clozapine (Clozaril) may include symptoms such as central nervous system depression and an accelerated heart rate. An overdose from olanzapine (Zyprexa) may include symptoms such as accelerated heart rate, central nervous system depression, coma, delirium, and low blood pressure. An overdose from quetiapine fumarate (Seroquel) may include symptoms such as accelerated heart rate, delirium, and low blood pressure. An overdose from risperidone (Risperdal) manifests primarily with an accelerated heart rate. An overdose from ziprasidone (Geodon) manifests primarily with an accelerated heart rate and sedation.

An overdose from an MAOI ADHD medicine may include symptoms such as agitation, coma, dizziness, drowsiness, fainting, hallucinations, headaches, high blood pressure, hyperactivity, irregular heart rate, respiratory depression, and seizures. An overdose from a MAOI medicine is rare and symptoms typically occur within 24 hours but may not manifest sometimes for 32 hours or more after ingestion.

Avoiding an Overdose

There are several common sense steps that can be taken to lessen the likelihood of having an overdose from the use of ADHD medications, particularly with respect to different age groups. With respect to preschool aged children in particular, it is recommended that ADHD medications, as well as of course other medications, should be kept in containers with child resistant caps, and that the containers should be stored, ideally locked, up high, and out of the sight and the reach of young children. If more than one adult distributes the ADHD medicine to a child, then a system should be established to prevent double dosing. The labels should be read carefully and fully understood. Further, children should be taught that medications are not candy and that they should only be taken when given by a parent or adult caregiver. With respect to elementary school aged children, it is also important that ADHD medications, as well as other medications, should be stored securely between doses, and that only parents or other adult caregivers should give the medicine to a child. For high school- and college-aged students and other young adults, it is important that individuals should not be allowed to take their own medications unless it is certain that they understand how to do so safely. Elderly individuals should keep their medications in original containers and not mix them with other medications, unless, of course, someone else is sorting their daily medications for them and placing them in a pill-minder. As around 40 percent of the elderly aged 65 years and older are taking five or more prescription medications, the chances of the medications interacting dangerously with one another is very high. Accordingly, it is important for the elderly, or their care takers, to communicate effectively with the individual's physicians, pharmacists, and other healthcare providers to make sure that there is no conflict, including attention to all dietary supplements taken as well as consideration of interactions from food and drink.

Chapter 7

Production, Distribution, and Regulation

The production, the distribution, and the regulation of respective attention deficit hyperactivity disorder (ADHD) medications is a complex, confusing, and evolving area of concern. The issues around production involve primarily the manufacturers of the various ADHD medications, including the generic formulations as well as the producers of illicit versions. There is a range of policy concerns relevant to this part of the story of ADHD medications, particularly those relating to the scheduling of drugs.

MANUFACTURERS OF ADHD MEDICATIONS

The various manufacturers of ADHD medications must navigate through a maze of production, distribution, and regulatory issues in order to be able to produce and supply medications to those with ADHD. One of the critical distinctions in this area is that between the brand name formulations and the generic versions of these ADHD medications. There are some important manufacturing and distribution issues that arise as well, including unique pharmacological designs. Finally, the illegal production of mainly psychostimulant drugs also impacts this area.

Brand Name versus Generic Medications

After a pharmaceutical company has invented a new drug and has filed for and has received patent protection for the exclusive right to manufacture, market, and sell that substance under a brand name for a finite period of time, which varies from one nation to another, but that is generally between 12 years and 20 years. At the end of that period, other companies can legally begin to manufacture, market, and sell generic versions of the substance under its chemical name. The company that first produced the brand name version of the particular medicine, hopefully, was able to recoup the typically substantial investments of time and money spent to create it, as well as the often considerable costs expended on advertising that substance to establish an awareness of and an understanding of the virtues of that substance to both lay and professional audiences.

Generic medications are versions of drugs that are chemically equivalent to brand name medications, but that are almost always sold at lower prices. The generic version of a medicine is required to contain the same active ingredients as the original brand name medicine. Generic medications are generally small molecule drugs compared to biologic agents or biosimilar agents, which tend to consist of larger, complex molecules. Thus the generic medications can be chemically and pharmacokinetically identical to their corresponding brand name medicine, while such exact duplication is impossible with biosimilar agents.

The extent of absorption and the rate of absorption of a bioequivalent generic medicine must not be significantly different from that of the original brand name medicine. According to the Hatch-Waxman Act of 1984, manufacturers of generic medications must file an Abbreviated New Drug Application (NDA) with the Food and Drug Administration (FDA) and must be able to demonstrate that the generic medicine is bioequivalent to the originally developed and approved brand name medicine. The generic medicine must also be equivalent to the original in its dose, safety, efficacy, intended use, and route of administration. This means that the generic must closely approximate the pharmacodynamic and the pharmacokinetic properties of the brand name medicine.

As soon as the patent protection of a new brand name medicine expires, many different companies may be interested in manufacturing generic versions. This competition generally tends to help drive down the prices. This also helps to guarantee a steady supply of the availability of that particular medication on the health market. However, as many pharmaceutical companies have become involved in producing generics and as more generics are being made and used, this has led to increased delays in getting generic medications through the FDA review process. In this vein, it has been noted that while three decades ago generic medications accounted for around 16 percent of all prescription drug products, today they amount to over 50 percent. In order to cope with this increased volume, the FDA in 2012 introduced the

Generic Drug User Fee Amendments, which were modeled after the earlier Prescription Drug User Fee Act, and that required manufacturers of generic medications to pay fees that could support the costs of administering the FDA review process. The availability of these fees has helped to expedite the process of reviewing generic medications for FDA approval. Yet as more and more generic medications are being produced in other countries using materials that are often imported there from several other countries, the ability to assume that the materials, facilities, and processes used to make respective generic drugs are of sufficient quality to guarantee their safety and efficacy has become severely strained. To help address these types of issues, several countries have entered into a collaborative group under the auspices of the World Health Organization known as the International Generic Drug Regulators Pilot. This pilot group was intended to assist each other by means of enhanced cooperation to make greater ease in regulating generic medications by, hopefully, establishing consistent standards and expectations, with more access to assess and review their production in member countries.

The total annual expenditures on all prescription medications in the United States currently is more than $325 billion; a substantial portion of which consists of the various ADHD medications. As a consequence, the American College of Physicians has released a new "best practices" advisory, which recommends that healthcare providers prescribe generic medications over brand name ones if possible. Part of their rationale is that the excessive cost of brand name medications is a major factor that contributes to lack of patient adherence, as well as that the underutilization of generic medications, including ADHD medications, is one of the reasons that U.S. per capita healthcare is higher than any other country, yet is not associated with improved outcomes in many areas. The price of prescription medications currently accounts for 17 percent of all healthcare costs. In fact, in the United States, the average per capita cost of prescription drugs, including ADHD medications, is about two times that of other developed nations; further, the total net cost of prescription medications rose by approximately 20 percent from 2013 to 2015. Unfortunately, government entities pay for about 40 percent of all prescription medications in the United States, which contributes to their escalated price structure, as well as driving up the size of the national budget. The primary reason for these rising costs is the excessive prices charged for brand name products protected by patents. Although these products may only account for 10 percent of all prescriptions in the United States, they make up almost three quarters (72%) of drug spending. The prices for the most common brand name drugs, including many ADHD medications, increased 164 percent from 2008 to 2015.

A sizeable barrier to greater use of generic medications is that many health-care providers hold negative perceptions about the safety and efficacy of generic medications, and that patients also hold preferences against and low expectations for generic medications. In fact, generic medications have generally been demonstrated to be not only as less expensive than brand name medications but also as equally effective and well proven. However, there have been some unusual exceptions to these standards. For instance, in 2012, it became necessary to close down several manufacturing facilities in India that were producing the ADHD medicine bupropion, which is sold here under the brand name of Wellbutrin, when it was discovered that their generic version was working less effectively than advertised, thus was not truly bioequivalent. It should be noted that the Affordable Care Act requires under its meaningful use criteria that all prescribers should be notified through electronic medical records systems of the formulary status of prescribed medications. In addition, the use of generic medications lowers the out of pocket consumer costs and thus promotes greater adherence.

Manufacturing and Distributing ADHD Medications

Application backlogs to the FDA for approval of generic formulations, including those for ADHD medications, can delay their entry to the market. The streamlining of the process of bringing generic medications to the market could substantially both help reduce drug costs and increase access for individuals who could benefit from them. However, many factors, besides FDA approval, impact market entry; these include, not only the number of manufacturers willing to produce such products along with mergers within the pharmaceutical industry, but also the availability of the raw materials and the demands for the respective products.

Unique Pharmacological Designs

Research is ongoing into the development of unique pharmacological designs that can be used to enhance the safety and effectiveness of ADHD medications, particularly the psychostimulant medications. For a considerable period of time, there has been a search for powerful but nonaddictive stimulants and other ADHD medications that would not be abused. New types of drugs are also under consideration, as well as other drugs that were previously used for other purposes, that might offer interesting possibilities for combination uses with ADHD medications. However, it is far too early to determine whether any of these will actually provide us with safe, effective, and nonaddictive alternatives.

There are numerous alternative formulation approaches than can be utilized to create unique pharmacological designs of respective ADHD medications. A simple strategy is to compose the formulation in a water soluble capsule rather than as a tablet form. The capsules can contain varied coated particles, such as beads or mini-tablets, of the active ingredients. These particles can be covered with an outer, delayed release coating and an inner, sustained release coating over a drug containing core. The delayed release coating could, for instance, allow the individual to sleep better if he or she were taking one of the more common ADHD medications, particularly the stimulant ADHD medications, such as the racemic amphetamine (Dyanavel XR), the enantiomer dextroamphetamine (Dexedrine), its prodrug lisdextroamphetamine dimesylate (Vyvanse), methamphetamine hydrochloride (Desoxyn), methylphenidate hydrochloride (Ritalin, Concerta), and mixed amphetamine salts (Adderall). The delayed release outer coating could consist of a plasticizer or of a pH dependent layer that is insoluble in a water solution, such as an acrylic polymer, hydroxylpropyl methylcellulose, or shellac. The inner, sustained release formulation could consist of a water permeable or a water insoluble coating, such as a cellulose ether derivative, a copolymer of acrylic acid, or an acrylic resin. The inner core could contain a disintegrant, like corn starch, potato starch, and a clay bentonite; an osmagent, like calcium bicarbonate, lithium sulfate, and sodium chloride; or a pore forming agent. This type of pharmacological design typically results in a low, but therapeutically appropriate level of the ADHD medicine in the blood plasma of the individual when she or he would typically wake up and prepare for the day or, in children, start the school day.

Another approach that can be used to reduce or prevent the abuse and the overdose of psychostimulant ADHD medications, like the amphetamines, is to covalently attach a chemical moiety to the respective drug. This particular pharmacological design strategy provides an abuse resistant alternative treatment for ADHD and related conditions. Under this approach the oral bioavailability of the ADHD stimulant medicine is maintained at therapeutically useful doses, while at higher doses of the ADHD psychostimulant, the bioavailability is substantially reduced, thus providing a method of reducing oral abuse liability. Due largely to the stimulating effects of the psychostimulant drug and their derivatives and analogs, they are highly susceptible to being abused. Legitimate users of these types of ADHD medications may easily develop drug tolerances, thereby become increasingly vulnerable to becoming accidental addicts as they increase their dosages in order to counteract their increased tolerance of the prescribed medications. Further, it is possible that individuals may inappropriately self-administer higher than prescribed amounts of the active drug or alter either the pharmacological product or the route of administration, such as by snorting, injecting, and smoking the drug, thereby resulting in immediate release of the psychoactive drug in greater than prescribed amounts. Unfortunately, extended release formulations of the ADHD psychostimulant medications have an even greater abuse liability relative to the single dose tablets, since these formulations contain higher concentrations of the respective active ingredient. By attaching a chemical moiety, which can be either a naturally occurring or synthetic substance, like a peptide or an amino acid, to the base psychostimulant ADHD medicine, it effectively reduces the pharmacological activity of that respective formulation. It is hoped that this approach may prevent or at least reduce the euphoric effect of the respective psychostimulant drug, which is associated with abuse and addiction. It may also, depending upon the particular technique utilized, substantially lower the toxicity of the unbound substance, thereby reducing the likelihood of producing an overdose. This pharmacological design approach also has the potential to be used with the myriad combination formulations of ADHD medications with other medications, such as is routinely done with those individuals with various comorbid conditions. These other medications that may be contained in combination with the ADHD psychostimulant formulations frequently are one of the nonstimulant ADHD medications discussed throughout this book, particularly the respective antidepressant ADHD medications such as the TCAs, the SSRIs, the MAOIs, and the antihypertensive ADHD medications, such as clonidine hydrochloride or guanfacine.

There are many other approaches that are currently being examined, as well as many more that have yet to be even imagined, which might someday yield even better ways to control and manage ADHD symptoms. Nutritional approaches, for instance, have long been considered as likely ways that could possibly provide effective management of some of the core symptoms of ADHD.

Illegal Production of Stimulants

The illicit production of stimulants, particularly methamphetamine, raises serious problems. Methamphetamine is a highly potent central nervous system stimulant occasionally used to treat ADHD. Unfortunately, methamphetamine is also a commonly abused and very addictive drug that can be easily, but dangerously, produced by converting chemical precursors such as pseudoephedrine, which is available in several over the counter cold and allergy products, such as that marketed under the trade name of Sudafed.

Methamphetamine and pseudoephedrine molecules only differ chemically by a single oxygen atom. There are two techniques popularly used by clandestine laboratories to remove this oxygen atom. One method utilizes red phosphorous and hydriodic acid, the other method, variously referred to as the Birch method or the Nazi method, utilizes anhydrous ammonic acid and a reactive metal. The ingredients for both methods are readily obtainable from many local stores, including Walmart.

Chemists have attempted to develop pseudoephedrine products that disrupt the extraction and conversion of pseudoephedrine into methamphetamine. One such product that has been released to deter illicit methamphetamine production is Nexafed, which is manufactured as a 30 mg tablet by Acura Pharmaceuticals Inc. employing a trademarked Impede Technology based on a mixture of polymers to result in a substantial reduction in methamphetamine extraction and conversion. The advent of tamper resistant pseudoephedrine products has aided legitimate consumers, pharmacists, and criminal justice agencies in reducing illicit methamphetamine production. Electronic tracking systems have also been implemented to support prevention efforts.

POLICY ISSUES

There are many policy issues that have been explored around concerns with the production, distribution, and regulation of drugs like ADHD medications. An early issue was that of the making and use of patent medications, which led to the passage of the influential Pure Food and Drug Act. Additional concerns, including those of illicit production and distribution, led to the formulation of several UN Conventions related to drugs. The modern production, distribution, and regulation of ADHD medications and other controlled substances are directed primarily under the clinical trials system. There have, of course, been other recent initiatives as well in this area.

Patent Medications

Patent medications were proprietary medications that were available without a prescription and that were typically manufactured and marketed under a trademark, but rarely under an actual patent. These proprietary medications originated in Great Britain under grants of favor to those who provided medications to the royal family. The term "patent" actually comes from "letters patent" that were issued in the late seventeenth century in Great Britain authorizing holders to use royal endorsements in advertising their medicinal products. In the eighteenth and nineteenth centuries, many drug formulations were sold under often sensational names and that typically made even more outrageous claims as to their purported effectiveness and cures. Some of these bizarre nostrums contained dubious and at times outright dangerous ingredients, yet the actual contents were usually not disclosed. These so-called patent medications included an array of myriad pills, capsules, powders, tonics, elixirs, teas, liniments, ointments, remedies, salves, and assorted other formulations. Many of these products invoked the mantle of Indian herb and root cures, which were held in high esteem by many segments of society; alcohol was often the chief active ingredient in many of these preparations. Some of these patent medications were administered to allegedly treat specific ailments, while many others claimed to be panaceas and cure-alls. Peddlers traveled the countryside dispensing these items and they could be readily ordered through the mail. Some were intended for women's problems, others for men's diseases, usually venereal diseases, and there were "soothing syrups" and others targeting children. Unfortunately, consumers were generally not informed as to the contents of what they were taking and giving to their loved ones, which not uncommonly might have included potent drugs like cocaine, opium, and morphine or even toxic substances such as mercury or lead. Public sentiment, aided by the growing Temperance movement, led to more and more calls for the disclosure of ingredients and an end to unrealistic and unsupported claims being made in advertisements. In 1881, the Proprietary Association, which was a trade organization of the producers of these patent medications, was formed primarily to lobby against any proposed legislation that would regulate them, prohibit deceptive advertising, and force the disclosure of ingredients.

Pure Food and Drug Act

Widespread concerns over the use of cocaine, opium, radium, and other substances, particularly those contained in patent medications and nostrums, led increasingly to public outcries for stricter controls. Accordingly, in 1906, the U.S. Congress passed the Pure Food and Drug Act that was signed into law by President Theodore Roosevelt, who had lobbied behind the scenes for it, as Public Law 59-384 (34 Stat. 768). The act created the FDA, which was given the authority to regulate aspects of drugs and food products. For example, it stipulated that products should be labeled identifying the contents and dosages of cocaine and other substances; it further prohibited interstate commerce in adulterated or mislabeled drugs. The efforts leading to the passage of this act were part of the Progressive reform movement. Passage of the act was part of the broader Progressive trend of having purported experts directing more health and social decisions, supposedly by means of application of the scientific method, so as to counter uninformed fads. Progressive leaders, many of whom were in the drug-manufacturing sector, saw it as in their own self-interest to pass such a law. Interestingly, various religious institutions, such as those affiliated with Protestant missionaries, seem to have been associated with several campaigns against drugs.

The Pure Food and Drug Act was amended on June 25, 1938, and expanded by the more comprehensive consumer-oriented Food, Drug, and Cosmetics Act to include the misuse and abuse of nonnarcotic medications under the FDA, which established standards of quality, identity, and container fill. The Durham-Humphrey Amendment of 1951 resolved what constituted a prescription. In 1962, the Harris-Kefauver Amendment to the Pure Food and Drug Act was enacted, which requires both extensive pharmacological and toxicological research before any drug can be tested in human beings; this established the modern clinical trial system in the United States that will be discussed further.

UN Conventions

International drug policy initiatives have been established to help control stimulants like cocaine and other drugs. The United Nations, on March 30, 1961, adopted the Single Convention on Narcotic Drugs, which attempted to simplify the maze of different national approaches to control drugs with one overall international agreement; it was amended in 1972. In 1968, the UN established the International Narcotics Control Board (INCB). The INCB was charged with implementing the drug policies of the United Nations, including the Single Convention on Narcotic Drugs of 1961. On February 21, 1971, the Convention on Psychotrophic Substances was adopted in order to establish an international control system for drugs. The UN Convention on Psychotrophic Substances of 1971 permitted legal protection for prescription use of many ADHD and other medications. On December 20, 1988, the UN Convention against Illicit Traffic in Narcotic Drugs and Psychotropic Substances was adopted to provide additional enforcement mechanisms for the two earlier UN conventions. This included allowing Interpol's Criminal Organization and Drug Sub-Directorate (CODSD) to work in cooperation with the United Nations to monitor international drug trafficking. The United Nations thus serves a major role in the formulation of policies and strategies to address drugs on a global scale. It must, however, also be recognized that the U.S. Congress has much greater influence over international drug trafficking than its counterparts in many other countries. The U.S. Congress is responsible for appropriating funds for, thereby maintains some degree of oversight over international drug control efforts. In the 1970s and 1980s, it was claimed that there were integral linkages between the trafficking in cocaine and other illegal drugs and U.S. security interests. The 1988 UN Convention is concerned primarily with the manufacturing, distribution, and possession of drugs; it also covers precursor substances typically used for the illegal production of drugs, such as pseudoephedrine and ephedrine used for making methamphetamine, as well as the materials and equipment used in such illicit production efforts. Another major objective of this Convention is to ensure an adequate international supply of controlled drugs for medical purposes, such as ADHD medications. It also has provisions for the extradition of drug traffickers and for transfer proceedings as well as creating mechanisms for controlled deliveries of ADHD and other medications.

CLINICAL TRIALS

Clinical trials provide the process by which new drugs, including new ADHD medications, are reviewed for approval consideration. This system consists of four major phases through which new pharmaceutical products must pass in order to be made available to those who need them. It is primarily the clinical trial process that grants us the confidence that our ADHD, and other, medications are safe and effective.

Background to Clinical Trials

Clinical trials are essentially research tests that are intended to evaluate how effective medical techniques are. Each clinical trial has a plan of action, or protocol, as to how the particular test will be conducted. This protocol must completely describe what will be done in the specific test, and describe each step that will be implemented as well as provide a justification of why each step is necessary. Every clinical trial has a specific set of conditions as to who can, as well as who cannot, participate. Clinical trials can furnish useful information about which pharmaceutical products or other medical interventions or devices should be further investigated with more rigorously designed studies.

The origins of modern clinical trials goes back at least to the eighteenth century when comparison groups were used to evaluate different treatment approaches, such as those treating scurvy by having British sailors eat citrus fruits. After a series of fatalities resulting from the use of a diethylene glycol solution of sulfanilamide, the Federal Pure Food and Drug Act was amended in 1938 requiring toxicity studies, as well as approval of a NDA, before a new medicinal substance could be marketed and distributed in the United States. The 1992 Prescription Drug User Fee Act and the subsequent Food and Drug Administration Modernization Act of 1997 have accelerated the drug approval process under the supervision of the Center for Drug Evaluation and Research (CDER).

Clinical trials are now typically used to evaluate the safety and effectiveness of a new medical treatment compared to the existing treatment available or to the current standard of care for a particular condition, including ADHD. These scientific studies generally involve active participation by human subjects to test the safety and effectiveness of new treatment approaches. Before a new medicine can be released for use in the United States, and in most of the rest of the developed world, it must first undergo a rigorous clinical trial process in order to determine if it is both safe and effective for use. However, not all clinical trials are necessarily intended to assess the safety and efficacy of a new pharmacological substance like an ADHD medicine. For instance, there are clinical trials that are fundamentally diagnostic in nature and designed in order to determine better ways to diagnose a serious disorder or illness, which could, for example, include a symptom like hyperactivity in children with autism who may have comorbid ADHD. There are screening clinical trials that are intended to find the best way to detect a particular condition or disorder; preventative trials to examine ways to prevent specific conditions or diseases, like ADHD after maternal alcohol consumption during pregnancy. There are also clinical trials that are primarily intended to find ways to better improve the quality of life for those experiencing respective conditions, of course, including ADHD and related issues. Clinical trials with different purposes would, naturally enough, have different research designs.

There are both publicly and privately supported clinical trials. Some common examples of industry sponsors of clinical trials include biotechnology, medical device, and pharmaceutical companies. Every year around 80,000 industry and federal sponsored clinical trials are conducted in this country using as many as 5,000 to 6,000 different research protocols. These research trials are conducted at many different types of sites, covering more than 10,000 different locations around the country, including independent research centers, doctor's offices, universities, and at private and public hospitals and medical centers. Millions of individuals participate each year as research subjects in these clinical trials and about 200,000 research professionals operate and manage these studies annually. Numerous clinical trials are also conducted each year in other countries around the globe. However, the results of clinical trials from other countries are not pooled generally, which could easily provide a greater data collection resources than any one nation could generate on its own, and this would efficiently provide enormous opportunities for extensive informed decision making in many areas.

A clinical trial typically is intended to examine a specific intervention or set of interventions, and it can even be referred to as an interventional study. The particular intervention could be a new drug or medical device; or it could involve different doses of a medicine or different ways to administer the drug, like an ADHD medicine administered as a transdermal patch rather than as a pill; or it could involve life style changes on the part of the research subjects, such as changes in their diet, exercise habits, or caffeine use. Another kind of approach is an observational study; variations of these types of clinical trials can include case only, case-control, case-crossover, cohort, community, and ecological studies. A critical feature is that all clinical trials are prospective in design, not retrospective; they can propose an intended effect, establish conditions that could test this possible relationship, and then assess the results, determining whether they support the hypothesis positively, negatively, or are unclear.

Clinical trials are designed as rigorously controlled research studies according to strict scientific procedures. They must control for as many variables as possible in order to clearly determine what the effects of a specific medicine or other treatment alternative is. In a clinical trial, the independent variable is manipulated by the researchers, such as whether or not the new drug being tested was administered to a particular part of the study sample. The dependent variable, on the other hand, is the outcome of the study, such as what the effects of a particular medicine are on a specific symptom of ADHD. When researchers are selecting samples of individuals with ADHD for clinical trials, whether of new ADHD medications or of other therapeutic approaches, it must be recognized that they are not necessarily a very homogenous group of individuals. Accordingly, attention should be directed to the particular sampling procedures that will be employed to, hopefully, construct a representative sample. In this vein, certain subgroups might need to be either somewhat reduced or expanded in order to get greater representativeness in the study sample, thus achieve more generalizable results. For example, individuals who have the anxious or hostile subtypes of depression are known found to be poor subjects in clinical drug trials since they typically have very high placebo response rates. On the other hand, individuals who have the withdrawn or disorganized subtypes of depressive disorder tend to be poor subjects in clinical trials of neuroleptic drugs since they typically respond poorly to both the placebo and the active drug. The exclusion of such subjects from samples means, of course, that the observed results of the clinical trial may not be as generalizable to persons with those particular types of conditions. In Europe, the European Medications Agency (EMA) is the general regulator of drugs, thus also of the clinical trials relating to them; it is, accordingly, somewhat analogous to the FDA in the United States. The EMA, naturally, has its own set of guidelines and policies regarding the conduct and utilization of clinical trials and their findings.

Phase I Clinical Trials.   It is thought that it may take up to 20 years and around $800 million to bring a new drug from its initial discovery through to the final marketing stage. It often takes around 10 years of testing in test tubes and on animal subjects before a new drug is potentially ready for initial human testing. It is recognized that only about 1 out of every 50 drugs that undergo preclinical testing will eventually be considered safe and effective enough for testing on human subjects. These preclinical investigations are usually conducted before Phase I studies can be initiated and they are typically conducted as either in vitro studies or as animal studies. There is then an extrapolation of the resulting preclinical safety data to human subjects. The results of laboratory and animal testing, as well as detailed study protocols, must then be submitted in an Investigational New Drug (IND) application to the FDA. If this application is not rejected by the FDA, then the actual clinical trial phases can be conducted. Of the new drugs that enter clinical trial phases, it has been found that only about one out of five will ever prove safe and effective enough to receive final FDA approval. Typically around 120 new medical approaches get FDA approval each year.

Clinical trials that are conducted for FDA approval in the United States are generally divided into four phases. Phase I studies typically involve a relatively small group, perhaps around 20 to 100 subjects who are usually normal, healthy individuals, such as college students, and these studies can last for up to a year. At the beginning of a clinical trial, baseline data typically are collected on participants. This usually includes collection of demographic data, such as age, gender, ethnicity, and racial background. Different baseline characteristics, of course, are likely to be collected depending on the particular nature of the clinical study. For example, a study of a potential ADHD medicine for adults is likely to record history of commonly associated problems, such as divorce, criminal arrests, motor vehicle infractions, prior use of both prescription and over the counter drugs, alcohol intake, and job loss. The primary purpose of Phase I clinical trials is to evaluate the safety of the approach, such as the bioavailability, dosage ranges, methods of administration, and rate of absorption of the substance in the body, as well as any possible toxicities. A major purpose of Phase I clinical studies is to determine safe dosage levels that can be administered before minor side effects, such as headaches or nausea, are likely to be experienced by users. Subjects in Phase I studies are typically compensated financially, particularly since there is a rather high probability that they will experience some unpleasant side effects. Phase I clinical trials are concerned primarily with estimating the maximally tolerated dose of the substance under study as well as determining its pharmacodynamics and pharmacokinetics. It is thought that around 70 percent of the new medical approaches submitted for review by the FDA will eventually be able to successfully pass Phase I testing.

Phase II Clinical Trials.   Phase II clinical trials are primarily concerned with evaluating various safety and efficacy issues for particular types of subjects. These studies, like those of Phase I, are relatively small studies, utilizing between a hundred and up to several hundred research subjects who have the condition being examined for the particular intervention. Phase II clinical trials usually take between one year and up to three years to conduct. Requirements for subjects to participate in Phase II clinical trials are generally stricter than for Phase I studies and subjects are usually randomly assigned to a control or to a treatment group. The control group might receive either a placebo or the standard treatment. Several different types of treatment groups may be used in a particular clinical trial. Commonly neither the research participants nor the researchers know who will get the treatment and who will not; this research strategy is referred to as a double blind study, which is designed to help eliminate as much bias as possible. During Phase II studies, different dosages of a medicine are typically explored. The main purpose of Phase II testing is to help determine if the new medicine, device, or treatment approach has sufficient efficacy or biological activity against the particular condition under study to warrant more extensive research and development efforts. It is thought that approximately a third of all drugs under development that begin clinical trials will pass Phase II and then are able to proceed on to testing in Phase III studies.

Phase III Clinical Trials.   Phase III clinical trials are generally larger and considerably more expensive to conduct than Phase I or Phase II studies. Phase III studies usually involve several hundred and up to several thousand subjects and typically last from two to four or even five years. The Phase III studies are frequently conducted in physician's offices and often involve a more diverse range of subjects than merely those for whom the treatment is actually intended. Researchers are likely to explore not only issues around safety and efficacy but also cost benefits, among different demographic subsets of participants, such as younger and older, female and male, various ethnic and racial groups, and individuals with mild, moderate, or severe forms of the particular disorder under study. Different dosage levels are usually explored in order to help determine maximum effectiveness while still having few adverse side effects. It is recognized that around 80 percent of medications that undergo Phase III testing will be able to successfully pass this stage.

After completing Phase III clinical trials, the research sponsor can submit an NDA to the FDA. It usually takes about a year review for the NDA to be considered; around 60 percent of the NDAs are eventually approved by the FDA. If the principal investigator made an agreement with the sponsor of a clinical trial that they would not publish or discuss the results the findings of the clinical study in any academic or scientific journal then an agreements document must be completed, according to Section 801 of the Food and Drug Administration Amendments Act (Public Law 110-85). An acceptable package insert must then be prepared through a cooperative effort between the FDA and the manufacturer; it should include approved indications, contraindications, precautions, warnings, adverse reactions, and so on. The medicine can then be produced and finally marketed for sale, but it is still only under conditional approval.

Phase IV Clinical Trials.   Phase IV clinical trials are conducted after the FDA has granted approval for the marketing of the new product. It is widely recognized that there may be many unanticipated adverse, as well as perhaps some beneficial effects that would generally only be detected after the medicine has been widely used, which is the reason that the FDA frequently suggests that Phase IV clinical studies be conducted. At any rate, the release of the new medicine is closely monitored by the FDA and patients are under close supervision. These Phase IV clinical trials often involve several hundred to several thousand test subjects, they are generally conducted at selected medical centers and administered by qualified healthcare professionals, and they generally take from 2 to 10 years to conduct. All healthcare providers who agree to participate in Phase IV clinical testing agree to participate in structured reporting, which pays attention to both the efficacy and the toxicity of the particular pharmacological product. It must be recognized, however, that studies of certain types of interventions, like those considering life style or behavioral changes or new medical approaches, might not fit neatly into the Phase I through Phase IV clinical testing paradigm.

Critiques of the Clinical Trial System

Many criticisms have been leveled at the clinical trial system. These generally relate to concerns over the degree of influence that pharmaceutical and other medical products companies have over the area, particularly with issues such as the selection of the sample of subjects participating in clinical trials and with matters of the publication and dissemination of the results of such studies.

Overview.   Critics have asserted that many clinical trials are seriously flawed and that the system within which they presently operate is not working as intended. Calls have been made for substantial reforms to the system. The basis of the problem, according to critics, is that the pharmaceutical or other related industries have been permitted to overly control and influence the process. An example of a flawed, but commonly used research design for a clinical trial is that of comparing the new substance under development against a placebo when, in fact, there is a perfectly good medicine that is already being used to treat the condition. Under such conditions, many medications would, not surprisingly, demonstrate higher efficacy than would a placebo, which by definition should have no actual therapeutic effect. Something, in fact almost anything, is likely to have a more profound impact than nothing, which is basically what a clinical trial against a placebo is designed to test. Another common flawed approach used in designing a clinical trial is to administer either an unusually high or an abnormally low dosage of a frequently used competing pharmacological product, thereby making it very likely to find either more severe side effects or insufficient therapeutic efficacy. While such biased approaches are allowed to be used to craft clinical trials for new ADHD medications, it is unlikely that major treatment improvements will be found.

Sample Selection.   Another commonly raised criticism of clinical trials is that related to concerns with the sample populations used in respective studies. Most clinical trials can be characterized as having a limited number of research subjects, which is generally rationalized for by claiming the excessive expense of utilizing much larger sample sizes. In addition, the participants selected for most clinical trials may not actually be very representative of the intended target population to whom a particular pharmacological product or other medicinal approach will actually be used on. In fact, it is not uncommon for a relatively young and healthy pool of subjects to be chosen for a clinical trial, even though the medical approach being investigated will eventually be used, if FDA approval is gained, with a considerably different population. Unfortunately, the unrealistic practice of choosing such nonrepresentative samples for application of the intervention being investigated is more likely to lead getting federal approval, since it is less likely that potential problems will be encountered, which might only become evident after wider exposure of the approach to groups with more diverse characteristics is involved.

Publication Concerns.   It is hardly surprising that pharmaceutical, or other similar medical industry, sponsored clinical trials might, in fact, be designed so as to be more likely yield positive results for the drug or other medical product being developed. What might, however, be somewhat less apparent is the extent to which the pharmaceutical and related industries excessively control, or at least influence, the eventual publication and dissemination of the results of such clinical trials. Unfortunately, they can, and often do, withhold negative results and further can otherwise manipulate factors that are usually assumed to be more neutral.

The selective publication of the results of only those clinical trials that indicate positive findings for the medical products produced by a respective pharmaceutical, or other related medical, company is very common. The fundamental problem is that pharmaceutical and similar companies are not obligated to publish all the results from all the clinical trials they actually conducted on a specific intervention. The missing results might well suggest that the pharmacological product or medical approach being examined is actually no better, or could even be worse, than other agents or approaches already being used. Unfortunately, this customary practice can result in the research literature available on the subject being overly biased with somewhat misleading and perhaps even asserting false positive findings. Although rules have been agreed upon, which state that the results of all clinical trials should be released and listed, there is no appropriate regulatory organization or body to oversee that such is, in fact, accomplished. Critics who have looked into the issue have actually found that the findings of clinical trials with negative results or even those that are just somewhat unflattering toward a potential pharmaceutical product are much less likely to be made available and declared. Unfortunately, the techniques and strategies utilized by the pharmaceutical and related industries to extol the image of their own products customarily go far beyond this degree of control.

There are actual publications designed by and paid for by the pharmaceutical and related medical companies that have the appearance of being an independent academic research journal, but in reality are not. Issues of these so-called publications are widely distributed by pharmaceutical representatives or mailed directly to physicians, who may diligently read them in the belief that they are legitimate scholarly, research journals that are simply tools that serve solely to market particular pharmaceutical or other medical products. The articles printed in these glossy publications typically claim to report on objective clinical trial data, but as the entire process has been set up by and for the respective company, all material contained therein will thus naturally promote its products.

There are also slightly more indirect pressures that the pharmaceutical or related companies apply upon the editors and publishers of allegedly independent medical research journals. It is well recognized that these companies will regularly purchase, for rather exorbitant prices, up to hundreds of thousands of reprints of articles published in prestigious journals if they extol the merits of their products. These expensive reprints are regularly and widely distributed by these companies to physicians and researchers at no charge under the superficial guise of professional development or of simply helping to spread research knowledge, but this prevalent practice is little more than overt advertising. The financial incentive for publishing such favorable articles is considerable, especially upon smaller academic journals, whose editors typically work part time, while usually maintaining full time academic positions with other commensurate responsibilities. In addition, pharmaceutical and related medical companies have long been known to hire ghost writers to prepare drafts of articles for submission to academic journals and then find a doctor or researcher who is willing to submit the glowing manuscript under his or her own name and credentials. If the article is accepted and published, the designated author can expect to then be hired to deliver those findings at professional conferences and at industry sponsored continuing medical education events often held at exotic locales. These academic presenters are generally supplied with talking points from the company on the exceptional virtues of the particular medical product being discussed. These trainings and related events are known to heavily influence what medications and other products the attendees will prescribe to their patients in the future as well as what products they will spontaneously promote to colleagues and trainees. Therefore, the overall results of perhaps a less than well designed clinical trial could easily become regarded as the state of the art approach for treating a particular medical problem, such as ADHD. This common practice of allowing industry-sponsored clinical trial data to remain largely under their control and to be used as they see fit to apply could, regrettably, and apparently has in certain cases already, have resulted in the demise of effective medical approaches with their being replaced by more expensive but less effective, if not even harmful, approaches. This approach is not only unethical but also can undermine the integrity of medical treatment and seriously threaten the ability of healthcare consumers to trust the advice given.

Recent Initiatives

The Center for Drug Evaluation and Research (CDER) of the FDA has established streamlined regulatory programs to expedite the review of new medications. For instance, in 2014, the FDA approved more novel new medications than it had in any of the previous 20 years. In fact, in 2014, the FDA approved 34 percent more new therapeutic drugs than it did in 2013. More than 75 percent of the novel medications were approved in the first cycle of review, without demands for additional information, which was more typical in the past, thereby extended the process. Further, nearly two thirds of these new pharmaceutical agents were approved in the United States under these new accelerated FDA approval programs before they were approved for use in other countries.

Since the late 1990s, the FDA has increasingly been requiring pharmaceutical companies to collect safety and efficacy data on new drugs that might at some point have pediatric applications. In 2012, the Safety and Innovations Act was enacted requiring the FDA to expand consideration of medications for use with individuals 17 years of age and younger. The EMA, acting on behalf of the European Commission, had already developed the Pediatric Regulation that took effect on January 26, 2007, and which, like the subsequent Safety and Innovations Act, established a system of both obligations and incentives to ensure that medications would henceforth be routinely researched, developed, and authorized to meet the therapeutic needs of children. These measures compel pharmaceutical companies to consider possible pediatric applications of medications they develop and to conduct research programs to improve the availability of high quality medications for children, including potential ADHD medications.

Greater attention has finally been paid in the last few years to the excessive influence that pharmaceutical and related companies have on physicians and other healthcare providers. It is recognized that measures that restrict meetings between pharmaceutical representatives and physicians and other healthcare providers, as well as those limiting the distribution of drug samples and of promotional materials, are associated with less influence on prescribing behavior. This has important financial ramifications for individuals who consume ADHD and other medications as the greater the influence such companies have upon healthcare providers the more likely it is that the rate of prescriptions for typically more expensive brand name medications will increase compared to that of the equally effective but lower priced generic versions of these medications. It has even been demonstrated, for instance, that such a seemingly innocuous activity as physicians receiving an industry sponsored meal promoting a brand name product significantly increases the probability that they will prescribe that product over the typically less expensive generic version. In fact, accepting more industry sponsored meals and costlier meals has been associated with even higher rates of brand name prescriptions. There are clearly inherent tensions between the self-interests of the profits of pharmaceutical and other healthcare companies and the affordability, independence, and integrity of medical care. Accordingly, it is increasingly becoming recommended that there be greater limitations imposed on the interaction between pharmaceutical and other medical products companies and healthcare providers, particularly physicians.

DRUG SCHEDULING

Drug scheduling is a system for the regulation of medications and other drugs that was established in the United States with the creation of the Controlled Substances Act. A brief review of the background to the Controlled Substances Act, as well as of the domains impacted by the act, helps to explain how significant its enactment was, including, of course, its formation of Schedules I, II, III, and IV for the listing of controlled substances.

Controlled Substances Act

The Controlled Substances Act, along with its latter amendments, combined together many separate drug laws into one sweeping federal statute that covered numerous aspects of drugs, from their use and abuse, prevention, and treatment, to pharmaceutical industry controls, and drug trafficking interdiction. The act was intended to serve as a wide-ranging federal approach to uniformly address varied aspects of drug use and abuse. This act and the broader Comprehensive Drug Abuse Prevention and Control Act, of which it is a part, collectively attempted to combine all the then existing federal drug laws into one single statute. These acts still serve as the major legal foundation that guide drug-enforcement efforts in the United States, as well as for regulating the manufacturing of medications. The act significantly changed the nature of federal drug policies in the United States.

Background to the Controlled Substances Act. The Controlled Substances Act created a new and very broad approach to how the United States deals with drugs. It was established at a time when the American public was extremely concerned about drugs and their associated problems, including that of drug-related crime. President Richard M. Nixon and others in key leadership positions then felt that their ability to wage a war on drugs was hindered by a perplexing network of laws, enforcement approaches, and regulatory bodies. The act was prepared under the direction of John Mitchell, the then U.S. Attorney General. The act was introduced to Congress on September 10, 1970, as H.R. 18583 by Harley O. Staggers, a Democratic assemblyman from West Virginia. The act was strategically intended to reorganize the confusing state of affairs around drugs into a comprehensive and effective federal approach.

The purpose of the Controlled Substances Act was to change and supplant numerous separate laws that covered myriad aspects of drug use and abuse. For example, the act repealed both the Harrison Narcotic Act of 1916 and many of the Drug Abuse Control Amendments of 1965, most of which were enacted to curtail illegal drugs. In fact, the act replaced more than 50 other separate pieces of drug legislation. An additional concern was that there was insufficient cooperation and coordination among many government agencies addressing drugs. Provisions were established to manage the development and testing of new medications and to guide how these could be covered by existing and revised regulatory processes. Then, on October, 27, 1970, the Controlled Substances Act of 1970 was signed into law by President Nixon as part of Public Law 91-513 (84 Stat. 1236), which is better known as the Comprehensive Drug Abuse Prevention and Control Act.

Domains Impacted by the Controlled Substances Act. The Controlled Substances Act specified processes by which drugs could be evaluated to determine whether they should be regulated. Prior to this, separate pieces of legislation had to be passed to cover particular drugs or drug classes, such as stimulants, depressants, and other substances with the potential for abuse. A revolutionary innovation of the act was its ability to include newly created substances into prior existing laws and regulations. This was considered a controversial approach when the act was first passed; earlier it had been believed that it would require passage of a constitutional amendment, such as that for the prohibition of alcoholic beverages, to stop people from using any substance.

The Controlled Substances Act and similar legislation granted expanded powers to police and other government agencies, such as for the search and seizure of drugs. For instance, in 1971, the Diversion Control Program was established to provide a specialized force that could investigate diversion of pharmaceutical products into the illegal drug trade. The act was amended in 1978 to allow criminal justice agencies to seize assets, including monies, property, and other resources, from anyone who got these proceeds from illegal drug sales. The U.S. Attorney General was authorized by Congress to delegate enforcement efforts and to establish regulations that are deemed necessary and appropriate to control drugs. Section 871a of the act requires the Attorney General to submit semiannual reports to congressional committees and organizations on investigation and prosecution efforts involving methamphetamine and scheduled precursor chemicals. This particular section was enacted as part of the USA PATRIOT Improvement and Reauthorization Act of 2005 during the administration of President George W. Bush.

Scheduling of Drugs.   The Controlled Substances Act (84 Stat. 1242) created five schedules for manufacturing, importing, distributing, possessing, and using certain substances, such as stimulants and other classes of ADHD medications as well as many of the chemical precursors used in making of these controlled substances. It also established procedures to study and possibly approve new drugs for marketing by examining their possible medicinal value, as well as their adverse side effects, including their potential for leading to addiction.

On May 1, 1971, the Controlled Substances Act went into effect, and it was initially enforced by the Department of Justice's Bureau of Narcotics and Dangerous Drugs, until 1973 when that agency was replaced by the Drug Enforcement Administration (DEA). Under Title 21, Chapter 13, Subchapter 1, Part B, the act places respective controlled substances into one of five schedules, which serves as a classification system for enforcement and regulatory purposes. These drug schedules are supposedly based on the accepted medical uses, the differing potentials for abuse and addiction, and the safety concerns for specific controlled substances. The schedule that a particular substance is placed in determines how it will be regulated and controlled.

Schedule I drugs are for those substances that are considered to be the most dangerous. Schedule I substances are those that have a high potential for abuse, that currently have no generally accepted medicinal use, and that lack an accepted level of safety, such that even under medical supervision, they cannot be safely used. Heroin, as well as DMT, LSD, mescaline, psilocybin, and other hallucinogens are all listed as Schedule I drugs.

Schedule II drugs also have a high potential for abuse, but they currently have accepted medicinal uses, even if with severe restrictions, and they can still lead to severe psychological or physical dependence. Schedule II drugs all require a prescription from a healthcare provider for their legal use. The psychostimulant ADHD medications such as the racemic amphetamine (Dyanavel XR), the enantiomer dextroamphetamine (Dexedrine), its prodrug lisdextroamphetamine dimesylate (Vyvanse), methamphetamine hydrochloride (Desoxyn), methylphenidate hydrochloride (Ritalin, Concerta), or mixed amphetamine salts (Adderall) are all currently listed as Schedule II drugs; as are other drugs such as cocaine, and painkillers like methadone and fentanyl.

Schedule III drugs have a lower potential for abuse than Schedule I or II drugs and although their use may lead to high psychological dependence or low to moderate physical dependence, they have accepted medical uses. A prescription is required for the legal use of all Schedule III drugs. Anabolic steroids, ketamine, and paregoric are examples of substances listed as Schedule III drugs.

Schedule IV drugs are those that are regarded as having a low abuse potential relative to substances in Schedule III, but limited psychological or physical dependence can still be developed, and these substances currently have accepted medicinal uses. A prescription is required for all Schedule IV drugs. The ADHD medications modafinil (Provigil) and armodafinil (Nuvigil), for instance, are listed as Schedule IV substances; other examples include the benzodiazepines, chloral hydrate, and phenobarbital.

Schedule V is used for those substances that are considered to be the least dangerous. Schedule V drugs have a lower abuse potential than those listed on Schedules I through IV, but their use can still lead to psychological or physical dependence; in addition, they currently have accepted medicinal uses. Lomotil and Robitussin A-C, for example, are a couple of substances listed as Schedule V products. Many Schedule V drugs do not generally require a prescription, while those listed on Schedules II, III, and IV all do require prescriptions.

The U.S. Department of Justice and the Department of Health and Human Services, including the FDA, collectively control substances under these five drug schedules. The Controlled Substances Act prohibits most drug offenses and lists a range of possible penalties, including fines and forfeitures, for those convicted.

The act acknowledges the likelihood that there may, from time to time, be a need for the addition, deletion, or transfer of substances from one schedule to another and has specific procedures for doing so. For example, the FDA is considering reclassifying hydrocodone compounds, like Vicodin, from a Schedule III to a Schedule II drug due to the increased levels of abuse. Any new drug or concerns over an existing drug can be considered on scientific and medical grounds. The DEA can consider any substance for inclusion into drug schedules based on information from the FDA and the National Institute on Drug Abuse (NIDA) as well as from criminal justice agencies, pharmaceutical companies, or others. This review will determine whether the substance should or should not be controlled under one of the five schedules or removed from them.

Legislation is enacted occasionally that amends the Controlled Substances Act. For instance, the Hillary J. Farias and Samantha Reid Date-Rape Prevention Act of 2000 placed gamma hydroxybutyrate on Schedule I. Similarly, the Synthetic Drug Abuse Prevention Act, which took effect in

July 2012, made 26 chemicals that are ingredients in synthetic drugs illegal; it made chemicals like mephedrone and methylenedioxypyrovalerone (MDPV), commonly referred to as "bath salts," Schedule I drugs.

The Controlled Substances Act significantly altered how the pharmaceutical industry operates with respect to how new drugs are developed and how all substances are manufactured and distributed, including import and export. For instance, it maintains and expands regulations that require how drugs are to be identified with specific symbols, primarily for use by pharmacists. Every year under the act, the U.S. Attorney General is charged with establishing production quotas for individual substances controlled in Schedules I and II, which thereby limits pharmaceutical production. The act also requires that the pharmaceutical industry keep selected drugs physically secure, such as by establishing strict standards for keeping thorough inventories and records. Provisions also exist to regulate selected operations of physicians, nurse practitioners, physician assistants, pharmacists, wholesalers, distributors, and others whose scope of service involves the dissemination or use of respective controlled substances. For example, prescriptions for ADHD and other medications must list the physician's DEA license number. The DEA registration system allows pharmaceutical manufacturers, researchers and healthcare professionals to access controlled substances on Schedules I, II, III, IV, and V.

Restrictions on Psychostimulants in the United States

Various restrictions on access to psychostimulant drugs have been established in the United States. Individual states initially and then finally beginning in 1914 the federal government passed legislation such as the Harrison Narcotics Act to regulate the importing and sale of cocaine and other drugs. Since 1956, amphetamines were only legally available in the United States by prescription. Numerous additional laws were passed as amendments to the Controlled Substance Act that put stimulants and other drugs into the various regulatory schedules. For instance, Adderall, a combination stimulant formulation commonly prescribed for treating ADHD, is listed as a Schedule II controlled substance.

Restrictions in Other Countries

Legislation has been passed in other countries similar to the Controlled Substances Act that broadly regulates the manufacturing and distribution of medications and controls illicit drug use and abuse. For instance, in 1971, the United Kingdom passed the Misuse of Drugs Act, and in 1996, Canada passed the Controlled Drugs and Substances Act, both of which are somewhat analogous to the Controlled Substances Act in the United States. These, and comparable laws elsewhere, were enacted to comply with treaty commitments made under agreements like the Single Convention on Narcotic Drugs (1961), Convention on Psychotropic Substances (1971), and UN Convention against Illicit Traffic in Narcotic Drugs and Psychotropic Substances (1988).

More narrowly focused laws have been passed in many countries specifically to address issues of abuse and addiction related to psychostimulant drugs. Norway, for example, has restrictions on prescribing psychostimulants to individuals with substance use disorders and to those who are in opioid maintenance treatment programs. From 1971 to 1995, the number of amphetamine-like psychostimulant drugs under regulatory control internationally increased about fivefold.

Chapter 8

The Social Dimensions of ADHD Medications

There are many social dimensions that are relevant to any thorough discussion of attention deficit hyperactivity disorder (ADHD). These include issues such as whether or not there is an over diagnosing of ADHD as well as issues such as the general controversies over the use of ADHD medications and why ADHD medications should be used if there are other treatments that work. There are also many different approaches that are used in treating individuals with ADHD. A closely related set of social dimensions are the differences observed in the prevalence rates of ADHD, which vary somewhat with respect to gender, racial, and ethnic group affiliation and for other special populations. A major social dimension is that of the involvement of the criminal justice system in areas related to ADHD and, in particular, ADHD medications. On the other hand, there are the numerous areas for which successes for those with ADHD have been observed, including in the educational and occupational realms. It is also important in this context to briefly note some of the many successful individuals who have had ADHD.

OVER DIAGNOSING OF ADHD

It is certainly true that there are some individuals, both children and adults, who have been diagnosed with ADHD who do not actually have it. Misdiagnosing could clearly result in perceived over diagnosing of ADHD. Individuals who have different disorders or illnesses that could cause them to present with a set of symptoms that appear similar to ADHD could easily be misdiagnosed as having ADHD. There are, in fact, myriad medical conditions that share symptoms with ADHD, and these could easily be confused and, if not appropriately ruled out, could possibly lead to over diagnosing. For instance, iron-deficiency anemia can cause feelings of irritability, difficulty concentrating, impaired cognition, and a short attention span in infants and children; this constellation of symptoms could easily be mistaken for ADHD. Similarly, hypoglycemia and other related nutritional deficiencies can cause many symptoms similar to those of ADHD, such as hyperactivity, difficulty sitting still, aggression, or low levels of concentration. Children with an intellectual disability or with an autism spectrum disorder can appear emotionally immature, exhibit limited social skills, and have school performance issues, all of which are also characteristic of individuals with ADHD. Likewise, children with autism or with sensory disorders when over stimulated can often become hyperactive. On the other hand, children with sensory disorders or with a hearing impairment can appear inattentive and may take risks without awareness of the dangers and also be accident prone. After having a mild absence seizure, a child can typically be confused or disoriented for several hours, which could also be mistaken for ADHD. Lead poisoning, as well as hypothyroidism, can manifest with diminished concentration, impaired memory, decreased cognitive skills, and poor academic performance, all of which are frequently observed in individuals with ADHD as well. Inattention can be caused by many factors, such as by medical conditions like a thyroid disorder or even by transitory events like just having had an argument with a significant other. These, and additional conditions, could contribute to the misdiagnosis of ADHD, which could contribute to an appearance of over diagnosing.

Immaturity may be another factor that contributes to some over diagnosing of ADHD. A study of kindergarten students found that 10 percent of the youngest individuals in class—that is, those born in August—were diagnosed with ADHD, while only 4.5 percent of the oldest individuals in class—that is, those born in September—were so diagnosed. Further, those who were born in August were twice as likely as those who were born in September to be prescribed stimulant ADHD medications. A related study in Iceland reported that the youngest third of the class was 50 percent more likely both to be diagnosed with ADHD and to be prescribed with ADHD stimulant medications.

Many professionals actually believe that ADHD is, in fact, under diagnosed. In fact, although ADHD may be somewhat over diagnosed in children, it is clearly under diagnosed in adults, particularly in older adults. It is estimated, for instance, that somewhere from 20 percent to 30 percent of all adult psychiatric patients diagnosed with anxiety, depression, or chemical dependence probably also have, generally undiagnosed, ADHD. In fact, many adults who have been diagnosed with a psychiatric disorder also have ADHD. However, many times the comorbid ADHD is unrecognized or at the very least under treated. It is challenging to make a differential diagnosis of adult ADHD since many of its symptoms overlap substantially with other psychiatric conditions. Further, the current *Diagnostic and Statistical Manual of Mental Disorders*, Fifth Edition's (*DSM-5*) diagnostic criteria may make it difficult to conduct an appropriate diagnosis of someone with ADHD symptoms that might also be accounted for by other psychiatric conditions. This is at least partly due to the fact that not all adults could readily provide evidence of a history of symptom onset during childhood. ADHD is often comorbid among individuals with conditions like anxiety, mood, substance abuse, and impulse-control disorders. In addition, ADHD can negatively impact the expression of other comorbid psychiatric disorders, and it can also make it more difficult for individuals to comply with treatment regimens. On top of this, unrecognized ADHD symptoms could easily be mistaken for poor treatment response in these other comorbid disorders. This all goes to underscore the critical importance of appropriately managing the ADHD, which is, of course, most often accomplished by means of prescribing ADHD medications. This is most likely to help stabilize the individual's daily functioning and thereby facilitate a fuller recovery.

CONTROVERSIAL USE OF ADHD MEDICATIONS

Serious concerns have been raised about the large numbers of children and others taking various medications for ADHD even before the disorder was fully recognized. Medications have been administered to treat what we now call ADHD since at least 1937 with the studies by Charles Bradley (1937) on the effects of racemic amphetamine (Benzedrine) on children with behavioral problems.

In 1955, methylphenidate, which was initially synthesized in 1944 and is better known by its trade name of Ritalin, was developed and first approved for use by the Food and Drug Administration (FDA) for treating hyperkinetic behaviors, as ADHD was then known. Beginning in the middle of the 1950s, it was prescribed for treating depression, lethargy, and narcolepsy. Since the middle of the 1960s, it has been one of the primary pharmacological treatments for ADHD. It has also been used for treating stroke. Methylphenidate hydrochloride (Ritalin) has been found to increase the ability of individuals with ADHD to focus their attention and to reduce the behavioral disruptions and impulsivity associated with the disorder. During the decade from 1985 to 1995, methylphenidate (Ritalin) production in the United States increased almost eightfold, reaching over 10 tons annually. By 1995, about 6 million prescriptions for Ritalin were being written each year in the United States, and approximately 2.5 million American children were using the drug annually. In fact, the United States then accounted for more than 90 percent of the manufacture and consumption of methylphenidate (Ritalin). From 1990 to 2005, production of methylphenidate (Ritalin) increased sixfold in the United States. In 2004, for instance, 29 million prescriptions for psychostimulants were written in the United States; of these, 14.5 million were for methylphenidate (Ritalin).

In 1996, the United Nations issued a warning about the controversial extensive use of methylphenidate (Ritalin) for treating what at that time was referred to as Attention Deficit Disorder (ADD). The United Nations noted that an influential special interest association of parents had received substantial financial contributions from the major U.S. pharmaceutical producer of the drug and, not surprisingly perhaps, was intensely promoting its use. Since then other groups of parents and physicians have actively campaigned against Ritalin and the other ADHD medications, citing the potential dangers that the use of these substances could possibly lead to, particularly including their abuse and even dependence, as well as to other potentially serious long-term health problems, and questions have also repeatedly been raised as to their long-term efficacy. For example, studies of the effects of Adderall, a combination amphetamine formulation, on individuals without ADHD failed to find any reliable improvements in several measures of cognitive ability, even though the subjects reported that they felt that their academic performance was enhanced. On the other hand, many parents, physicians, healthcare providers, and other interested individuals contend that these ADHD medications have been safely used for many decades and that such administration has afforded individuals with ADHD considerable benefits and usually an improved quality of life. For example, 70 percent to 80 percent of children diagnosed with ADHD exhibit improved task behavior, improved attention span, and reduced impulsivity while they are on ADHD stimulant medications.

In the early 1990s, around 1 percent to 3 percent of all school-age children in the United States were taking an ADHD stimulant medicine for treating ADHD; at that time, over 11 million prescriptions for stimulant medications were being written in the United States each year. The use of ADHD medications globally rose threefold from 1993 to 2003; however, taking inflation into account, global spending on ADHD medications increased ninefold, up to

$2.4 billion in 2003. Although use and spending grew in both developing and developed countries, the United States, Canada, and Australia exhibited significantly greater-than-predicted increases in use as well as in spending, the latter mostly due to switching to more expensive, longer-acting formulations of ADHD medications.

There have clearly been dramatic increases in the numbers of prescriptions being written for ADHD medications. Of the roughly 6.4 million children diagnosed with ADHD in the United States, approximately half are taking various ADHD medications. In 2015, there were 49.1 million prescriptions written in the United States for ADHD medications. This total represents a 21 percent increase over that from 2008. In 2010, 46 percent of the prescriptions for ADHD medications were written for individuals aged 20 years and above, which represents a 42 percent over those written in 2008. Prescriptions for adults with ADHD increased 53.5 percent from 2008 to 2012; the greatest increase was among females from the ages of 26 years to 34 years, which rose by 86 percent. In 2015, there was a 32 percent increase over that from 2008 in prescriptions for ADHD medications for men aged 20 years to 59 years; there was also a 38 percent increase in prescriptions for women the same age over the same time period; in 2015, there were 8.2 million prescriptions for men and 11.4 million for women in the same age range.

It is widely acknowledged that the more ADHD medications are available, the more likely it is that they will be abused. The strong association between the availability of and the abuse of respective substances has been conclusively demonstrated for many drugs, including, but certainly not limited to, drugs like nicotine, alcohol, cocaine, and opioids. In a related vein, it is generally understood that over a third of individuals who receive ADHD medications legally have been asked to trade or sell their medications to those without prescriptions. Currently, over 4.2 million individuals are prescribed ADHD stimulant medications. While more than 19 million legal prescriptions for amphetamines alone were filled in the United States in 2000, the increases in illicit nonprescription stimulant drug abuse became a much greater societal problem.

Dramatic increases have been reported for other classes of ADHD medications. The number of children taking antipsychotic medications has nearly tripled in the last decade to decade and a half; from 2001 to 2007 alone the number doubled. Annual global sales of antipsychotic medications as of 2007 are over $20.4 billion each year. In the United States alone, annual sales of antipsychotic medications were about $2.8 billion in 2003; and, by 2011, the total annual U.S. sales reached $18.2 billion. In 2007, more than 389,000 children and adolescents in the United States were prescribed the atypical antipsychotic medicine risperidone (Risperdal); of that total 240,000 individuals were 12 years of age or younger; some as young as 2 years old, and most were taking the medicine off label for treatment of ADHD. Since 2006, the number of prescriptions for antipsychotic medications written by pediatricians has increased almost 25 percent, and from 2005 to 2009, the use of antipsychotic medications in children and adolescents increased about 85 percent, again primarily for off-label treatment of ADHD.

WHY USE MEDICATIONS IF OTHER TREATMENTS WORK?

ADHD medications sometimes do not work for certain individuals. Nevertheless, we know from decades of research that they do work most of the time for most individuals. Unfortunately, the initial use of ADHD medications, or of any medicine for that matter, is not always as desired. At times the particular ADHD medicine tried is the problem, or perhaps the dosage, both of which can be adjusted through a careful process trial and error with proper monitoring to find a better solution. At other times though the expectations for the ADHD medicine might be unrealistic, this typically is handled by means of psychoeducation.

There is widespread reluctance to prescribe or to use ADHD medications, particularly the psychostimulant medications, in spite of the numerous studies that have shown both safety and efficacy. Just as every individual differs with respect to myriad physiological and psychological factors, not every individual with ADHD will necessarily take the same medications or even any medicine. Treatment approaches are complex and will naturally vary among respective individuals. Accordingly, it is very important to discuss all ADHD treatment options available with healthcare providers and their patients.

The use of medications to treat ADHD is generally to be recommended, and while medications alone may not fully address the underlying reasons that an individual develops ADHD, the use of these medications can generally help to keep the symptoms under control as other treatment approaches are introduced and implemented. Examples of medications that may be presented as part of a treatment approach to ADHD include the central nervous system stimulant medications, such as amphetamine (Evekeo, Dyanavel XR), dextroamphetamine (Dexedrine), lisdextroamphetamine (Vyvanse), methamphetamine (Desoxyn), and methylphenidate (Ritalin) and antidepressant medications, like the tricyclic antidepressants (TCAs), such as amitriptyline (Elavil), desipramine (Norpramin), and nortriptyline (Pamelor), and the selective serotonin reuptake inhibitors (SSRIs), such as fluoxetine hydrochloride (Prozac), fluvoxamine (Luvox), nefazodone (Serzone), paroxetine (Paxil), and sertraline (Zoloft), may also be used in treating ADHD. In other circumstances, other classes of drugs can also be used to help reduce and manage symptoms of ADHD; these can include the antihypertensive alpha 2 agonist medications, like clonidine hydrochloride (Kapvay, Catapres) or guanfacine hydrochloride (Intuniv, Tenex); the beta blockers, like atenolol (Tenorim), nadolol (Corgard), and propranolol (Inderal); the anticonvulsant medications, such as carbamazepine (Tegretol) and valporic acid (Depakote); the eugeroics, like modafinil (Provigil) and armodafinil (Nuvigil); the monoamine oxidase inhibitors, such as moclobemide (Amira), phenelzine (Nardil), and tranylcy-promine (Parnate); the antipsychotics, like clozapine (Clozaril), haloperidol (Haldol), olanzapine (Zyprexa), pimozide (Orap), quetiapine fumarate (Seroquel), risperidone (Risperdal), and thioridazine; and cholinergic agents, like nicotine. All of the stimulant medications mentioned previously have been approved by the FDA for treating ADHD. Several of the nonstimulant medications were approved by the FDA in 2003 for treating ADHD; the approved nonstimulant ADHD medications include atomoxetine (Strattera), clonidine (Kapvay), and quanfacine (Intuniv); use of most of the other medications is done off label for treating ADHD.

If the ADHD medications are working properly, most individuals will soon begin to experience things such as sustained focus, less impulsivity, improved mood, more attention to details, better memory, and even better sleep. However, if the individual is not feeling any of these positive signs, or if they are experiencing uncomfortable side effects, such as nausea, headaches, or loss of appetite, then they should talk with their healthcare provider.

Although ADHD medications are the recommended front line of treatment in the United States for children and adolescents above preschool age, such is not the case in many other countries. For example, in the European Union (EU) countries, the practice guidelines state that ADHD medications should only be used if the behavioral therapies are tried first and determined not to be sufficient to manage the ADHD symptoms. In these and in many other countries, accordingly, the practice is to initiate treatment with behavioral therapies and to only add medications if the behavioral therapies were inadequate to fully address the individual's needs. On the other hand, the American Academy of Pediatrics guidelines and the American Psychological Association both recommend that the first line of treatment in the United States for young children aged two years to five years should be behavioral therapy, which should be tried before medications are prescribed. Unfortunately, this is not always the practice followed; younger children in the United States are routinely being prescribed off-label use of various ADHD medications, including the atypical antipsychotic and other potent medications, before behavioral therapies have been tried.

TREATMENT APPROACHES

There are two major approaches used in the treatment of individuals with ADHD; these are pharmacological and behavioral strategies, respectively. The pharmacological approach, of course, uses the respective ADHD medications that are discussed in this work. There are many varied types of medications that are regularly prescribed to decrease the specific symptoms typically associated with ADHD. However, by far, the most commonly prescribed type of medications for ADHD is that of the central nervous system stimulants. On the other hand, 10 percent to 30 percent of children and adults with ADHD do not either respond well to or cannot tolerate the side effects associated with stimulant medicine treatment and, therefore, typically move on to the nonstimulant ADHD medications as an alternative treatment approach that can be employed. Some of these, like the TCAs and bupropion (Wellbutrin), usually help with the distractibility and hyperactivity issues, but they do not generally address impulsivity adequately; accordingly, alpha 2 agonist antihypertensive medications like clonidine hydrochloride (Kapvay, Catapres) or guanfacine hydrochloride (Intuniv, Tenex) may then be used as a second-line medicine. The anticonvulsant ADHD medications, such as carbamazepine (Tegretol) and valporic acid (Depakote), appear to be particularly helpful in controlling impulsivity. Some individuals with ADHD have found that use of an anticonvulsant medicine along with a psychostimulant medicine can be effective. These nonstimulant medications tend to be long-acting medications.

Compliance is a major issue in the utilization of pharmacological treatment, particularly an area of concern when used with children with ADHD. Use of longer-acting ADHD medications, such as those that permit once a day dosing, have been shown to have marked advantages with respect to compliance over shorter-acting formulations. Other advantages that have been found with the use of longer-acting medications are higher rates of symptom remission as well as less stigmatizing as administration during the school day is not necessary.

Behavioral psychotherapeutic strategies, of which there are many, have generally been found to be most effective when used in combination with the use of ADHD medications. Behavioral approaches can be very helpful in reducing uncertain expectations as well as in assisting with greater organization. Schools working in concert with parents in applying behavioral therapy or modification programs, such as behavioral classroom management and parent training, can be helpful in creating supportive, mutually reinforcing environments to ensure that consistency is in place to increase the likelihood that individuals with ADHD can maintain attention and focus as necessary. The use of Cognitive Behavioral Therapy (CBT) and ADHD medications together appears to improve overall functioning more than when either is used alone. The use of CBT, or related behavioral treatment approaches, can sometimes be frustrating since many individuals do not have the patience or the organizational skills to comply with their directives, which certain ADHD medications can make much more likely.

Treatment, as much as possible, should be individualized in addressing ADHD or any other condition for that matter. In particular, the dosages of respective ADHD medications usually need to be adjusted to the needs of different individuals. Adjusting the dosage quickly can help boost the individual's confidence in the treatment and its effectiveness. Longer-acting, once-daily-administered ADHD medications are preferable to cover the entire day at school or work and into the evening. Some individuals may require shorter-acting "booster" doses for even coverage. At any rate, it is critically important for informed decision making that a clear presentation of the potential risks as well as of the potential benefits associated with a particular plan of care for ADHD be made. It is recommended that healthcare providers focus on the absolute risk increase or reduction of a particular treatment choice and that use of graphics be employed when possible, rather than using broad qualitative descriptors or relative risk values, which most lay individuals find confusing. Other alternative treatment strategies for helping individuals with ADHD include dietary and lifestyle changes as well as the use of assorted meditation and biofeedback techniques.

In the 1990s, the Multimodal Treatment Study of Children with ADHD was funded by the National Institute of Mental Health to examine longer-term effects of ADHD medications. This multimodal study randomly assigned 579 children aged 7 years to 9.9 years who were diagnosed with ADHD to one of four possible treatment modalities. One group was administered ADHD stimulant medications; another received behavioral therapy; one got both ADHD stimulant medications and behavioral therapy, and the last continued to get the community care that they had been receiving prior to the study. The last group was the control group. After 14 months of treatment, those subjects in the group that were administered ADHD stimulant medications and those in the group getting both an ADHD stimulant medicine and behavioral therapy demonstrated more improvements in core ADHD symptoms than those in the other two groups; with respect to academic achievement, parental and child relations, social skills, and teacher and parental satisfaction, those in the group that received the combination of ADHD stimulant medications and behavioral therapy demonstrated the most improvements compared to those receiving their regular standard treatment. However, after three years, those in all four treatment groups were virtually indistinguishable in all measured respects. There was no lasting benefit evident on every attribute measured, such as test scores, grades, and social adjustment. Subsequent evaluation after another eight years confirmed that there were no significant differences evident between those in any of the four treatment groups. Many subsequent studies tracking subjects for three or more years found similar results to those reported for the Multimodal Treatment Study of Children.

DIFFERENCES IN RATES OF ADHD

There are many reasons that might explain why substantial differences are observed in the prevalence rates of ADHD. These certainly include an array of diagnostic concerns as well as differences due to issues related to society, gender, racial and ethnic membership, and those of assorted special populations.

Diagnostic

There have been, for various reasons, substantial increases in the number of individuals diagnosed and treated for ADHD around the world. The prevalence rates of ADHD diagnoses in the United States, accordingly, have progressively been increasing. For example, in 1995, there were 2,357,833 children in the United States diagnosed with ADHD, which is twice the number of children who were diagnosed in 1990. From 1997 to 2006, the diagnostic prevalence rate among children and adolescents aged 4 years to 17 years increased an average of 3 percent per year, and, from 2003 to 2011, the diagnostic prevalence rate increased about 5 percent per year. Over the past decade, in fact, the number of children and adolescents aged 4 years to 17 years in the United States diagnosed with ADHD has risen about 40 percent; this increase has given the United States the highest prevalence rate of ADHD diagnosis in the world. Currently, more than 10 percent or more than 1 out of every 10 children and adolescents under the age of 17 years in the United States are diagnosed with ADHD. For example, the prevalence of ADHD diagnosed among children and adolescents aged 4 years to 17 years in 2003 was 7.8 percent; in 2007 it was 9.5 percent, and in 2011 it was 11 percent.

While ADHD is generally diagnosed in childhood, the symptoms may persist into adulthood, and there are many adults today who were children at a time when ADHD was not as widely diagnosed as it currently is and thereby may likely have never been diagnosed. ADHD symptoms can appear as early as between the ages of 3 years and 6 years, and they can continue through adolescence and into adulthood. Most children with ADHD today are diagnosed during their elementary school years. For an adolescent or adult to receive a diagnosis of ADHD, the symptoms must have been present before the age of 12 years.

Social Issues

It is well understood that different societies have their own cultural set of expectations and values that substantially impact how a diagnosis of ADHD may be made and accepted as well as what treatment options may be practically possible. These factors influence us as well in this country. For instance, in the early 1990s in the United States, after the reauthorization of the Individuals with Disabilities Education Act (IDEA), ADHD was added as a diagnostic category that could make a child eligible for special education services at primary and secondary schools. After that the prevalence rate of ADHD diagnoses increased by about 30 percent to 40 percent at schools around the country. Of course, that does not mean that more individuals were suddenly having ADHD but simply that many more were being diagnosed so as to be able to access services.

Diagnosis rates for ADHD vary by geographical region within the United States. The highest prevalence rates are generally found in the southeastern United States, while the western and southwestern United States generally have the lowest prevalence rates. From 1998 to 2009, the ADHD diagnostic prevalence rates increased approximately 10 percent in the Midwest and in the South. Prevalence rates also vary substantially by state and even by county within the same state. For instance, in 2011, the prevalence of ADHD diagnoses among children and adolescents aged 4 years to 17 years in Colorado was 5.6 percent, while in Kentucky it was 14.8 percent. Similarly, in 2011, the prevalence rates of those diagnosed with ADHD stimulant medications were 47 percent in Nevada and 86.2 percent in Nebraska. Overall, the proportion of children and adolescents aged 4 years to 17 years who were taking medications for ADHD increased 28 percent from 2007 to 2011. In 2007, it was reported that 4.8 percent of youth 4 years to 17 years old were taking medications for ADHD; by 2011 it had increased to 6.1 percent. This is about a 7 percent average annual increase in the taking of ADHD medications.

If left untreated, or if treated ineffectively, ADHD can be a serious social problem. Around 52 percent of untreated adolescents and adults with ADHD abuse alcohol or other drugs of abuse, including several of the ADHD medications. Nearly a fifth (19%) of adults with ADHD smoke tobacco products, compared to approximately 10 percent of the general population. About 46 percent of untreated young adolescent males with the hyperactive subvariant of ADHD are arrested with a felony charge before reaching the age of 16 years, and about 21 percent of adults with ADHD will be arrested for a felony offense. Individuals with untreated ADHD have more emergency room visits and many more medical visits, as well as getting injured far more often, than other individuals.

Gender

It is widely acknowledged that boys are somewhat more likely than girls to be diagnosed with ADHD, at least during childhood and adolescence. In fact, the percentage of children and adolescents aged 5 years to 17 years has progressively been increasing among both boys and girls, but it has consistently been higher among boys. In this regard, boys, at 13.3 percent, are currently more than twice as likely as girls, who are at 5.6 percent, to have a current ADHD diagnosis. In addition, about one-fifth (20%) of American high school males have been told that they have ADHD. The ADHD diagnostic prevalence rate has, like many other ADHD-related statistics, been progressively increasing; from 1998 to 2000, it was 9.9 percent for boys, which increased from 2007 to 2009 to 12.3 percent; while for girls it was 3.6 percent from 1998 to 2000, and it increased to 5.5 percent from 2007 to 2009. Female children and adolescents are more likely than males to be diagnosed with the predominantly inattentive ADHD subtype; in addition, they are more likely than young females without ADHD to have anxiety, mood, and conduct disorders as well as lower IQ and achievement scores. In this regard, it has been found that young females with ADHD are five times more likely than young males to be diagnosed with depressive disorders and three times more likely to be treated for depression before receiving their ADHD diagnosis. The unbalanced sex ratio for ADHD diagnosing among children and adolescents seems to be at least partially remedied by the higher rate of self-referrals for an ADHD evaluation by adult women compared to men. During their lifetimes, 12.9 percent of males and 4.9 percent of females will be diagnosed with ADHD. Whatever gender differences may exist, it appears that fundamentally males and females with ADHD are far more similar than they are different. There clearly are no sex-specific ADHD profiles.

The research available seems to suggest that treatment approaches, including pharmacological treatment, for ADHD are equally effective for males and females. However, there is a tendency for referral bias, as more males are referred to treatment than females.

Racial/Ethnic Groups

There are clearly underlying cultural and ethnic differences behind ADHD as well as of the use of ADHD medications. White children, for instance, are much more likely than their Latino peers to be identified as having ADHD. However, the differences in ADHD diagnostic prevalence rates narrowed between most racial and ethnic groups from 1998 to 2009. There are also substantial differences within respective ethnic groups. For example, with respect to Latino countries, there are considerable differences in the rates of ADHD diagnosis, such that children in Mexico are about 5 times more likely than those in Puerto Rico to be diagnosed with ADHD and they are about 10 times more likely to be so designated than those in Cuba. The racial and ethnic variation with respect to the diagnosis prevalence rates within the United States is considerable. While 9.6 percent of white individuals are diagnosed with ADHD, the prevalence rate among African American individuals is 10.5 percent; it is 6.4 percent among Native American/Alaska Native individuals, 4.9 percent among Hispanic individuals, and 1.4 percent among Asian individuals. From 2001 to 2010, the prevalence rate of ADHD diagnosis among African American girls increased 90 percent. The highest prevalence rate of ADHD diagnosis is actually among individuals who identify as being of multiple races, which is at 11.6 percent. The overall prevalence rate among all individuals is 9.4 percent.

These ethnic differences also play out in the rates of the use of ADHD medications. It is estimated that about 76 percent of white children diagnosed with ADHD in the United States take ADHD medications, while about 56 percent of African American children diagnosed with ADHD and only about 53 percent of Latino children diagnosed with ADHD take these same ADHD medications.

Special Populations

There are many different special populations that have been examined with respect to the prevalence of ADHD diagnosing. There are some, albeit minor, gender differences. For instance, males with ADHD tend to be diagnosed more often with conditions such as oppositional defiant disorder (ODD) and conduct disorder (CD), while females are more likely to be diagnosed with separation anxiety disorder. Adult men with ADHD are more likely to be incarcerated than women with ADHD.

Individuals diagnosed with a disability other than ADHD are far more likely than their peers to also be diagnosed with ADHD. For instance, we know that approximately 20 percent to 30 percent of all school-age children with ADHD may also have a specific learning disability (SLD). It is also recognized that around 20 percent to 40 percent of all children with ADHD may eventually develop CD. From a third (33%) to one-half (50%) of all children with ADHD will also have a diagnosis of ODD. In a study related to these issues, it was reported that among younger U.S. elementary school–age students, 5 years to 11 years old, who had successfully committed suicide, nearly 60 percent (59.3%) had received a diagnosis for ADHD and they were also less likely than their adolescent counterparts, aged 12 years to 14 years, to experience symptoms or to be diagnosed with either depression or dysthymia, and among whom less than a third (29%) received an ADHD diagnosis. Further, we know that about 25 percent to 40 percent of individuals with ADHD may also have an anxiety disorder. Similarly, it is known 25 percent to 40 percent of individuals with ADHD may also have bipolar disorder. At any rate, depression is about three times more common in individuals with ADHD; in fact, up to 70 percent of individuals with ADHD are treated for depression at some point in their life.

The socioeconomic status of an individual's family of origin also can significantly influence an individual's chances of being diagnosed with ADHD. From 1998 to 2009, for instance, the ADHD diagnostic prevalence rates increased most among children and adolescents from families with household incomes below the poverty level. In addition, from 2008 to 2011, two-year-old to five-year-old children covered by Medicaid were twice as likely to receive clinical care for ADHD, generally consisting of prescriptions for ADHD medications, than were children of similar ages covered by employer-sponsored health insurance plans.

CRIMINAL JUSTICE INVOLVEMENT

The use and abuse of psychostimulant drugs, particularly methamphetamine, are related to crime in many different ways. Long-term abuse of methamphetamine at higher dosages than used for therapeutic purposes, such as for treating ADHD, can frequently lead to the development of amphetamine psychosis, which impairs judgment and the ability to control feelings of anger and frustration that often results in violent outbursts disproportionate to the context. In popular public discourse, in Australia at least, a routine linkage is asserted for the use of methamphetamine and the appearance of severe psychological psychosis. When, for instance, a drug deal for methamphetamine is perceived to have gone bad, violence and even murder often result. In a similar vein, when a clandestine methamphetamine laboratory is raided, firearms, explosives, and other weapons are typically found.

Qualitative studies have endeavored to examine factors associated with illicit methamphetamine initiation. For example, in-depth interviews conducted in South Africa identified several major themes relating to methamphetamine initiation. These themes, respectively, were prevalence of users and distributors made the drug convenient and highly accessible; increased popularity fostering social pressure to initiate use; lack of employment and recreation opportunities leading to boredom and curiosity over rumored effects; gang membership leads to methamphetamine use and distribution, particularly in impoverished communities; and, finally, initiation of methamphetamine use is described by some participants as a coping response to deal with cumulative stress and psychological burdens.

Methamphetamine users in various places have reported perceived benefits of use, which contribute to more regular, widespread illicit use. Young men in the Philippines, for instance, feel that methamphetamine use gives them more stamina, strength, confidence, disinhibition, improved mood, and need for less sleep; they even refer to it as a *pampagilas* or literally a "performance enhancer." Similarly, young people in northern Thailand regard use of methamphetamine, which they refer to as *ya ba* (literally "crazy drug"), as a fashionable signifier of participation in a modern consumer economy.

Illicit stimulants are widespread throughout much of the world and have become a serious global problem for criminal justice entities in many countries; for instance, in Southeast Asia this is a pervasive problem. In an area of northern Thailand, eastern Myanmar, and Western Laos, known as the Golden Triangle, which was initially associated with illicit opium and heroin trafficking, methamphetamine and related psychostimulant trafficking, in particular, is rampant. The precursor chemicals used for producing methamphetamine, like pseudoephedrine and ephedrine, are produced in chemical plants in neighboring China and then smuggled into Myanmar and neighboring countries. Ethnic militia groups in Myanmar produce methamphetamine from these precursor substances to finance their military operations. In fact, around 30,000 tons of methamphetamine are produced annually in illegal laboratories in Myanmar. The methamphetamine is then smuggled from Myanmar to northern cities in Thailand, such as notoriously to Chiang Mai, which serve as transit hubs for traffickers to collect and then further distribute. For instance, in 2014, Thai authorities seized over a million *ya ba* pills in Chiang Mai. *Ya ba* pills are a combination of methamphetamine and caffeine, which can be smoked or swallowed, and are, as mentioned previously, particularly popular in Thailand. *Ya ba* is heavily used not only by drug addicts but also by certain kinds of workers, such as taxi drivers, and its use is known to sometimes result in drug psychosis and extreme anxiety. The methamphetamine component produces a rapid high, and the caffeine component prolongs the effect. It is estimated that about one billion *ya ba* pills are consumed annually in Thailand alone.

There has been strong international cooperation directed to help control diversion of precursor substances. Since 1988, the International Narcotics Control Board, a UN-affiliated agency, has been supplying pre-export records from large-scale manufacturers of the precursor substances used to make amphetamines and methamphetamine-related drugs. More than 70 countries have adopted these measures, which allow better tracking of the distribution and use of these substances. In the United States, the Chemical Diversion and Trafficking Act of 1988, which was an amendment to the Controlled Substances Act, imposed tighter restrictions on the availability of precursor substances, essential chemicals for illicit production, and machines used to produce tablets and capsules. Electronic tracking and reporting of this process was implemented in 2006, which substantially enhanced real-time tracking and enforcement efforts. In an effort to disrupt illicit methamphetamine markets, Mississippi is one of the few states that have enacted regulations that require a prescription for purchase of pseudoephedrine-based medications. Although such an approach may help reduce the number of small domestic methamphetamine laboratories, as Mississippi reported a 77 percent reduction in such small laboratories over the two years after passing their prescription-only precursor control law, it seems that total methamphetamine availability remained relatively unimpacted.

Methamphetamine abuse has become a major illicit drug problem in the United States and around the world as well. About 12 million individuals in the United States have tried methamphetamine. Some individuals consume methamphetamine by means of a legal prescription, usually for treating ADHD, but many others do so through illicit means. Methamphetamine was supplied for decades by localized clandestine trafficking and manufacturing operations—initially mainly by Mexican organized criminal groups and by motorcycle gangs. More recently, transnational criminal organizations have stepped in to gain control over most of the methamphetamine supply in the United States, and, accordingly, methamphetamine remains widely available.

The National Survey on Drug Use and Health (NSDUH) estimates that each year around 353,000 individuals in the United States aged 12 years or older abuse methamphetamine. The Drug Enforcement Administration (DEA) estimates that the lifetime prevalence of illicit methamphetamine use is around 4 percent of the U.S. population. However, it is recognized that the lifetime prevalence rates of methamphetamine vary substantially in the United States by ethnicity. The American ethnic group that currently reports the highest levels of methamphetamine use is that of Native Hawaiians and Pacific Islanders at around 2.2 percent; the second-highest rate, 1.9 percent, is among those who report themselves to be multiracial; and the third-highest group is that of Native Americans at 1.7 percent. The prevalence rates are lower among other ethnic groups with whites at 0.7 percent, Asians at 0.2 percent, and African Americans at 0.1 percent.

There was a widespread moral panic about crystal methamphetamine in the United States from about 1996 to 2008, which shifted from about 2005 to 2008 to a secondary moral panic over the use of crystal methamphetamine in the gay community and its link to the spread of HIV/AIDS and, possibly, to the emergence of a super lethal strain. It has been reported that 1 out of every 10 gay men in San Francisco, California, for instance, have tried methamphetamine; gay men still have the highest rate of HIV infection. Likewise, there have been indications from other countries, such as Australia, where gay and bisexual men typically report high rates of methamphetamine use, both for crystal and powder forms of the drug.

The arrest rates for methamphetamine possession have risen and fallen over time. In 1996–1997, the methamphetamine arrest rate was reported to be 5 percent. This rate then peaked in 2000–2001, when it reached 11 percent, and, it has been declining substantially each year since. Nevertheless, about 9 percent of teenagers (around 1.9 million) in the United States report that they have misused or abused methylphenidate hydrochloride (Ritalin) or amphetamines (Adderall) in the past year.

There have been dramatic increases in the use of illegal methamphetamine. In 1998, there were 3,441 seizures of illicit methamphetamine laboratories in the United States; by 2004, there were 17,956 laboratory seizures. In 2005, the costs of methamphetamine abuse in the United States, including costs of clandestine laboratory site cleanups, drug arrests, incarceration and parole suspension, lost productivity, lowered quality of life, premature death, property damage, health care, hospitalization, and custodial care of children, were estimated to be about $23.4 billion per year. In 2011, over 10,000 clandestine methamphetamine laboratories were found in the United States. Each one of these laboratories creates environmental hazards that typically require extremely costly and time-consuming cleanup. For example, from 1998 to 2012, one program in Missouri processed about 16,000 methamphetamine laboratory incidents that produced 280 tons of hazardous wastes that had to be properly and expensively disposed of.

Much of the illegal methamphetamine consumed in the United States is produced and trafficked by Mexican drug cartels. In fact, somewhere around 80 percent of methamphetamine in the United States is currently supplied by Mexican cartels with transnational connections. In support of this fact, there was a 75 percent increase from 2002 to 2004 in seizures of methamphetamine at ports of entry between the United States and Mexico.

Likewise, between 2007 and 2009, seizures of methamphetamine along the Mexican-U.S. border increased by 87 percent. The Sinaloa Mexican cartel began trafficking methamphetamine to reduce its reliance on cocaine from Colombia. Mexican methamphetamine is currently up to 90 percent purity and is less than half the price of competitors.

Comprehensive Methamphetamine Control Act

On October 3, 1996, the then U.S. president William Jefferson Clinton signed into law the Comprehensive Methamphetamine Control Act (PL 104-237). This law was intended to address the rising abuse of methamphetamine in the United States, primarily by attempting to prevent the illegal manufacturing of methamphetamine while still allowing for its legal use for treating ADHD and other conditions. The act granted the DEA the authority to regulate precursor substances for methamphetamine and other amphetamines, such as pseudoephedrine, both inside and outside of the United States. Further regulation of these products to curtail methamphetamine production was established under the 2005 Combat Methamphetamine Epidemic Act, which imposed severe monthly purchase restrictions and behind-the-counter safe-keeping measures on pseudoephedrine and related products.

The 1996 Comprehensive Methamphetamine Control Act consists of five titles that provide measures to address the related problems. Under Title I of the Comprehensive Methamphetamine Control Act, the U.S. attorney general and the secretary of state are to coordinate international drug enforcement efforts to decrease the importation of methamphetamine and its precursor substances into the United States from other countries.

Title II of the Comprehensive Methamphetamine Control Act provides measures to control the manufacture of methamphetamine in the United States; for example, chemicals, such as iodine and hydrochloric gas, that are used in the production of methamphetamine, are to be closely monitored; the attorney general is charged to study their diversion; and, they were added as Schedule II chemicals of the Controlled Substances Act. Further, under Title II greater penalties were imposed on the manufacture and possession of equipment used to make controlled substances; a first conviction could result in fines of up to $30,000 and/or imprisonment for up to 10 years, while a subsequent violation can result in fines of up to $60,000 and/or imprisonment for up to 20 years; any business found guilty of distributing a listed chemical, product, material, or equipment used for producing a controlled substance could be fined up to $250,000 for the first violation and up to double the previous penalty for subsequent violations. In addition, Title II holds that anyone convicted for manufacturing methamphetamine can be subjected to pay restitution for cleanup of clandestine laboratory sites, which can be very costly.

Under Title III of the Comprehensive Methamphetamine Control Act, the penalties for the trafficking and manufacturing of methamphetamine and its precursors were substantially increased. Title III of the act specifically requires that the U.S. Sentencing Commission increase the offense level for offenses involving Schedule I chemicals by at least two levels and stipulate under the sentencing guidelines of both the Controlled Substances Act and the Controlled Substance Import and Export Act. This provision, accordingly, increased the maximum penalty for possessing a listed chemical with the intent to distribute or manufacture knowing that it would be used to make a controlled substance from 10 years to 20 years.

Title IV of the Comprehensive Methamphetamine Control Act added phenylpropanolamine and pseudoephedrine to ephedrine as precursor chemicals. A maximum threshold of 24 g was set for a single transaction of an over-the-counter sale of any of these chemicals or their derivatives. Further, any transaction involving any of these three substances and the Postal Service or other carrier must be provided to the attorney general on a monthly basis.

Title V of the Comprehensive Methamphetamine Control Act created the Methamphetamine Interagency Task Force, which is responsible for designing and evaluating the education, prevention, and treatment practices related to methamphetamine and other synthetic psychostimulants. A public health monitoring program was also established to monitor methamphetamine and related substance abuse concerns across the United States.

The Combat Methamphetamine Epidemic Act of 2005 was passed by the U.S. Congress in March 2006 as Title VII of the USA PATRIOT Improvement and Reauthorization Act of 2005 (PL 109-177). It amended the Controlled Substances Act to regulate and intensified restrictions on retail purchases of products that contain ephedrine, pseudoephedrine, and phenylpropanolamine as these can all be used in the illicit production of methamphetamine and amphetamines. The Combat Methamphetamine Epidemic Act prohibits individuals from purchasing more than 3.6 g/day, or more than 9 g over 30 days, of the precursors ephedrine or pseudoephedrine; this act also requires that any products containing these precursor substances can only be sold from behind the counter and that purchasers must present a state-issued form of identification and, further, must sign a logbook at the point of purchase. Importers of these precursor substances must also maintain a chain of custody record from the foreign manufacturers to the delivery to U.S. retail stores for sale. The Methamphetamine Production Prevention Act of 2008

(PL 110-415) was passed to require electronic logbook systems to control the retail sales of these precursor substances. The DEA acknowledges that these regulations stimulated a rash of small-capacity laboratories, referred to variously as "one pot" or "shake and bake" operations, that essentially provide little more than the personal quantity level of production for addicts utilizing small quantities of legally purchased pseudoephedrine tablets. The "one pot" method typically involves the pseudoephedrine tablets being crushed and converted in a single vessel, usually a plastic soda bottle. This relatively low level of illicit methamphetamine production makes it much more difficult for criminal justice agencies to monitor and control.

ADHD MEDICATIONS USED AS STUDY AIDES

It may not be that surprising that the use of stimulant ADHD medications, in particular, like a mixed amphetamine formulation (e.g., Adderall) or a methylphenidate hydrochloride (Ritalin), is somewhat higher among college students than it is among their same-age noncollege peers as these substances are often used by students to remain alert and awake so that they can complete course assignments and to help study for examinations. For instance, we know that full-time college students are about twice as likely as are non-full-time college students to abuse amphetamines (Adderall). Further, these substances are often abused because of the euphoric effects as well as their energizing potential. In addition, we know that college students who abused amphetamines (Adderall) are about three times as likely to abuse marijuana, about five times as likely to abuse prescription pain-killers (e.g., hydrocodone, hydromorphone, oxycodone, or oxymorphone), and about eight times as likely to abuse prescription tranquilizers (e.g., benzodiazepines).

Sharing and Misuse in High School and on College Campuses

The Monitoring the Future study is an ongoing, annual survey of U.S. secondary school students, college students, and young adults concerning their behaviors, attitudes, and values related primarily to alcohol, tobacco, and other drug use, including specific ADHD medications. Each year over 50,000 questionnaires are completed by a sample of students and young adults who comprise a representative target sample of Americans of the same age group.

In 2012, U.S. high school students, college students, and noncollege young adults all had comparable annual prevalence rates of illicit drug use, around approximately 18 percent. By 2014, however, college student illicit drug use exceeded that of 12th graders, which is attributable largely to college students' greater use of amphetamines without a physician's prescription. In recent years, amphetamine use without a prescription has increased substantially among college students, rising from a 5.8 percent annual prevalence in 2008 to 11.1 percent in 2012, but it has not increased substantially since, reported at 9.7 percent in 2015.

In 1999, the first year that the Monitoring the Future study asked questions about methamphetamine use separately from other stimulant drugs, 4.7 percent of American high school seniors reported use of methamphetamine in the previous 12 months. By 2009, the use within the previous year of methamphetamine by American high school seniors declined to 1.2 percent. By 2015, the use within the previous year of methamphetamine by American high school seniors declined to 0.6 percent.

Amphetamine use is somewhat higher among college students than among the same-age noncollege young adults. The annual prevalence rate of amphetamine use among college students in 2015 was 9.7 percent, while it was 8.1 percent for the noncollege sample. More specifically, the annual use of the mixed amphetamine formulation ADHD medicine Adderall without a prescription was higher for college students at 10.7 percent compared to the noncollege sample at 7.1 percent; this pattern has been consistent for at least the past five years. Likewise, the past-year nonmedical use of Adderall remained stable at 6.2 percent for U.S. 12th-grade students in 2016—the same rate as had been reported by the 2015 sample. However, the use of methylphenidate (Ritalin) was the same at 2 percent across both college student and the noncollege sample. Thus, use of Adderall without a prescription was reported by more than five times as many U.S. college students in 2015 as Ritalin. It seems highly likely that the increased use of these psychostimulant drugs is attributable to the interest in using them to improve academic performance.

The perceived harmfulness questions for Adderall were added to the young adult surveys for the first time in 2012. The results indicated that the perceived risk of using Adderall once or twice was around 30 percent among young adults in 2012. By 2014, the perceived risk of occasional Adderall use had risen to 35.9 percent among 27- to 30-year-olds, while the perceived harmfulness of taking Adderall occasionally hovered around 44 percent to 45 percent among 27- to 30-year-old young adults from 2012 to 2015. Similarly, in 2016, when U.S. 8th-grade students were asked if occasional nonmedical use of Adderall is harmful, that is, if there is a "great risk" associated with it, 35.8 percent said yes, which rose from the 32 percent reported in 2015.

SUCCESS FOR PEOPLE WITH ADHD

Many people with ADHD in the past and currently and, hopefully, many more in the future can be highly successful individuals. The possibility of individual success is much likely for those individuals with ADHD who are the recipients of accommodations and services in the various arenas of their life, particularly within the educational and workplace realms.

Educational Issues

Educators acknowledge that somewhere from 10 percent to 20 percent of any average school-age population of children will have difficulties with academic work. In fact, it is likely that in any typical elementary or secondary school classroom, there are at least two children or youth who are seriously affected by ADHD to the point that it is causing them problems. The reasons for these difficulties are manifold. Some of these children and adolescents will have difficulties in maintaining their attention, in sitting still, and in responding before they have thought their answers through. These are the children who have ADHD.

ADHD can certainly make school even more challenging than it is for those without the condition. Around a third (33%) of individuals with ADHD never finish high school, compared with a national average of about 8.7 percent.

Workplace Issues

Employers have consistently reported that employees with ADHD have lower levels of work performance, impaired task completion, lack of independent skills, and poorer relationships with coworkers and supervisors. These and related issues typically lead to higher rates of unemployment, frequent job changes, and, consequently, lower socioeconomic status of adults with ADHD. Nevertheless, adults with ADHD often have developed coping skills that allow them to survive in the workplace. For example, an individual with the hyperactive subtype of ADHD might appear to be an employee who is overworking or who has an atypical competitive drive compared to other coworkers. Adult workers with ADHD often have learned coping mechanisms that permit them to pass as well as having discovered other ways to adjust their work environments to suit their needs, such as being able to rely on other coworkers for assistance and selecting careers and work environments that accommodate their particular repertoire of symptoms.

A recent economic impact study estimated that up to 83 percent of the overall annual incremental costs of ADHD, which are thought to be somewhere between $143 billion to $266 billion, are incurred by adults, which would be between \$105 billion and \$194 billion per year. Workplace issues, primarily those of productivity and income losses, represent the largest share of the costs of adult ADHD to the American economy—accounting for somewhere between \$87 billion and \$138 billion each year. For example, workers with ADHD are more likely to have at least one sick day per month compared to fellow workers without ADHD. The World Health Organization estimates that untreated adults with ADHD lose an average of 22 days of job productivity each year. We know that adults with ADHD are 18 times more likely to be disciplined at work for perceived behavior problems and are 60 percent more likely to lose their jobs than their colleagues without ADHD. It has been found that adults with ADHD, on average, earn from \$5,000 to \$10,000 less each year compared to their peers who do not have ADHD. These costs contribute to the societal costs of ADHD, which are estimated to amount to somewhere from \$12,005 to \$17,454 annually per individual in this country alone.

Successful Individuals with ADHD

Many individuals with ADHD, whether they took ADHD medications or not, have been successful in a wide array of areas. This includes numerous individuals who have contributed in myriad ways to making the world a better place in a vast array of fields of endeavor, such as explorers, entertainers, artists, musicians, business leaders and entrepreneurs, political leaders, scientists and inventors, authors, and athletes. However, it is somewhat difficult to state with certainty that a particular individual in the distant historic past, long before the condition of ADHD was even recognized, actually had ADHD or not. Nevertheless, when we review surviving biographical or autobiographical details available about the life of a specific historical person, we can make a reasonable assessment as to whether he or she exhibited characteristics indicative of an individual with ADHD.

Some very notable explorers had qualities consistent with individuals who have ADHD, and they may have benefited from having the condition in order to have been able to develop and maintain their visionary pursuit of the unknown. Some of the better-known explorers who probably had ADHD include individuals such as Christopher Columbus (1451–1506), the Italian navigator and sailor whose voyages across the then unknown Atlantic Ocean begun in 1492 initiated the European colonization of the New World; Sir Walter Raleigh (ca. 1554–1618), the soldier and adventurer who helped establish the English colony near Roanoke Island in present-day North Carolina; and, Captain Meriwether Lewis (1774–1809) and Second Lieutenant

William Clark (1770–1838), who jointly shared command of the famed *Corps of Discovery* through its adventurous May 1804 to September 1806 perilous journey across the newly acquired U.S. western territories.

Entertainers from many areas, such as acting and comedy, are well-represented celebrities who probably had or have ADHD. Contemporary comedians who have stated publicly that they have ADHD, which may help with their sponta- neity and professional creativity, include Howie Mandel (1955–), James Eugene "Jim" Carrey (1962–), and Patrick McKenna (1960–). Some of the celebrity chefs and restaurateurs who have publicly declared that they have ADHD include James Trevor "Jamie" Oliver (1975–) and Alexis Hernandez (1976–), a contestant on *The Next Food Network Star*. Karina Smirnoff (1978–), a professional ballroom dancer and regular on the television series *Dancing with the Stars*, has also acknowledged being diagnosed as an adult with ADHD and says that she is able to channel her high energy levels into her work.

Famous artists are also included among the ranks of some well-known indi- viduals who probably had ADHD. This may be partly attributed to the fact that some individuals with ADHD appear to demonstrate higher levels of cre- ative thought and achievement than those of individuals without ADHD. Artists who appear to have had ADHD include Leonardo da Vinci (1452– 1519), the Italian Renaissance painter, sculptor, architect, engineer, and scien- tist; Vincent van Gogh (1853–1890), the Dutch postimpressionist painter; Pablo Picasso (1881–1973), the Spanish painter, sculptor, ceramicist, and graphic artist; and, Salvador Dalí (1904–1989), the surrealist Spanish painter.

Many noted musicians have probably had, have had, or have ADHD and appear to have the creativity that often accompanies it. This includes famous classical musicians, such as the Austrian composer Wolfgang Amadeus Mozart (1756–1791) and the German composer Ludwig van Beethoven (1770–1827). Other musicians who probably also had ADHD include Elvis Presley (1935–1977), the King of Rock and Roll; Stevie Wonder (1950–), the stage name of Stevland Hardaway Morris, the legendary Motown/Pop/ Soul/Rock and Roll singer, songwriter, multi-instrumentalist, and record pro- ducer; and Kurt Cobain (1967–1994), the Nirvana lead singer, guitarist, and songwriter. Among the contemporary musicians who have publicly admitted to having ADHD are Justin Randall Timberlake (1981–), a Grammy- winning singer, songwriter, actor, and record producer; Solange Piaget Knowles (1986–), a singer, songwriter, actress, and model; and, Phillip Manuel (1953–), a New Orleans Jazz vocalist. Justin Bieber (1994–), the popular Canadian singer and songwriter, admits to taking Adderall.

American business leaders and entrepreneurs who probably had ADHD include Andrew Carnegie (1835–1919), Frank Winfield Woolworth

(1852–1919), Henry Ford (1863–1947), Walter "Walt" Elias Disney (1901–1966), Howard Robard Hughes (1905–1976), Malcolm Forbes (1919–1990), and Ted Turner (1938–). A few contemporary entrepreneurs who have publicly stated that they have ADHD include Sir Richard Charles Nicholas Branson (1950–), the British tycoon and founder of the Virgin Group consisting of over 400 companies; David Neeleman (1959–), the Brazilian American who founded three commercial airlines, Jet Blue Airways, Morris Air, and Azul Brazilian Airways; and, Paul Orfalea (1947–), the founder of Kinko's copy chain stores. Some of this success may be partially attributed to the fact that some individuals with ADHD demonstrate higher levels of spontaneous idea generation than typical of most individuals with ADHD.

Several political leaders from the past have exhibited behaviors consistent with that of individuals with ADHD. Several American presidents probably had ADHD, including Abraham Lincoln (1809–1865), Theodore Roosevelt (1858–1919), Thomas Woodrow Wilson (1856–1924), Dwight David Eisenhower (1890–1969), and John Fitzgerald Kennedy (1917–1963). In addition to Eisenhower, other famous military generals who likely had ADHD include Napoleon Bonaparte (1769–1821), George Smith Patton (1885–1945), and Herbert Norman Schwarzkopf (1934–2012). Other political figures who have publicly stated that they have ADHD include Kendrick Meek, the U.S. representative from Florida's Seventeenth Congressional District from 2003 to 2011; James Carville (1944–), the American political commentator and media personality; and, Glen Lee Beck (1964–), the conservative American television and radio host and commentator.

Many scientists and inventors, who tend to be highly inquisitive and can approach a subject from a novel perspective, probably have also had ADHD. This could certainly include the famous theoretical physicist Albert Einstein (1879–1955), his illustrious predecessor the English physicist and mathematician Sir Isaac Newton (1642–1727), and his predecessor the Italian astronomer, mathematician, and physicist Galileo Galilei (1564–1642). Among the well-known American inventors who probably had ADHD are Benjamin Franklin (1706–1790), brothers Orville (1871–1948) and Wilbur Wright (1867–1912), Alexander Graham Bell (1847–1922), and Thomas Alva Edison (1847–1931). The English mathematician and writer Charles Lutwidge Dodgson (1832–1898), who is better known by his pen name of Lewis Carroll, also exhibited signs highly indicative of ADHD.

Authors, including poets and playwrights, are well represented among successful individuals who probably had ADHD. Famous poets who probably had ADHD include the English poet Samuel Taylor Coleridge (1772–1834), the

English Romantic poet Lord George Gordon Noel Byron (1788–1824), and the American poets Emily Dickinson (1830–1886), Robert Frost (1874–1963), and Anne Harvey Sexton (1928–1974). Playwrights who likely had ADHD include the Irish playwright and writer Oscar Fingal O'Flahertie Wills Wilde (1854–1900), the Irish playwright George Bernard Shaw (1856–1950), and the American playwright Thomas Lanier "Tennessee" Williams (1914–1983). Other well-known writers who probably also had ADHD include the Danish writer of fairy tales Hans Christian Anderson (1805–1875), the American transcendentalists Ralph Waldo Emerson (1803–1882) and Henry David Thoreau (1817–1862), the English novelist and poet Charlotte Brontë (1816–1855), the French novelist Jules Verne (1828–1905), and the American writer Samuel Langhorne Clemens (1835–1910), who is better known by his pen name of Mark Twain. Among contemporary writers who have publicly announced that they have ADHD are Jenny Lawson, a well-known Internet blogger and author of *Let's Pretend This Never Happened*, and Katherine Ellison, a Pulitzer Prize–winning foreign correspondent and author of several books, including *Buzz, A Year of Paying Attention*.

Numerous athletes from many different sports and related activities are known to have ADHD. Some of this may be explained by the fact that some individuals with ADHD appear to be able to hyper-focus more than is typical of most individuals without ADHD. Michael Fred Phelps II (1985–), for instance, the most successful Olympic athlete ever with 28 medals, has publicly stated that he has ADHD and takes ADHD medications. Similarly, Simone Arianne Biles (1997–), the American gymnast who won four gold medals at the Rio Olympics, has acknowledged that she also takes ADHD medicine, as has Cammi Granato (1971–), who was captain of the gold medal–winning U.S. Women's Ice Hockey team at the 1998 Winter Olympics at Nagano, Japan; Adam Kreek (1980–), Canadian Olympic gold medalist rower at the 2008 Beijing Olympics; and, Louis Smith (1989–), the British gymnast and silver medalist at the 2012 London Olympics. Many other athletes have also publicly acknowledged that they have ADHD. This includes Gregory James LeMond (1961–), the professional road cyclist and three-time winner of the Tour de France (1986, 1989, and 1990) and Terry Bradshaw (1948–), who played quarterback for the Pittsburgh Steelers of the National Football League. Professional golfers with ADHD include Bubba Watson (1978–) and Payne Stewart (1957–1999). Current professional football athletes who have publicly stated that they take ADHD medications include individuals such as Josh Freeman (1988–), quarterback for the Tampa Bay Buccaneers; Virgil Green (1988–), Denver Broncos tight end; and, Andre Brown (1986–), New York Giants running back.

Chapter 9

The Future of ADHD Medications

These are exciting times for the future of attention deficit hyperactivity disorder (ADHD) medications and other associated treatments. In order to come up with new and better ADHD medications, and other nonpharmacological treatment approaches as well that can be used along with or without ADHD medications, it is critically important that we learn more about and more fully understand what ADHD actually is. Toward this ultimate end, there are many scientific technological resources that can be utilized to help us learn more about the brain and the nature of its functioning with respect to individuals with ADHD. A diverse field of research endeavors is opening up new areas that can potentially be considered as possible additions to the arsenal available in addressing ADHD. These developments will help us not only to better understand ADHD but also to better treat individuals with ADHD.

Ongoing research provides exciting glimpses as to what the future may hold in the varied areas of ADHD medications. Investigators are currently studying several approaches to simplify and improve the traditional dosage regimens. Potent, well-tolerated multiple drug combinations have the potential, for instance, for coformulation as single tablet regimens. There are investigational ADHD drugs in development, some of which fit within the existing drug classes of ADHD medications discussed in this work and some that do not. Other researchers are studying novel drug administration systems, such as that of weekly subcutaneous injections. Given the tremendous amount of progress that has been made over the past few decades, ongoing and future research will undoubtedly yield new and hopefully more effective options for the management of ADHD.

The discussions in this text, at least in part, have been predicated upon the assumption that having a fuller understanding of the past, particularly with respect to the history and evolution of our understanding of ADHD, will help us to generate new solutions and also to develop additional resources to better comprehend the issues surrounding this area of concern. In a like manner, having a better understanding of the various issues impinging upon the current situations related to ADHD and the assorted medications used to treat it should, hopefully, help prepare us to create better ways to more effectively address associated issues in the future. A significant area of concern in this matter is that of the various disability laws that address the rights of individuals with ADHD and related disabilities. This greater historical awareness should provide us with a more informed basis upon which to craft forthcoming choices and decisions regarding how we might best proceed to cover related areas such as policy, particularly those including measures that provide accommodations for individuals with ADHD.

LEARNING MORE ABOUT ADHD

A critical first step necessary in adequately helping someone with ADHD is in having a full understanding of the background and nature of the condition, including its causes, signs, and symptoms, as well as of the factors most associated with treatment success. An array of promising scientific technologies is being drawn upon in this collective research agenda. The findings of these research studies will help direct future successful developments within the fields used in treating individuals with ADHD. An awareness of the various assessment tools that are available to help diagnose whether an individual has ADHD or not, as well as for a more refined assessment of how the respective characteristics of the varied subtypes of ADHD are present or not in a particular individual, could of course be very useful in deciding what, if any, treatment approaches might be productively applied to treating a particular individual with ADHD.

Scientific Technologies and Other Advances

There are numerous fields of scientific endeavor and other related areas that can offer valuable insights that may further help us to better improve how we attempt to assess and more effectively address ADHD. There are, in fact, entirely new and emerging areas of research that may yield significant opportunities to help us better understand ADHD and ADHD medications.

Pharmacogenetics, which is the identification of the genetic variations that can help predict, either positively or negatively, the response that a particular individual will have to a particular ADHD medicine, is a new but rapidly emerging field. It has been suggested, in this vein, that ADHD has a 0.8 degree of inheritability and that up to 80 percent of the phenotypic variation observed among individuals with ADHD can be attributed solely to genetics. As noted in an earlier chapter, the concordance of ADHD in monozygotic twins is significantly greater than it is in dizygotic twins, which strongly suggests that there are substantial contributions from genetics to the development of ADHD in respective individuals. It appears that several different genes are likely to be involved in this expression, several of which have already been identified, and it is generally agreed that ADHD is one of the most heritable psychiatric disorders. Thus, it is to be expected that pharmacological responses to ADHD medications should also be largely influenced by genetic variation among individuals. Several genes have been reported to be associated with responses to ADHD medications; these include the adrenergic alpha 2A receptor gene (ADRA2), catechol-O-methyltransferase (COMT), dopamine receptor D4 (DRD4), SNAP-25, and the serotonin transporter genes. Similarly, individuals who carry a variant of the CHRNA4 gene, which is associated with the nicotinic acetylcholine receptor system, and who are exposed to certain forms of environmental risks, such as psychosocial adversity, or prenatal alcohol or tobacco consumption, may respond differently to respective ADHD medications. On the other hand, a couple of studies failed, for example, to find an association between methylphenidate hydrochloride (Ritalin) treatment in adults with ADHD and the DAT1 or the ADRA2 genes. Nevertheless, administration of the popular ADHD medicine methylphenidate hydrochloride (Ritalin) appears to be positively associated with the functioning of the hypothalamic-pituitary-adrenal axis in individuals with ADHD, at least as measured by salivary cortisol levels, which have been significantly positively correlated with several measures of neuropsychological performance.

Related research has suggested that precision ADHD medications may be developed in the future that could help to reduce the impact of genetic risk factors for ADHD. Genetic risk factors for brain development that may lead to ADHD might converge in particular regulatory pathways. This appears to relate mainly to promoter and enhancer activity of genetic factors in the development of the human brain. If we can determine how this works more precisely, then we might someday be able to better identify the specific biological processes that are affected and then possibly be able to target them with precisely designed medications.

An array of neuroimaging modalities is now available to help examine brain structure and function in individuals with ADHD. Structural brain-imaging techniques, such as magnetic resonance imaging (MRI) studies, can help better evaluate variables such as brain size, composition, organization, and volume, while functional brain-imaging approaches can help to explain activity of the brain as one is engaged in certain tasks. An MRI utilizes magnetic fields and radio waves to create either two-dimensional or three-dimensional images of the brain and other body parts; it has the advantage of not using radiation or radioactive tracer materials. For instance, numerous studies have reported that individuals with reduced volume in several regions of the brain, such as the amygdala, the basal ganglia, the caudate nucleus, the cerebellum, the frontal lobes, the hippocampus, the nucleus accumbens, and the putamen, are more likely to have ADHD. However, it must also be acknowledged that there is generally a large range of individual variability in the volumes of respective brain regions, and we certainly are not at a point where an MRI can be used for conclusive diagnostic purposes for ADHD. Studies have further suggested that there are subtle structural differences in select regions of the brains of individuals with ADHD, such as a smaller right anterior prefrontal cortex and less white matter in the right frontal lobes, which could possibly cause problems with focused or sustained attention. There also appear to be asymmetries in the caudate nucleus, which could possibly cause problems with self-control as it integrates information from different parts of the brain and supports cognitive functioning, including memory. A related observation is that children with ADHD are more likely to be maturationally delayed with respect to both brain volume and cortical thickness and structure. Diffusion tensor imaging (DTI) is a relatively new approach that can be used to assess brain structure in individuals with ADHD, particularly for examining white matter integrity across brain regions, which is known to be associated with measures of both attention and impulsivity.

Computed axial tomography (CAT), also referred to as computed tomography (CT), scanning is a structural imaging approach that utilizes a series of x-rays to create images of the brain; it is most useful for evaluating brain injuries. As ADHD is not the result of a structural problem in the brain, but primarily a functional, neurochemical issue, CAT/CT scans and other structural techniques have limited applicability in treating ADHD, except perhaps in ruling out other possible conditions for diagnostic purposes.

Functional neuroimaging techniques, on the other hand, measure the physiological functioning of the human brain. Functional neuroimaging provides information about the activity levels in specific areas of individual's brains, usually comparing activity before and during task performance. A functional MRI, for instance, shows the degree of oxygen uptake associated with areas of high neuronal activity. Functional MRI studies, in this regard, have indicated that there often is disrupted brain function in areas known to be related to neuropsychological processes associated with ADHD. More specifically, reduced frontostriatal activation and increased activation in the medial frontal and parietal regions are related to motor inhibition, which is common in many individuals with ADHD, although the latter may be caused by the use of stimulant medications. Under activation of the anterior cingulate and of the inferior prefrontal cortex is associated with interference inhibition, another feature characteristic of some individuals with ADHD. Similarly, under activation of the left inferior and of the dorsolateral prefrontal cortex is associated with attention vigilance, another common ADHD characteristic. Likewise, under activation of the inferior ventrolateral, the prefrontal, the parietal, the temporo-occipital, and of the cerebellar regions of the brain appears to be associated with deficits of working memory, another feature implicated in many individuals with ADHD.

Diffuse optical tomography (DOT), also referred to as diffuse optical imaging (DOI), is another imaging approach that utilizes near-infrared light waves to create images of the brain or of other parts of the body. This particular functional imaging technique is based on the optical absorption of hemoglobin, which tends to vary in direct relation to the oxygenation status of different regions of the brain reflecting areas where greater activity occurs based on greater levels of blood flow. DOT is comparable in application to functional MRI studies.

Positron emission tomography (PET) imaging techniques are used to examine metabolic processes in the brain. PET-CT (positron emission tomography-computed tomography) combine the PET scan with an x-ray CT scan to generate sequential, three-dimensional images of the biochemical activity in the brain to create a single superimposed image. PET scans utilize radioactive, metabolically active isotopes injected into the blood and accumulate differentially in various regions of the brain to measure levels of neurotransmitter activity. PET imaging studies have characterized individuals with ADHD as having deficits in the release of dopamine in the limbic and caudate regions of the brain, which clearly can be remediated by the use of ADHD stimulant medications particularly, such as dextroamphetamine (Dexedrine), lisdextroamphetamine (Vyvanse), methamphetamine hydrochloride (Desoxyn), and methylphenidate hydrochloride (Ritalin). PET imaging that indicates deficits in the norepinephrine transporter system has been used to suggest that atomoxetine hydrochloride (Strattera), a selective norepinephrine reuptake inhibitor, could be particularly useful in treating those sorts of individuals with ADHD.

Single photon emission computed tomography (SPECT) is a neuroimaging technique that utilizes gamma ray emitting radioisotopes to create two-dimensional and three-dimensional images of active regions within the brain. SPECT scans use radioactive isotopes that have half-lives that make them more widely available and are easier to handle and thus are generally considered safer to use than those employed in PET scanning.

There are many other techniques that are have been used to study the brains and brain activity of individuals with ADHD. For example, electroencephalography (EEG), which measures patterns of brain wave activity, is a commonly used technology; however, magnetoencephalography (MAG), which creates detailed images of neuronal activity, may be a more useful approach for examining issues more relevant for assisting an individual with ADHD. An even more relevant approach is the quantitative EEG that measures the ratio of the slow theta brain waves to the fast beta waves, with a pattern of under arousal in areas of the cortex, which is referred to as cortical hypoarousal, frequently used to help diagnosis ADHD, and that further helps to predict which individuals will likely respond well to stimulant ADHD medications.

Innovations in fields such as quantum computing and synthetic biology may soon permit us to eventually engineer optimal pharmacological products that can best be used to treat a condition such as ADHD with the least undesired side effects. These sorts of endeavors along with more sophisticated genetic screening may bring us closer to realizing the potential of actually individualizing treatment approaches, particularly those pharmacologically based ones such as with the use of respective ADHD medications.

There are also many opportunities to explore for better ways to reduce and prevent the abuse of ADHD medications and others through various social media platforms, such as Facebook and Twitter. Social media–based approaches have the potential to enhance substance abuse screening, prevention, and treatment efforts with minimal expense. These social media–based efforts also afford potential opportunities to be better able to understand areas such as ADHD medicine use patterns and prevailing attitudes toward various substances in respective subpopulations.

Use of digital interactive and other forms of electronic social media is dramatically increasing and has been associated with both health benefits and risks. The American Academy of Pediatrics issued new guidelines in 2016 concerning the potential risks and benefits of exposure to electronic media in young children. The varied benefits, supported by research findings, include early learning opportunities, increased social contact and support, the introduction of new ideas and knowledge, and the ready availability of appropriate health-related prevention, education, and promotion. The numerous risks associated with exposure to electronic media include negative impacts on attention and learning; decreased sleep and physical activity patterns; increased prevalence of many health problems like obesity and depression; threats to confidentiality and personal privacy; as well as possible exposure to inappropriate, inaccurate, or unsafe content and contacts. Nevertheless, young children, starting at around the age of 18 months, can begin to learn from digital media with high quality programming.

There are, of course, numerous other fields of scientific endeavor that may yet yield better understandings, technologies, and other assorted benefits that may prove of use in addressing ADHD. It is difficult to completely identify beforehand where these innovations will come from. If history teaches us anything in this field, it is that significant new developments can come from the apparently least likely of places. We must simply remain optimistic and open to the possibilities for better applications and more informed insights. In fact, with no doubt, we can be rest assured that our current understandings of ADHD will change in the future and at the very least will continue to be revised.

Research Findings

Research into the myriad possible causes of ADHD, the nature of ADHD, and areas of effective management and treatment is an area of diverse ongoing scientific endeavors that is shedding new light upon several areas that may offer opportunities to prevent as well as to better treat ADHD. There are several factors that appear to increase the risk for an individual having ADHD. For instance, it seems that a postterm birth, that is, after 42 weeks of gestation as compared to the normal 40 weeks, substantially increases the chances of developing a behavioral problem later in life, including ADHD. Similarly, poor prenatal nutrition, such as a maternal diet consisting mostly of highly processed foods that are typically high in both fats and sugars, is also associated with greater risk for the development of ADHD. Secondhand smoke exposure is another factor that is associated with a higher prevalence of ADHD. Repeated, but not single, anesthesia exposure at young ages also appears to escalate the risk for developing ADHD. Children who experience family and other environmental stressors, as well as traumatic experiences, including mental illness, poverty, and exposure to violence, are more likely to be diagnosed with ADHD. For instance, a significant genetic influence has been found on the association between childhood trauma and the severity of inhibitory deficits in children with ADHD. It is suspected that the male biasness of ADHD may be partially explained by sexually dimorphic effects in genes predisposing one to develop ADHD. At any rate, it is well established that many children with Fetal Alcohol Spectrum Disorders (FASD) also have comorbid ADHD. These are just a few examples of the many varied risk areas that recent research efforts have implicated as increasing the likelihood of an individual having ADHD.

Policy researchers have examined how various treatments for ADHD are authorized and reimbursed by respective healthcare plans. One such policy area that substantially impacts the use of ADHD medications is that authorizing and reimbursing respective treatments. Those healthcare plans or state programs, like Medicaid, that require prior authorization before particular ADHD medications can be prescribed are particularly such types of policies. Prior authorization policies for ADHD medications mean that healthcare plans or state programs must review a physician's prescription request before coverage for an ADHD medicine is given. In the past couple of decades, the number of children and adults who are prescribed ADHD medications has dramatically increased. Therefore, many state Medicaid programs have implemented prior authorization policies for pediatric and adult use of ADHD medications. These particular policies, of course, vary somewhat from state to state, and there is presently no comprehensive federal mandate. At any rate, there are now 27 states that currently manage access to ADHD medications for children.

The costs of treating ADHD directly and the personal and societal costs associated with it can be substantial. Researchers estimate that the combined annual cost of treating ADHD in the United States is about $31.6 billion. This estimate includes the healthcare costs for individuals with ADHD related specifically to their diagnosis, for the healthcare costs for the family members of individuals with ADHD related specifically to the diagnosis of their family members, and for the work absences among adults with ADHD and for those of family members of individuals with ADHD. It is unclear, at this point, how changes, if any, to the Affordable Care Act (ACA) will impact the assessment and treatment of ADHD as well as of substance use and other related issues. Similarly, it is still too early to evaluate the effects of the Medicare Access and CHIP Reauthorization Act, which functions in a complementary way to the ACA and was intended to help move the country from volume-based to value-based Medicare reimbursement, upon ADHD and related substance use issues. At any rate, better prevention and treatment of individuals with ADHD could produce sizeable financial savings to society and substantially reduce the suffering of individuals and their families from untreated ADHD and associated problems, including those of substance use.

Several research studies have examined the prevalence, potential causes, and consequences of ADHD medicine nonadherence. As ADHD medications are known to alleviate many aspects of the condition and as it is well recognized that medication nonadherence increases the likelihood of subsequent treatment failure, a better understanding of this phenomenon is very important. Research studies of pharmacy claims and treatment statistics indicate that the prevalence of ADHD medicine discontinuation or nonadherence ranges from 13.2 percent to 64 percent. It is understood, for instance, that the use of immediate-release psychostimulant ADHD medications, such as dextroamphetamine (Dexedrine), is associated with higher rates of nonadherence, more than that of extended-release formulations of the same medicine. However, long-term consequences of ADHD medicine nonadherence are not as well understood, and, in addition, most studies in this area have examined nonadherence in children with ADHD, but few have examined nonadherence among adults with ADHD. There clearly is a need for many future research studies considering a broad array of issues related to ADHD medications.

Many research studies have produced voluminous findings that help us better understand and address ADHD and its treatment, including the use of respective ADHD medications. For example, the Project to Learn About ADHD in Youth (PLAY) is a 10-year-long population-based research project that is funded by the Centers for Disease Control and Prevention (CDC) and conducted by the University of South Carolina and the University of Oklahoma Health Sciences Center to better understand the public health impacts of ADHD. For instance, from the findings of PLAY, and from related research studies, we now know that children with ADHD are more than twice as likely as children without ADHD to have another psychiatric disorder in addition to ADHD. In fact, more than half (60%) of children with ADHD have another psychiatric disorder, and about a quarter (25%) have two or more other psychiatric disorders. Further, children with ADHD and either conduct disorder or oppositional defiant disorder (ODD) are more likely to have difficulties with school and friendships and to get into trouble with the police. PLAY has also collected and analyzed data on trends in ADHD medications and related treatments.

Assessment Tools and Strategies

There are many different types of assessment tools and strategies available for help in evaluating who may or may not have ADHD. Several behavioral scales, particularly those to be completed by parents and teachers familiar with the individual, are available, such as the Conners' Rating Scales, the Behavior Assessment System for Children (BASC), and the SNAP-IV. Conners' Parent Rating Scales, for instance, are typically completed by the child's parents and ask about the child's ADHD-related symptoms. The Conners' Teacher Rating Scales are completed by teachers to evaluate the child's ADHD symptoms in the classroom setting. The BASC is for use for children and adolescents between the ages of 4 years and 18 years. The SNAP-IV Teacher and Parent Rating Scale is a 90-item instrument completed with a Likert-type scale ranging from "Not at All" to "Very Much"; it gauges emotional behaviors and physical symptoms at home and in the classroom.

The Development and Well-Being Assessment (DAWBA) is a standardized instrument for assessing common mental health problems, including ADHD, in children aged 5 years to 17 years. It consists of a package of interviews, questionnaires, and rating techniques, which can all be rapidly scored. The DAWBA interviews can be administered by computers or by human beings and can include interviews with the parents, with the child, and with the teachers of the child. The parent interview can be administered in about 50 minutes, and the child interview can be administered in about 30 minutes; it has been most widely used in Great Britain.

The Concomitant Difficulties Scale (ADHD-CDS) is a brief tool intended to assess the presence of some of the more important comorbid conditions that often appear in association with ADHD, such as impaired academic achievement, disruptive behavior, emotional management, fine motor coordination, motivational management, time management, sleep habits, and quality of life. The 13-item ADHD-CDS is intended to be completed by parents or by guardians, and it has demonstrated good sensitivity for various ADHD profiles and high convergent validity.

There are also several self-report scales that the individual suspected of having ADHD usually completes for himself or herself. These sorts of instruments include the Adult ADHD Self-Report Scale (ASRS) Symptom Checklist, which will be discussed later in this chapter, the Conners Abbreviated Symptom Questionnaire (ASQ), and the Weiss Functional Impairment Rating Scale Self-Report (WFIRS-S). The ASQ is a brief instrument, which has good sensitivity and specificity, and it has high diagnostic accuracy. The WFIRS-S is a 57-item assessment instrument that evaluates how an individual is actually able to function; it has high internal consistency and excellent sensitivity to symptom change and improvement.

Other assessment instruments are designed to be completed by clinical interviewers, such as Barkley's Quick-Check for Adult ADHD Diagnosis and the Brief Semi-Structured Interview for ADHD in Adults. Barkley's Quick-Check for Adult ADHD Diagnosis is an 18-item instrument that was designed by R. A. Barkley and H. R. Murphy and that can be administered for either current or retrospective reporting; it uses a Likert scale from 0 to 3, respectively "Rarely or Never" to "Very Often"; a symptom is considered to be present if the response of "Often" or "Very Often" is given. This instrument produces six scores; the first three scores are the summations of the item scores, respectively, for inattention, hyperactive-impulsive, and a total ADHD score for the retrospective responses; and then another three scores are for the current responses. The Brief Semi-Structured Interview for ADHD in Adults is a 33-item instrument developed by the National Association for Continuing Education (NACE).

A commonly employed practice is to initially administer a general screening instrument and then for those individuals whose scores suggest they may have symptoms of ADHD, to follow up with a more sophisticated instrument, and if still warranted, then a more in-depth evaluation. For instance, the ASRS, which was developed by the World Health Organization, is a highly validated, six-item screening tool for adult ADHD, which typically can be completed in about one minute, making it acceptable to use in most general practitioner settings; it demonstrates high sensitivity and moderate specificity. Individuals who screen positively on the ASRS would commonly then be administered a more specific instrument, such as the more in-depth assessment provided by the Conners' Adult ADHD Rating Scale Self Report: Short Version (CAARS-S:S), a 26-item instrument. Individuals scoring positively on the CAARS-S:S would then generally receive a more thorough personalized medical examination, including a detailed personal history looking for signs and symptoms of ADHD, as well as an evaluation for any coexisting conditions.

A comprehensive assessment of ADHD should usually include multiple strategies, including self-report rating scales; rating scales from other sources, most typically parents and teachers; a structured clinical interview, with a thorough patient history; a complete medical examination, particularly to exclude conditions that can manifest with a lack of attention, such as a central nervous system infection, cerebral-vascular disease, hypothyroidism, and Reye's syndrome; structured tasks of attention; and, structured tasks of impulsivity. Numerous tests are currently available as structured tasks of attention and/or impulsivity; such instruments include the Continuous Performance Tests (CPTs), the Matching Familiar Figures Test (MFFT), the Stroop Word-Color Association Test, and the Wisconsin Card Sort. Many healthcare professionals, such as psychiatrists, psychologists, therapists, and some general practitioner physicians, are trained to appropriately diagnose ADHD. At any rate, the sorts of ADHD rating tools that were discussed here are helpful both for the purposes of assessment and for ongoing treatment monitoring.

DISABILITY LAWS

Neuropsychiatric disorders, including ADHD, are the most common reason for disability in the United States, and since 2010, mental disorders and substance use disorders are the leading causes of disability around the world. In the future how we respond to and how we better serve individuals with ADHD and other special needs will be largely shaped by the various bodies of disability law. The rights of individuals with ADHD to have access to their medications are also protected under some of these laws. Accordingly, a brief review of the chief relevant laws that address disability issues is called for here.

The rights of individuals with disabilities, including ADHD, are protected under several laws. The two main federal pieces of legislation that cover the rights of individuals with disabilities are the Americans with Disabilities Act (ADA) and Section 504 of the Rehabilitation Act of 1973. There are many other federal laws that protect the rights of individuals with a disability, such as the Architectural Barriers Act, the Fair Housing Act, and the Individuals with Disabilities Education Act (IDEA). In addition, there are many varied state, county, and local ordinances that also extend further legal protections to individuals with a disability and their families.

Americans with Disabilities Act

The ADA of 1990 expanded the types of institutional and service provider responsibilities beyond earlier legislation for providing reasonable accommodations to individuals with a disability. The ADA (PL 101–336) is essentially a civil rights statute and as such serves as a comprehensive antidiscrimination law for persons with disabilities across the life span. The ADA prohibits discrimination on the basis of disability in employment, state and local government, public accommodations, commercial facilities, transportation, and telecommunications; it thus extends to virtually all sectors of society and every aspect of daily living. To be protected by the ADA, one must have a disability or have a relationship or association with an individual with a disability. An individual with a disability is defined by the ADA as a person who has a physical or mental impairment that substantially limits one or more major life activities; a person who has a history or record of such impairment; or a person who is perceived by others as having such an impairment. The ADA does not specifically name all of the impairments that are covered. Although the original text of the ADA does not specifically mention ADHD, it is covered as a "mental or psychological disorder." Further, the severity of an individual's ADHD is assessed as an impairment based on its limiting impairment without the potential alleviation following the use of ADHD medications.

The right to equal access to postsecondary education is covered under the ADA. However, it does not require colleges and universities to accept or accommodate everyone who has disabilities. Students with disabilities such as ADHD must satisfy the standards required by the college or university for all students. Students with disabilities must also be able to perform the "essential academic and technical standards of the program" with or without reasonable accommodations.

Section 504 of the Rehabilitation Act

Section 504 of the 1973 Rehabilitation Act is a federal civil rights law (PL 93-112). Section 504 states that "no qualified individual with a disability in the United States shall be excluded from, denied the benefits of, or be subjected to discrimination under" any program or activity that receives federal financial assistance. Requirements include reasonable accommodation for employees with disabilities, program accessibility, effective communication with people who have hearing or visual disabilities, and accessible new construction and alterations. Thus, students with disabilities may, when necessary, get accommodations on their behalf within the academic setting under Section 504.

Section 504 requires that no person with a disability may be excluded from a program because of the lack of an appropriate aid; however, it does not require that colleges must have all potential aids available at all times. Although architectural accessibility for individuals with disabilities is an important feature of Section 504, a completely barrier-free environment is not mandated. Therefore, nondiscriminatory placement in the "most integrated setting appropriate" is called for, and for most individuals with ADHD, this would generally be in regular classrooms and work environments; although a reasonable accommodation for testing situations for some individuals with ADHD would be in a separate, quite room.

On July 26, 2016, the U.S. Department of Education's Office for Civil Rights (OCR) issued further guidance to help clarify the obligation of schools to provide students with ADHD with equal educational opportunity under Section 504 of the Rehabilitation Act of 1973. It reminds schools that they must provide parents with due process that includes allowing them to appeal any decisions concerning the identification, evaluation, or educational placement of a student with ADHD.

Fair Housing Act

The Fair Housing Act prohibits housing discrimination on the basis of disability as well as race, color, religion, sex, familial status, and national origin. Its coverage includes private housing, housing that receives federal financial assistance, and state and local government housing. It is unlawful to discriminate in any aspect of selling or renting housing or to deny a dwelling to a renter or buyer because of the disability of that individual, an individual associated with the renter or buyer, or an individual who intends to live in the residence.

Individuals with Disabilities Education Act

The IDEA requires public schools to make themselves available to all eligible children with disabilities for a free appropriate public education in the least restrictive environment appropriate to their individual needs. The IDEA was formerly known as Public Law 94-142 and is also known as the Education for All Handicapped Children Act. The IDEA guarantees that each student with a handicap must get a culturally unbiased and valid assessment of his or her special needs; it is by means of this provision that most individuals receive their diagnosis of ADHD. IDEA requires public school systems to develop appropriate Individualized Education Programs (IEPs) for each child with special needs. However, the IDEA does not directly apply to students who are enrolled in institutions of higher education, nor do IEPs. The specific special education and related services outlined in each IEP reflect the individualized needs of each student in public schools and may not be appropriate for those in college.

SUBSTANCE USE AND ABUSE LAWS

In addition to the various disability laws just reviewed, there are numerous other laws relating to aspects of substance use and abuse that will affect how we can deal appropriately with the myriad and complex issues related to the use and abuse of ADHD medications. Two of the most significant pieces of legislation related to this area of concern, the Pure Food and Drug Act and the Controlled Substances Act, were summarized earlier in Chapter 7; and, another more recent law, the Comprehensive Methamphetamine Control Act, was discussed in Chapter 8. There have been and will continue to be other laws passed in the future that will in various ways impact how we address issues around ADHD medications and various forms of substance use and abuse.

The 21st Century Cures Act, which was signed into law on December 13, 2016, by President Barack Obama, is a recent example of such a measure. The Cures Act is intended to improve prescription drug monitoring programs, implementation of prevention activities, training for healthcare providers, and expanding access to treatment. It also amends the Federal Food, Drug, and

Cosmetic Act to establish processes by which the Food and Drug Administration (FDA) can utilize patient experience data to consider in the risk benefit assessment of new drugs, including new ADHD medications. It also established the Council for 21st Century Cures, a nonprofit corporation that is intended to accelerate the discovery, development, and delivery of innovative cures, treatments, and preventative measures.

FUTURE CHANGES IN HOW MEDICATIONS ARE USED TO TREAT ADHD

The future, of course, has yet to be written with respect to changes in how varied medications may be used to better treat individuals with ADHD. Nevertheless, there are many promising bright rays of light that are just beginning to shine through and that may hopefully in the future provide greater enlightenment as how to best address ADHD. These potentialities include possibly new ADHD medications and the creation of novel drug delivery systems, both for existing as well as future ADHD medications, as well as hopefully in gaining a better understanding of how to most effectively combine the use of ADHD medications along with other treatment approaches. Furthermore, perhaps we will acquire new insights that will help us to disentangle the nearly virtual indivisibility that exists presently between ADHD and being prescribed ADHD medications.

New Medications

Research into new medications for ADHD and other conditions is a perennial focus for pharmaceutical companies and for other investigators. In the United States, the scheduling of drugs and the clinical trial system for the development and testing of new medications is regulated primarily under the Controlled Substances Act, as was more thoroughly discussed in Chapter 7. Similar comprehensive legislation pertaining to drugs has been passed in many other countries. For instance, in 1971, the United Kingdom enacted the Misuse of Drugs Act, and in 1966, Canada passed its own Controlled Drugs and Substances Act. These and similar laws passed in other countries were enacted to help respective nations to comply with the treaty commitments that were made under assorted international agreements such as the Single Convention on Narcotic Drugs (1961), the Convention on Psychotropic Substances (1971), and the UN Convention Against Illicit Traffic in Narcotic Drugs and Psychotropic Substances (1988). These sorts of laws and international agreements help to regulate and control the development and production, as well as curtail the misuse and abuse, of existing drugs and of new substances that may be of assistance in the management and treatment of ADHD and related conditions.

Researchers are continuously evaluating the use of novel pharmacological agents for treating ADHD and similar conditions. For instance, the potential of cholinergic drugs, like the acetylcholinesterase inhibitors, such as donepezil and tacrine, is being explored for treating ADHD. In a similar vein, novel nicotinic analogues, such as ABT-418, are also under experimental examination as potential ADHD medications. Likewise, studies are currently underway of NFC1, a glutamatergic agonist, which primarily appears to have both acceptable safety and efficacy for treating ADHD. NFC1 essentially targets the glutamatergic pathways that have been found to be dysfunctional in many individuals with ADHD. This sort of drug would not target the entire brain, as, for example, methylphenidate (Ritalin) or a combination amphetamine formulation (Adderall) do and therefore are often associated with a considerable array of undesired side effects, but the action of this new class of drugs is expected to be more focused.

Nitric oxide is a diatomic with a very short half-life after it is produced and released and that is involved in modulation of neurotransmission and of several other physiological processes. It is an endogenously produced substance and as such is a potential therapeutic agent for varied conditions, perhaps including ADHD. Nitric oxide is created by the action of the enzyme nitric oxide synthase, and the resulting nitric oxide affects different pathophysiological systems, including the cardiovascular system, the peripheral nervous system, and, of most concern here, the central nervous system. Medications that enhance the production of or block the degradation of nitric oxide synthase could, accordingly, potentially help influence neuronal transmission, which is an integral component of ADHD.

Another group of drugs under consideration as possible ADHD medications are those that raise the levels of the orexins. The orexin-producing cell bodies in the hypothalamus have projections that spread out widely within the central nervous system. The orexins act mainly as excitatory neurotransmitters. These neuropeptides have been found to regulate arousal and promote wakefulness, similar to the effects of the eugeroic ADHD medications, like modafinil (Provigil), adrafinil (Olmifons), and armodafinil (Nuvigil), and thus are being examined for their potential uses in treating ADHD.

These are but a few selected examples of the vast array of the potential classes of substances research into which may yield uses for new medications for treating individuals with ADHD. It is extremely difficult, if not actually impossible, to predict where the next new ADHD drugs may come from, but it is encouraging to recognize at least that there are ongoing efforts to look for them. It should also be duly noted that there are many, many medications that are already developed and currently in use for assorted other conditions that may upon further consideration in the future be shown to also be efficacious in treating symptoms of ADHD.

Novel Delivery Systems

Alternative drug delivery systems are now also being explored that may possibly offer improved management of ADHD symptoms. A unique drug delivery system, for instance, was created for a particular methylphenidate formulation that was released in 2000 and that is presently marketed under the trade name of Concerta. It consists of a capsule that is coated with a relatively small amount of methylphenidate that is thus available for immediate release, but as the capsule moves progressively through the gastrointestinal tract, it absorbs more water that, in turn, causes a gel located in the bottom of the capsule to slowly expand, which gradually pushes out more of the methylphenidate dose through a small laser drilled hole, which is situated in the top of the capsule. This multifaceted process results in a novel drug delivery system that allows the therapeutic dose of the methylphenidate to last for approximately 12 hours in a normal healthy individual. Concerta has a low abuse potential since the capsule is difficult to open and the contents have to be processed by a complex extraction process to separate out the pure methylphenidate active ingredient.

Transdermal drug delivery systems are currently available, and other alternative systems are already under development for selected ADHD medications. For example, a transdermal selegeline (Emsam) delivery system is currently being developed such that it essentially bypasses the intestinal mucosa, which contains considerable levels of the MAO enzyme subtype A that serves to more rapidly break the drug down. Under such a drug delivery system, foods containing tyramines and other ingredients that must generally be restricted for users of many monoamine oxidase inhibitors (MAOIs) would no longer be problematic. Further the side effects profile of the MAOIs used this way seems to be more favorable than that of traditional drug delivery systems. Transdermal patch delivery systems have been developed for many ADHD medications. However, there are several disadvantages to the use of this delivery technique. One of the most commonly cited disadvantages to the use of a transdermal patch is the high rate of contact dermatitis, which often results. Problems with transdermal patch adherence are also particularly common in humid environments with physically active individuals. Patch replacement is routinely necessary, for instance, after extended swimming or physical exertion. These sorts of inconveniences that are commonly associated with the use of a transdermal patch typically lead to reduced compliance. One novel technique that is under consideration is to administer an ADHD medicine by means of a new transdermal delivery system, such as that which uses microneedles, which are attached to an adhesive patch. These tiny needles create micrometer-sized porous holes through the skin for the active pharmacological agent to pass through more easily into the body; such small needle holes do not create any perceived pain sensation, yet they permit ready drug delivery. Drug permeation can be further enhanced in this approach if the active ingredient is encapsulated in backing layers that circumvent the premature closure of the miniature holes created by the microneedles. This type of drug delivery system could be used, for example, on very young children. It also would permit a larger dose of the respective ADHD medicine to be delivered faster, which could, in turn, help reduce the chances of causing skin irritations, as sometimes happens with traditional transdermal patches.

The development of drug delivery systems that are more difficult to abuse is an important area of concern. The need for such deterrent systems is indicated by the alarming prevalence rates of abuse of the varied ADHD medications, particularly the respective psychostimulant ADHD medications. In this regard, the annual National Survey on Drug Use and Health (NSDUH) collects data on substance use and substance misuse among Americans aged 12 years and older, representing over 265 million individuals. The past-year misuse of stimulants, like the popular ADHD medications marketed as Adderall and Ritalin, was reported in the NSDUH by 5.3 million individuals in the United States in 2015. Further, the past-year initiation of stimulant abuse was reported by 1.3 million individuals in the United States in 2015. These types of statistics clearly indicate the need for more effective abuse-prevention strategies, of which tamper-resistant drug delivery systems could be a crucial part. Myriad pharmacological abuse-deterrent approaches are accordingly under consideration already. One of the sorts of approaches being examined is the development of altered capsule and tablet formulations that make it more difficult to crush the pharmacologically active contents of the capsule or tablet into a powder so that they can be snorted, swallowed, or injected. These altered formulations would present substantial barriers to the routes of administration most typically used by substance abusers. However, no prevention strategy is going to be effective when we live in a society that tolerates the disturbing increase in the use of psychostimulants without prescriptions, which is a direct consequence of the dramatic rise in the use of ADHD psychostimulant medications as evidenced by the approximately 21 million individuals in the United States aged 12 years or older who were prescribed these substances in 2015. This statistic reflects trends that have been developing for some time. For example, medication sales data for ADHD medications from the IMS Health's National Disease and Therapeutic Index database from 1998 to 2005 for adolescents aged 13 years to 19 years indicate a 133 percent increase for amphetamine products, like Adderall; a 52 percent increase for methylphenidate products, like Ritalin; and, an 80 percent increase for both together. Over the same eight-year time period, for the same age population, there was a 76 percent increase in the number of calls related to the intentional abuse or intentional misuse of these substances to the American Association of Poison Control Center's National Poison Data System. The rising abuse of these ADHD prescription medications clearly reflects the increase in their availability. The very strong positive relationship that is observed between availability and abuse has been seen time and again with many different substances, including alcohol, tobacco, and opiates, and thus should be of no surprise when looking more closely at ADHD medications, particularly the psychostimulant ADHD medications, such as amphetamine (Evekeo, Dyanavel XR), dextroamphetamine (Dexedrine), lisdextroamphetamine (Vyvanse), methamphetamine (Desoxyn), and methylphenidate (Ritalin).

Better Understanding of Combining Medications with Other Treatments

The use of ADHD medications in combination with other treatment approaches is an area that can potentially be of extreme importance in the near future. As effective as any respective ADHD medicine may, or may not, be, this area of combined treatment approaches is highly likely to yield substantially enhanced results when these ADHD medications are administered concurrently with other treatment modalities. Findings from numerous studies of brain neuroplasticity suggest that the use of these additional treatment approaches will help individuals with ADHD not only to achieve greater brain health but also to lead healthier lives overall.

A growing body of research evidence strongly suggests that a combination of ADHD medications and lifestyle changes can be most effective in treating ADHD symptoms. Conjunction treatments can include simple but very beneficial healthful lifestyle choices, such as staying properly hydrated, getting enough sleep, learning how to meditate, and getting regular physical exercise.

Certainly, it would be very helpful for any individual who needs an ADHD medicine to also be following a set of lifestyle choices that would contribute to his or her optimal healthful living. These personalized choices would not only help to promote the overall health of the individual, but they would also help to foster a scenario where the ADHD medications would be most likely to attain their maximal therapeutic efficacy.

A good night of sleep is critically important to everyone, including individuals taking an ADHD medicine. Individuals with ADHD generally sleep poorly and sleep less than those without ADHD. Attention and the ability to focus and concentrate decrease for all of us as our sleep becomes more restless. In fact, mental function, in general, is less effective in individuals who do not get normal, restful sleep. Establishing regular sleep routines, like going to bed and waking up at the same general time each day, helps our brains work best at all ages. The National Sleep Foundation reports that up to 80 percent of adolescents do not get enough sleep. Children who are sleep deprived typically lack focus and may demonstrate symptoms of hyperactivity. Eating large meals and drinking alcohol or caffeinated beverages close to bedtime can also disrupt sleep patterns. In fact, excessive alcohol use at any time can result in neuronal loss and declining brain volume; compared with light drinkers, heavy drinkers, those consuming six to nine alcoholic drinks once a week throughout adolescence, have significantly smaller gray matter volumes in the bilateral anterior cingulate cortex, the right orbitofrontal and frontopolar cortices, the right superior temporal gyrus, and the right insular cortex. This is particularly troubling as we now know that the brain continues developing into the middle of 20s and that interfering with this normal development by engaging in heavy drinking can have serious adverse long-term effects. Tobacco smoking and the use of other drugs of abuse also accelerate brain function declines as we age, particularly contributing to memory loss.

Maintaining regular physical activity also helps to improve brain functioning in all individuals, including those who are taking an ADHD medicine. Studies indicate that individuals who exercise regularly have higher levels of gray matter in their brains. Regular physical exercise, particularly as we age, helps to prevent many illnesses and poor health conditions, such as diabetes, high cholesterol, hypertension, obesity, and stroke, that can lead to loss of memory and mental agility. Regularly performing complex mental activities, such as puzzles and word games, also helps to prevent these declines in mental function. It has been suggested that maintaining patterns of regular physical activity helps to stimulate the release of brain derived neurotrophic factor (BDNF) that helps promote healthy neurons, which, in turn, helps to increase cognitive factors like memory, processing time, and attention. Exercising regularly additionally has been shown to significantly improve our ability to focus and concentrate as well as to stimulate the growth of new brain neurons.

Proper nutrition is also clearly important to all individuals, including, of course, those individuals with ADHD. Although the studies to date are not entirely conclusive in this area, considerable speculation has been directed at varied nutritional factors, such as the relative levels of fiber, sugar, and food additives, as well as pesticides, in the food consumed as potentially contributing to the etiology and maintenance of symptoms of ADHD. Low glycemic foods help to deliver a steady supply of sugar to the blood, which makes it easier for an individual with ADHD to control their behaviors and to improve performance. Sugars, by the way, include all the monosaccharides and disaccharides added to foods and beverages as well as all the natural sugars like those contained in milk, fruit, honey, and syrups. The use of nutritional supplements may also be beneficial. The taking of Omega-3 fatty acids, for instance, has been found to help decrease inflammation and to improve mood, which could clearly be of assistance in helping individuals with ADHD; they also seem to help improve cognitive skills, such as concentration and focus. Omega-3s delivered in a phospholipid composition, specifically meaning formulations in which phosphatidylserine is attached to the Omega-3s (PS-Omega-3s), appear to result in a greater reduction of ADHD symptoms compared to those delivered in a triglyceride formulation. Further, as mentioned in the first chapter, low levels of Omega-3s are a factor associated with ADHD. Other nutritional supplements may also be helpful, such as taking zinc to help reduce hyperactivity and impulsivity or magnesium to help with sleep and relaxation.

Dehydration is also well known to affect our ability to concentrate; it impairs memory and is highly associated with mood swings and fatigue. About 55 percent to 65 percent of the average human body is made up of water. When you start to get thirsty, your kidneys send less water to the bladder, which darkens the urine. Body temperature increases as we sweat less; our blood becomes thicker and flows more sluggishly; heart rate must increase to maintain appropriate oxygen levels to the brain as well as to the rest of the body. Keeping properly hydrated and well-nourished is certainly key to optimal brain function and health in general, including reducing the adverse impacts of ADHD.

Reducing levels of stress is also a wise health choice for our brains and for allowing an ADHD medicine to work optimally. Higher levels of the stress hormone cortisol, for instance, make it more difficult to retrieve information from our memory stores. Stress-related inflammation, as measured by C-reactive protein levels, can also adversely impact brain health. Learning how to meditate may help many individuals with ADHD be able to concentrate better; they also appear to have less depression and anxiety. Mindfulness, intentionality, and maintaining a positive attitude are some of the many other lifestyle approaches that are positively associated with better brain health and, therefore, with less difficulties associated with symptoms of ADHD.

Many individuals with ADHD have a distorted sense of time and thus have a tendency to be out of synchrony with their everyday contexts. This desynchronization results in extreme performance deficits. If we measure and define our treatment targets through real contexts and implement them with appropriate timing details, we are far more likely to attain treatment success. Since symptoms and treatment efficacy for respective ADHD medications are known to vary with respect to different times of the day, when to take a particular medicine should be considered carefully. Chronotherapy, that is timing the administration of medications in accord with an individual's internal clock, or his or her circadian rhythm, could possibly lead to more optimal therapeutic results from ADHD medications with less adverse side effects.

Use of digital interactive and social media is dramatically increasing and has been associated with both health benefits and risks. The American Academy of Pediatrics issued guidelines in 2016 concerning the potential risks and benefits of exposure to electronic media in young children. Benefits, supported by research, include early learning opportunities; increased social contact and support; introduction of new ideas and knowledge; and the ready availability of appropriate health prevention, education, and promotion. The numerous risks of early exposure to electronic media include negative impacts on attention and learning; decreased sleep; greater prevalence of many health problems like obesity and depression; threats to confidentiality and privacy; as well as possible exposure to inappropriate, inaccurate, or unsafe content and contacts. Nevertheless, young children, starting at about the age of 18 months, long before they start use of ADHD medications, can begin to learn from digital media and from high-quality media programming.

The very young, that is those four to five years of age, are a group of individuals that should only be given ADHD medications if behavioral therapy approaches were tried and found not to be successful. As noted previously, the American Academy of Pediatrics' clinical practice guidelines recommend that behavioral therapy be prescribed as the first line of treatment. In particular, parent training approaches have been found to be the most effective for this age group. Parent training behavioral therapy is known by many different names, including Behavioral Parent Training, Behavioral Management Training for Parents, Parent Behavioral Therapy, and Parent Training. Some of the various programs of parent training that have been found to be effective in reducing symptoms of ADHD are Helping the Non-Compliant Child, Incredible Years Parenting Program, New Forest Parenting Programme,

Parent-Child Interaction Therapy, and Positive Parenting Program (Triple P). These types of parent training programs teach parents the skills that they need to encourage and reward positive behaviors in their children; using a system of rewards and consequences can effectively help change behavior, particularly with immediate and positive feedback to structure situations in ways that support desired behavior. The use of relatively simple behavioral techniques, such as keeping to routines, making lists of tasks and activities, using reminder notes, assigning special places for important items to be routinely placed, and breaking down large tasks into more manageable smaller units, can be helpful for both children and adults with ADHD. Behavioral therapy not only gives parents the strategies and skills to help their children, but it has also been shown to be as effective as ADHD medications for treating symptoms of ADHD in preschool children. Further, preschool children typically experience more side effects from ADHD medications than older individuals, and, in addition, the long-term effects of the use of most ADHD medications have not been well studied in these younger-aged individuals.

There are many alternative therapeutic techniques, such as those described earlier in the second chapter, like acupuncture, biofeedback, hypnosis, and massage that can be very helpful for some individuals when used in combination with ADHD medications. There is, of course, a vast array of other techniques that have promise and may also be shown in the future to be helpful in enhancing treatment success for individuals with ADHD. Music therapy, for instance, has been shown to help individuals with ADHD to improve their attention and focus, to reduce their hyperactivity, and to strengthen their social skills. Transcranial electromagnetic stimulation is a noninvasive technique that has been shown to improve the precision of memory recollection, which can be an issue for some individuals with ADHD and it is hoped may, in the future, be found to positively augment the use of ADHD medications.

ADHD medications appear to make the greatest differences nearly immediately for the vast majority of individuals living with ADHD. The typical process that is followed to introduce an individual to a new ADHD medicine is titration, where you start with the smallest dose as a baseline and then increase this gradually until either a therapeutic response is attained or until the side effect profile becomes undesirable. Physicians typically adjust dosages of ADHD medications every three to seven days in this titration process. Initially, this is fundamentally a system of trial and error as different medications are introduced and tried. However, as time goes on, other factors seem to more significantly come into play, like the positive connections that the individual with ADHD has with significant others, such as parents, teachers, and healthcare providers.

Individuals with ADHD will often benefit from combination treatments because they often have other comorbid psychiatric problems. Among young children, conduct disorder and ODD are the most common psychiatric comorbidities; among older children, adolescents, and young adults, antisocial personality disorder, bipolar disorders, depression, and substance use disorders appear to be the most common comorbid conditions. Anxiety, binge eating behaviors, premature death, and suicidality are just a few of the other variables that research has identified as being more likely among individuals with ADHD. In addition, individuals with ADHD can also benefit from careful and continuous long-term monitoring and treatment. Finally, ADHD medications have been found to be the most effective in treating ADHD when not used as stand-alone treatments. In fact, when used in combination, many ADHD medications may be even more effective than when used alone. For instance, several studies indicated that when the antihypertensive alpha 2 agonist guanfacine hydrochloride (Intuniv) is administered in combination with the stimulant medicine methylphenidate (Ritalin), the cognitive effects are greater than when either is used alone. The ways that behavior is managed at home, school, and elsewhere are also essential; accordingly, we must also work to change the ways that children with ADHD are taught and regarded. Further, social stigma is far more likely to raise its ugly head if the individual with ADHD is left untreated; effective treatment can generally help alleviate both the problem itself and the stigma often associated with it.

The notion that ADHD and other "disabilities" can be socially constructed has been raised in many theoretical and practical discussions, and it overrides the understanding of social stigma just noted. The cultural, organizational, and technological factors that affect the recognition of ADHD as a condition are part of the far larger trend of the medicalization of the range of human behaviors. A cultural underpinning of the medical models of any disorder is the assumption that there is a generally recognized normative range of behaviors. However, when the actions of an individual depart from this accepted norm, the medicalization response is typically to define it as indicative of an existing pathology, disease, or disorder, which, consequently, would merit diagnosis and treatment. The history of the varied diagnostic labels formulated as the precursors of what is today identified as ADHD clearly supports the understanding of ADHD as a socially constructed notion.

The response to prescribe a respective ADHD medicine to an individual when he or she crosses the blurred range between acceptable and unacceptable behaviors is accordingly seen as part of the far wider trends within society to medicalize behavior. The ever-broadening classes of drugs used to medicate symptoms of ADHD to increasingly encompass more and more individuals under the diagnostic umbrella of ADHD bear testimony to the trend to accommodate the apparent incongruities in the presenting behaviors of individuals diagnosed with ADHD.

The rampant escalation in the numbers of individuals diagnosed with ADHD and consequently prescribed the varied ADHD medications has been observed to be a worldwide phenomenon. This is a further indication in support of the concept of the social construction of the disorder. The geographical disproportionalities that were not long ago seen in the prevalence of ADHD and of the concomitant prescribing of psychostimulant ADHD medications, in particular, have somewhat been diminishing more recently, perhaps attributable in no small measure to the hegemonic expansion of the diagnostic predisposition to conform to Western medicine and to its dominant pharmaceutical tendencies in this era of ever-increasing globalization.

This brief review has hopefully shown some of the vast potential that a better understanding of how to combine the use of respective ADHD medications with other varied treatment approaches promises to offer. The future of ADHD medications is certainly difficult to predict, but if the current trends in this general area are any indication, then we can optimistically look forward to profound developments that will both help to revitalize and to enhance the lives of individuals living with ADHD.

Directory of Resources

ATTENTION DEFICIT DISORDER ASSOCIATION (ADDA)

ADDA is an international nonprofit, tax-exempt [501(c)(3)], entirely volunteer run, organization that provides information, networking opportunities, and resources to support adults with ADHD.

Contact: Attention Deficit Disorder Association
P.O. Box 103
Denver, PA, 17517
1(800) 939-1019
www.add.org

CENTERS FOR DISEASE CONTROL AND PREVENTION (CDC)

The U.S. CDC is charged with protecting America from health, safety, and security threats. To accomplish its objective, the CDC provides health information, including that related to ADHD and ADHD medicines.

Contact: United States Centers for Disease Control and Prevention
1600 Clifton Road
Atlanta, GA, 30329
1-800-CDC-INFO (1-800-323-4636)
www.cdc.gov/

CHILDREN AND ADULTS WITH ATTENTION-DEFICIT/ HYPERACTIVITY DISORDER (CHADD)

CHADD is a national nonprofit, tax-exempt [501(c)(3)] organization that provides advocacy, education, and support for individuals with ADHD.

Contact: Children and Adults with Attention-Deficit/ Hyperactivity Disorder
4601 Presidents Drive, Suite 300
Lanham, MD, 20706
1(303) 306-7070
www.chadd.org

DRUG ENFORCEMENT AGENCY (DEA)

The DEA is part of the U.S. Department of Justice. It is the major federal agency responsible for domestic enforcement of U.S. drug policy, including both for prescribed medicines and for illicit drug abuse.

Contact: United States Drug Enforcement Agency
800 K Street, NW, Suite 500
Washington, DC, 20001
1-202-1305-8500
www.dea.gov/

FOOD AND DRUG ADMINISTRATION (FDA)

The U.S. FDA is responsible for protecting the public health by assuring that foods and drugs, including painkiller medications, are properly labeled and sanitary; with respect to drugs and medical devices, the FDA is responsible for ensuring that they are both safe and effective.

Contact: U.S. Food and Drug Administration
10903 New Hampshire Avenue
Silver Spring, MD, 20993
1-888-INFO-FDA (1-888-463-6332)
www.fda.gov/

NARCOTICS ANONYMOUS (NA)

NA is a 12-step fellowship of men and women seeking recovery from drug addiction.

Contact: NA World Services
P.O. Box 9999

Van Nuys, CA, 91409
1(818) 773-9999
www.na.org

NATIONAL ALLIANCE FOR THE MENTALLY ILL (NAMI)

NAMI is the nation's largest grassroots mental health organization dedicated to helping individuals affected by mental disorders build better lives. It helps promote awareness of and provides support and education for individuals affected by mental illness, including ADHD.

Contact: National Alliance for the Mentally Ill
3803 N. Fairfax Drive, Suite 100
Arlington, VA, 22203
1-703-524-7600
TTY: 703-516-7227
Helpline: 1-800-950-6264
www.nami.org

NATIONAL INSTITUTE OF MENTAL HEALTH (NIMH)

The NIMH is the leading national agency for research on mental disorders, including ADHD. It is concerned with the prevention and treatment of mental disorders through basic and clinical research.

Contact: National Institute of Mental Health
6001 Executive Boulevard
Bethesda, MD, 20892
1-866-615-6464
TTY: 301-443-8431
www.nimh.nih.gov/

NATIONAL RESOURCE CENTER ON ADHD (NRC)

The NRC is a national clearinghouse for evidence-based information on ADHD. It is funded through the CDC National Center on Birth Defects and Developmental Disabilities (NPHPRC) and operates as a program of CHADD.

Contact: Children and Adults with Attention-Deficit/ Hyperactivity Disorder
4601 Presidents Drive, Suite 300
Lanham, MD, 20706
1(800) 233-4050
www.help4adhd.org

SUBSTANCE ABUSE AND MENTAL HEALTH SERVICES ADMINISTRATION (SAMHSA)

SAMHSA is part of the U.S. Department of Health and Human Services. The primary mission of SAMHSA is to improve the availability and quality of substance abuse prevention, treatment, and mental health services. SAMHSA encompasses the Center for Substance Abuse Prevention (CSAP), the Center for Substance Abuse Treatment (CSAT), and the Center for Mental Health Services as well as its Office of Applied Studies. Collectively, it is the major federal agency in the U.S. supporting substance abuse treatment and prevention and mental health initiatives.

Contact: Substance Abuse and Mental Health Services Administration
1 Choke Cherry Road
Rockville, MD, 20857
1-877-SAMHSA-7 (1-877-726-4727)
TDD: 1-800-487-4889
www.samhsa.gov/

TREATMENT LOCATOR:

Treatment Referral Routing Service Helpline
1-800-662-Help (4357)
http://www.samhsa.gov/find-help/national-helpline

UNITED STATES DEPARTMENT OF JUSTICE: AMERICANS WITH DISABILITIES ACT

The U.S. Department of Justice oversees the federal enforcement, certification, regulatory, coordination, and technical assistance activities as required by the Americans with Disabilities Act (ADA).

Contact: United States Department of Justice
Americans with Disabilities Act
Information and Technical Assistance
950 Pennsylvania Avenue, NW
Washington, DC, 20830-0001
1-800-514-0301
TTY: 1-800-514-0383
www.ada.gov/

Glossary

Abuse: The intentional continued consumption of any drug despite recognition of the harmful consequences of such problems.

Action potential: The rapid change in electrical potential between the inside and the outside of a neuron, which when attained as sodium rushes in, results in depolarization with an electrical impulse transmitted down the length of the axon; it is an all-or-nothing process either resulting in activation or not firing at all.

Addiction: A primary chronic disease, characterized by relapse, in which compulsive drug seeking and use predominates, even after serious negative consequences are experienced and understood to result from such use; its development and manifestations can be influenced by environmental, genetic, and psychosocial factors.

Adrenergic: Related to activation of neurons and organs controlled by the catecholamine neurotransmitter epinephrine or similar substances, such as norepinephrine.

Afferent: System to transmit pain signals and other neuronal impulses from the periphery into the center, such as from a sensory ending to the central nervous system.

Agonist: A substance that binds to a receptor site and activates it by mimicking the action of other substances that also binds there.

Amine: Any member of a broad class of organic compounds that contain a nitrogen atom, including the catecholamine neurotransmitters, like dopamine, epinephrine, and norepinephrine; amino acids; and many synthesized medicines, like the TCAs, amphetamines, and opiates.

Amygdala: A part of the limbic system of the brain, located in the temporal lobe of the cerebral hemisphere, that functions in generating feelings of pain, pleasure, and fear.

Antagonist: A substance that binds to a receptor site and blocks its action preventing a drug or neurotransmitter from activating it.

Autonomic nervous system: The part of the peripheral nervous system that regulates the internal organs and glands.

Axon: A fibrous structure that transmits signals and other neuronal impulses away from the cell body to neurons or other structures, such as glands or muscles.

Basal ganglia: Part of the forebrain important for consciously control of motor activity, including the caudate nucleus and the putamen.

Behavioral therapy: A therapeutic approach based on the principles of classical and operant conditioning to help individuals to change problematic or self-defeating behaviors.

Bioavailability: Extent of the availability of a particular drug after oral administration, which is expressed as a percentage of the dose taken.

Biogenic amines: Internally produced organic substances that are critical to brain functioning; they can be subdivided into the catecholamines and the indolamines.

Biotransformation: The processes by which the body, usually in the liver, alters the chemical structure of a substance so that it can be eliminated, typically by excretion through the urine.

Brain stem: That part of the brain closest to the spinal cord through which signals are transmitted; some of the most basic natural functions are controlled here, like respiration and heart rate. It consists of the medulla, pons, and the midbrain.

Caudate nucleus: That part of the corpus striatum which has a shape with a long extension, like a tail.

Central nervous system: A part of the nervous system, specifically the brain and spinal cord, that serves to centrally process information from the sensory systems and to select an appropriate response.

Cerebrum: The upper part of the human brain, divided into two hemispheres, which controls most cognitive, motor, and sensory processes.

Catecholamines: A group of biogenic amines derived from phenylalanine that contain a catechol nucleus, such as dopamine, epinephrine, and norepinephrine.

Cholinergic: Neurons and neural pathways related to activation controlled by the neurotransmitter acetylcholine, particularly the parasympathetic nerve fibers.

Clinical trial: An experimental study designed to determine if a medicine or other medical intervention is safe and effective.

Cognitive behavioral therapy: A treatment approach that helps individuals change the way they think and behave by changing their ways of thinking.

Corpus striatum: That part of the human brain situated at the base of each cerebral hemisphere.

Dendrite: A fibrous structure that transmits signals and other neuronal impulses toward the cell body; one neuron can have many hundreds of dendrites, each of which can potentially receive signals from adjacent neurons.

Depolarization: The increase in the action potential across the membrane of a neuron, which is accompanied by the build-up of positive charges inside the cell reversing its charge or polarity.

Dopaminergic: Related to cells stimulated by the neurotransmitter dopamine.

Downregulation: The process by which the number of receptor sites on a neuron is reduced, thereby decreasing its sensitivity to stimulation.

Efferent: A system to transmit signals and other neuronal impulses away from the center to the periphery, such as from the spinal cord to a muscle.

Enzyme: A protein that affects a specific molecule, and thereby substantially accelerates the rate of a particular chemical reaction in the body.

Extrapyramidal symptoms: Various signs of the dysfunction of the extrapyramidal system, frequently associated with side effects of certain psychotropic drugs; they include drooling, involuntary postures, motor inertia, muscular rigidity, restlessness, shuffling gait, and tremors.

Gate control theory: A theory that posits a gate along the spinal cord that either allows signals to transmit to the brain or else blocks them.

Indolamines: A group of biogenic amines that have both an indole ring and an amine group chemical structure, such as serotonin and tryptophan.

IUPAC name: The IUPAC name is the systematic, recommended and preferred nomenclature for a respective organic chemical compound as recommended by the International Union of Pure and Applied Chemistry.

Limbic system: The interconnected group of structures in the brain that control emotions and motivation; it includes the amygdala, hypothalamus, and the septum.

MAOIs: A group of medicines that inhibit the enzymes that break down neurotransmitters, like dopamine and serotonin, and thereby increase the levels of these neurotransmitters.

Mesolimbic system: The interconnected system in the brain controlled by dopamine and running from the ventral tegmental area to the nucleus accumbens and that is responsible for reward.

Misuse: Consumption of, in this case, any painkiller drug in any manner or for any purpose other than that recommended or prescribed by a health care professional.

Myelin sheath: White lipid and protein covering of an axon; provides the white matter for the brain and spinal cord and helps increase the speed of an action potential.

Neuron: A nerve cell in the brain and nervous system that transmits chemical and electrical impulses.

Neurotransmitter: A chemical substance that enables signal transmission between neurons and related structures, such as norepinephrine, dopamine and serotonin.

Pharmacodynamics: The effects, in this case, of a particular ADHD medicine on the body.

Pharmacokinetics: The effects of the body on, in this case, a particular ADHD medicine.

Physical dependence: A physiological state of adaptation that results from chronic use of a drug, where tolerance is generally developed, and one in which withdrawal symptoms typically manifest when use is dramatically reduced or ceased. It can occur with any type of chronic use, either appropriate or inappropriate use, of a drug.

Plasma protein binding: The affinity of a drug to chemically bind to proteins in the blood, particularly albumin.

Polydrug abuse: The abuse of two or more drugs at the same general time.

Pons: That part of the brain stem situated between the medulla and the midbrain and serving as a bridge between the right and left halves of the cerebellum.

Postsynaptic potential: A change in the potential of a neuron's membrane that received a transmission signal from another neuron.

Prescription abuse: Use of a drug without a prescription, or use in any way other than that prescribed; used interchangeably with nonmedical use.

Putamen: A large, lateral part of the lenticular nucleus of the corpus striatum.

Receptor site: A structure on the surface of a neuron that allows only specific neurotransmitters or other substances, such as a psychoactive drug or its derivatives, to fit into it and thereby activate it to create an action potential.

SNRIs: A group of medicines that limit the reuptake of serotonin and norepinephrine, thereby selectively increasing their levels in the body.

SSRIs: A group of medicines that selectively increase the amount of serotonin by inhibiting its reuptake.

Stimulant: Any substance which when administered increases arousal, blood pressure, heart rate, respiration, and so forth.

Striatum: Part of the corpus striatum consisting of the caudate nucleus and the putamen.

Substantia nigra: A large nucleus located in the midbrain containing dark melanin pigmented cells and responsible for motor functions.

Substitution: Practice of administering any substance with the intent of replacing it for the misuse or abuse of, in this case, any ADHD drug.

Sympathomimetics: Drugs that act to stimulate or mimic the activities of the sympathetic branch of the autonomic nervous system, such as by increasing heart rate, blood pressure, and respiration.

Synapse: The minute space at the junction between two or more neurons where neurotransmission or inhibition of signals occurs.

TCAs: A group of medicines that selectively increase the levels of norepinephrine and serotonin in the body, and they also tend to block the action of acetylcholine.

Thalamus: Inner part of the cerebrum responsible for integrative and sensory functions.

Tolerance: A situation of adaptation where increasingly greater amounts of a substance are required to produce a similar effect experienced during earlier use with a lower amount.

Vesicle: A small sac-like structure of a neuron that contains a neurotransmitter or its precursor substances produced by the neuron.

Withdrawal: A constellation of unpleasant physical and psychological effects that appear when chronic use of a particular type of substance that an individual became habituated to is abruptly reduced or stopped; symptoms might include abdominal pain, convulsions, delirium, tremors, and vomiting.

Bibliography

Adler, L., & Cohen, J. (2004). Diagnosis and evaluation of adults with attention-deficit/hyperactivity disorder. *Psychiatric Clinics of North America* 27(2), 187–201.

Amen, D.G. (1995). *Windows into the A.D.D. mind: Understanding and treating attention deficit disorders in the everyday lives of children, adolescents and adults.* Fairfield, CA: Mind Works Press.

Amen, D.G. (2013). *Healing ADD: The breakthrough program that allows you to see and heal the seven types of attention deficit disorder.* New York: Berkley Books/Penguin Random House.

American Psychiatric Association. (1952). *Diagnostic and statistical manual of mental disorders* (DSM-I). Washington, DC: Author.

American Psychiatric Association. (1968). *Diagnostic and statistical manual of mental disorders* (DSM-II). Washington, DC: Author.

American Psychiatric Association. (1980). *Diagnostic and statistical manual of mental disorders* (DSM-III). Washington, DC: Author.

American Psychiatric Association. (1987). *Diagnostic and statistical manual of mental disorders* (DSM-III-R). Washington, DC: Author.

American Psychiatric Association. (1994). *Diagnostic and statistical manual of mental disorders* (DSM-IV). Washington, DC: Author.

American Psychiatric Association. (2000). *Diagnostic and statistical manual of mental disorders* (DSM-IV-TR). Washington, DC: Author.

American Psychiatric Association. (2013). *Diagnostic and statistical manual of mental disorders* (DSM-5). Washington, DC: Author.

Archer, D. (2015). *The ADHD advantage: What you thought was a diagnosis may be your greatest strength.* New York: Avery/Penguin Random House.

August, G.J., & Garfinkel, B.D. (1993). The nosology of attention-deficit hyperactivity disorder. *Journal of the American Academy of Child and Adolescent Psychiatry* 342, 155–165.

Banaschewski, T., Roessner, V., Dittmann, R.W., Janardham Santosh, P., & Rothenberger, A. (2004). Non-stimulant medications in the treatment of ADHD. *European Child and Adolescent Psychiatry* 13(Sup. 1), i102–i116.

Barkley, R.A., Fischer, M., Newby, R.F., & Breen, M.J. (1988). Development of multimethod clinical protocol for assessing stimulant drug response in children with attention deficit disorder. *Journal of Clinical Child Psychology* 17, 14–24.

Barkley, R.A. (1990). *Attention deficit hyperactivity disorder: A handbook for diagnosis and treatment.* New York: Guilford Press.

Barkley, R.A. (1997). *ADHD and the nature of self-control.* New York: Guilford Press.

Barkley, R.A. (2004). Driving impairments in teens and adults with attention deficit/hyperactivity disorder. *Psychiatric Clinics of North America* 27(2), 233–260.

Barkley, R.A., & Peters, H. (2012). The earliest reference to ADHD in the medical literature? Melchior Adam Weikard's description in 1775 of attention deficit (*Mangel der Aufmerksamkeit, Attentio Volubilis*). *Journal of Attention Disorders* 16(8), 623–630.

Beard, G. (1869). Neurasthenia, or nervous exhaustion. *Boston Medical and Surgical Journal* 3, 217–221.

Berger, M. (1981). Remediating hyperkinetic behavior with impulse control procedures. *School Psychology Review* 10(3), 405–407.

Bhowmik, A.D., Sarkar, K., Ghosh, P., Das, M., Bhaduri, N., Sarkar, K., Ray, A., Sinha, S., & Mukhopadhyay, K. (2017). Significance of dopaminergic gene variants in the male biasness of ADHD. *Journal of Attention Disorders* 21(3), 200–208.

Biederman, J., & Faraone, S.V. (2004). The Massachusetts General Hospital studies of gender influences on attention-deficit/hyperactivity disorder in youth and relatives. *Psychiatric Clinics of North America* 27(2), 225–232.

Biederman, J., Newcorn, J., & Sprich, S. (1991). Comorbidity of attention deficit hyperactivity disorder with conduct, depressive, anxiety, and other disorders. *American Journal of Psychiatry* 148, 564–575.

Bradley, C. (1937). The behavior of children receiving Benzedrine. *American Journal of Psychiatry* 94, 577.

Brunton, L.B., Lazo, J.S., & Parker, K.L. (Eds.). (2010). *Goodman and Gilman's: The pharmacological basis of therapeutics.* New York: McGraw-Hill.

Brzeczko, A.W., Leach, R., & Stark, J.G. (2013). The advent of a new pseudoephedrine product to combat methamphetamine abuse. *American Journal of Drug and Alcohol Abuse: Encompassing All Addictive Disorders* 39(5), 284–290.

Burgard, D.A., Fuller, R., Becker, B., Ferrell, R., & Dinglasan-Panlilio, M.J. (2013). Potential trends in attention deficit hyperactivity disorder (ADHD) drug use on a college campus: Wastewater analysis of amphetamine and ritalinic acid. *Science of the Total Environment* 450–451, 242–249.

Conners, C.K. (1963). The effects of methylphenidate on symptomology and learning in disturbed children. *American Journal of Psychiatry* 120, 458–464.

Conners, C.K., & Delamater, A. (1980). Visual-motor tracking by hyperkinetic children. *Perceptual and Motor Skills* 51(2), 487–497.

Cortese, S., Kelly, C., Chabernaud, C., Proal, E., Di Martino, A., Milham, M.P., & Castellanos, F.X. (2012). Toward systems neuroscience of ADHD: A meta-analysis of 55 fMRI studies. *American Journal of Psychiatry* 169, 1038–1055.

Courtwright, D.T. (2001). *Forces of habit: Drugs and the making of the modern world.* Cambridge, MA: Harvard University Press.

Crichton, Alexander. (1798). *An inquiry into the nature and origin of mental derangement: Comprehending a concise system of the physiology and pathology of the human mind. And a history of the passions and their effects.* Vol. 2. London: T. Cadwell, Junior, and W. Davies.

DeSantis, A.D., Webb, E.M., & Noar, S.M. (2008). Illicit use of prescription ADHD medications on a college campus: A multimethodological approach. *Journal of American College Health* 57(3), 315–324.

Doyle, R. (2004). The history of adult attention-deficit/hyperactivity disorder. *Psychiatric Clinics of North America* 27(2), 203–214.

Edwards, R.P., Alley, R.P., & Snider, R.P. (1971). Academic achievement and minimal brain dysfunction in mentally retarded children. *Exceptional Children* 37(7), 539–540.

Evans, R.W., Clay, T.H., & Gualtiere, C.T. (1987). Carabamazepine in pediatric psychiatry. *Journal of the American Academy of Child and Adolescent Psychiatry* 26, 2–8.

Faraone, S.V. (2004). Genetics of adult attention-deficit/hyperactivity disorder. *Psychiatric Clinics of North America* 27(2), 303–321.

Ford, S.M., & Roach, S.S. (2010). *Roach's introductory clinical pharmacology.* Philadelphia, PA: Lippincott Williams & Wilkins.

Freeman, R.D. (1976). Minimal brain dysfunction, hyperactivity, and learning disorders: Epidemic or episode? *School Review* 85(1), 5–30.

Goodman, B., & Volkow, N.D. (2008). ADHD medication and drug abuse. *Attention* 15(3), 10–12.

Hallowell, E.M., & Ratey, J.J. (2006). *Delivered from distraction: Getting the most out of life with attention deficit disorder.* New York: Ballantine Books.

Hallowell, E.M., & Ratey, J.J. (2011). *Driven to distraction: Recognizing and coping with attention deficit disorder.* New York: Random House.

Halkitis, P.N. (2009). *Methamphetamine addiction: Biological foundations, psychological factors, and social consequences.* Washington, DC: American Psychological Association.

Hines, J.L., King, T.S., & Curry, W.J. (2012). The adult ADHD self-report scale for screening adult attention deficit hyperactivity disorder (ADHD). *Journal of the American Board of Family Medicine* 25(6), 847–853.

Hinshaw, S.P., & Scheffler, R.M. (2014). *The ADHD explosion: Myths, medication, money, and today's push for performance.* New York: Oxford University Press.

Hoffmann, H. (2015). *Struwwelpeter 2000.* Trans. By C. Blyth. Kingston, ON: Iolair Publishing.

Huang, S., Hu, H., Sanchez, B.N., Peterson, K.E., Ettinger, A.S., Lamabrid-Figueroa, H., Schnaas, L., Mercado-Garcia, A., Wright, R.O., Basu, N., Cantonwine, D.E.,

Hernandez-Avila, M., & Tellez-Rojo, M.M. (2016). Childhood blood lead levels and symptoms of attention deficit hyperactivity disorder (ADHD): A cross-sectional study of Mexican children. *Environmental Health Perspectives* 124(6), 868–874.

James, William. (1890). *The Principles of psychology*. New York: Henry Holt & Co.

Janicak, P.G., Marder, S.R., & Pavuluvi, M.N. (2010). *Principles and practice of psychopharmacology*. Philadelphia, PA: Lippincott Williams & Wilkins.

Jensen, P.S. (2004). *Making the system work for your child with ADHD*. New York: Guilford Press.

Justus, K. (2016). Learning to plan and be organized: Executive function skills for kids with AD/HD. *School Library Journal* 62(12), 133–134.

Katzung, B.G. (Ed). (2007). *Basic and clinical pharmacology*. New York: McGraw-Hill Companies, Inc.

Kaye, S., & Darke, S. (2012). The diversion and misuse of pharmaceutical stimulants: What do we know and why should we care? *Addiction* 107, 467–477.

Kellogg, J.H. (1915). *Neurasthenia: Or, nervous exhaustion*. Battle Creek, MI: Good Health Publishing Co.

Kelly, E. (2009). *Encyclopedia of attention deficit hyperactivity disorders*. Santa Barbara, CA: Greenwood Press/ABC-CLIO.

Knights, R.M., & Hinton, G.G. (2004). Minimal brain dysfunction: Clinical and psychological test characteristics. *Intervention in School and Clinic* 4(4), 265–273.

Kolb, B., & Whishaw, I.Q. (1985). *Fundamentals of human neuropsychology*. New York: W.H. Freeman and Company.

Kramer, P.D. (1993). *Listening to Prozac: A psychiatrist explores antidepressant drugs and the remaking of the self*. New York: Viking/Penguin Books.

Laufer, M.W., Denhoff, E., & Solomons, G. (1957). Hyperkinetic impulse disorder in children's behavior problems. *Psychosomatic Medicine* 19(1), 38–49.

Mayes, R., & Rafalovich, A. (2007). Suffer the restless children: The evolution of ADHD and paediatric stimulant use 1900–80. *History of Psychiatry* 18(72, Part 4), 435–457.

Mick, E., Faraone, S.V., & Biederman, J. (2004). Age-dependent expression of attention-deficit/hyperactivity disorder symptoms. *Psychiatric Clinics of North America* 27(2), 215–224.

Mickle, T., Krishnan, S., Moncrief, J., & Lauderback, C. (2005). *U.S. Patent Application No. 11/089,056.*

Molina, B.S., Hinshaw, S.P., Swanson, J.M., Arnold, L.E., Vitiello, B., Jensen, P.S., . . . Houck, P.R. (2009). The MTA at 8 years: Prospective follow-up of children treated for combined-type ADHD in a multisite study. *Journal of the American Academy of Child and Adolescent Psychiatry* 48(5), 484–500.

Morrison, J.R., & Stewart, M.A. (1973). Evidence for a polygenetic inheritance in the Hyperactive Child Syndrome. *American Journal of Psychiatry* 130, 791–792.

Murray, J.B. (1987). Psychophysiological effects of methylphenidate (Ritalin). *Psychological Reports* 61, 315–336.

Nissen, S.E. (2006). ADHD drugs and cardiovascular risk. *New England Journal of Medicine* 354(14), 1445–1448.

Otasowie, J., Castells, X., Ehimare, U.P., & Smith, C.H. (2014). Tricyclic antidepressants for attention deficit hyperactivity disorder (ADHD) in children and adolescents. *Cochrane Database of Systematic Reviews*, doi:10.1002/1461858.CD006997.pub2.

Palmer, E.D. (2001). An early description of ADHD (Inattentive Subtype): Dr. Alexander Crichton and "Mental Restlessness" (1798). *Child Psychology and Psychiatry Review* 6, 66–73.

Park, S., Kim, B.-N., Kim, J.-W., Shin, M.-S., Yoo, H.J., & Cho, S.-C. (2017). Interactions Between early trauma and catechol-O-methyltransferase genes on inhibitory deficits in children with ADHD. *Journal of Attention Disorders* 21(3), 183–189.

Parker, C. (2013). *New ADHD medication rules: Brain science and common sense.* Virginia Beach, VA: Koehler Books.

Pliszka, S.R. (1992). Comorbidity of Attention-Deficit Hyperactivity Disorder and overanxious disorder. *Journal of the American Academy of Child and Adolescent Psychiatry* 31, 197–203.

Reiff, M.J., & S, Tippins. (2004). *ADHD: A complete and authoritative guide.* Elk Grove Village, IL: American Academy of Pediatrics.

Rief, S.F. (2003). *The ADHD book of lists: A practical guide for helping children and teens with attention deficit disorders.* San Francisco, CA: Jossey-Bass.

Ross, D.M., & Ross, S.A. (1976). *Hyperactivity: Research, theory, and action.* New York: John Wiley and Sons.

Routhier-Martin, K., Roberts, S.K., & Blanch, N. (2017). Exploring mindfulness and meditation for the elementary classroom: Intersections across current multidisciplinary research. *Childhood Education* 93(2), 168–175.

Ryan, J.B., Katsiyannis, A., & Hughes, E.M. (2011). Medication treatment for attention deficit hyperactivity disorder. *Theory into Practice* 50(1), 52–60.

Safren, S.A., Sprich, S., Chulvick, S., & Otto, M.W. (2004). Psychosocial treatments for adults with attention-deficit/hyperactivity disorder. *Psychiatric Clinics of North America* 27(2), 349–360.

Schatzberg, A.F., Cole, J. O., & DeBattista, C. (2010). *Manual of clinical psychopharmacology.* Arlington, VA: American Psychiatric Publishing.

Scheffler, R.M., Hinshaw, S.P., Modrek, S., & Levine, P. (2007). The global market for ADHD medications. *Health Affairs* 26(2), 450–457.

Seidman, L.J., Doyle, A., Fried, R., Valera, E., Crum, K., & Matthews, L. (2004). Neuropsychological function in adults with attention-deficit/hyperactivity disorder. *Psychiatric Clinics of North America* 27(2), 261–282.

Shaywitz, S.E., Cohen, D.J., & Shaywitz, B.A. (1978). The biochemical basis of minimal brain dysfunction. *Journal of Pediatrics* 92(2), 179–187.

Sleator, E.K, von-Newmann, A., & Sprague, R.L. (1974). Hyperactive children: A continuous long-term placebo controlled follow-up. *Journal of the American Medical Association* 229(3), 316–317.

Smith, A., Cubillo, A., Barrett, N., Giampietro, V., Simmons, A., Brammer, M., & Rubia, K. (2013). Neurofunctional effects of methylphenidate and atomoxetine in boys with attention-deficit/hyperactivity disorder during time discrimination. *Biological Psychiatry* 74(8), 615–622.

Spencer, T. Biederman, J., & Wilens, T. (2004a). Stimulant treatment of adult attention-deficit/hyperactivity disorder. *Psychiatric Clinics of North America* 27(2), 361–372.

Spencer, T. Biederman, J., & Wilens, T. (2004b). Nonstimulant treatment of adult attention-deficit/hyperactivity disorder. *Psychiatric Clinics of North America* 27(2), 373–383.

Stahl, S.M. (2013). *Stahl's essential psychopharmacology: Neuroscientific basis and practical applications.* New York: Cambridge University Press.

Still, G.F. (1902). The Goulstonian Lectures: On some abnormal physical conditions in children. *Lancet* 159(4102), 1008–1013.

Stolberg, V.B. (2006). A review of perspectives on alcohol and alcoholism in the history of American health and medicine. *Journal of Ethnicity in Substance Abuse* 5(4), 39–106.

Stolberg, V.B. (2007). A cross-cultural and historical survey of tobacco use among various ethnic groups. *Journal of Ethnicity in Substance Abuse* 6(3–4), 9–80.

Stolberg, V.B. (2009a). Comprehensive Drug Abuse Prevention and Control Act. In G.L. Fisher & N.A. Roget (Eds.). *Encyclopedia of substance abuse prevention, treatment, and recovery.* (pp. 224–225). Thousand Oaks, CA: SAGE Publications.

Stolberg, V.B. (2009b). Historical images and reviews of substance use and substance abuse in the teaching of addiction studies. *Journal of Teaching in the Addictions* 8(1–2), 65–83.

Stolberg, V.B. (2011a). The use of coca: A mild stimulant through prehistory, history, and ethnography. *Journal of Ethnicity in Substance Abuse* 10(2), 126–146.

Stolberg, V.B. (2011b). Comprehensive Drug Abuse Prevention and Control Act. In M.A.R. Kleiman & J.E. Hawdon (Eds.), *Encyclopedia of drug policy.* (Vol. 1, pp. 155–158). Thousand Oaks, CA: SAGE Publications.

Stolberg, V.B. (2011c). Narcotic Addict Rehabilitation Act. In M.A.R. Kleiman & J.E. Hawdon (Eds.), *Encyclopedia of drug policy.* (Vol. 2, pp. 541–543). Thousand Oaks, CA: SAGE Publications.

Stolberg, V.B. (2011d). United Nations Convention against the Illicit Traffic in Narcotic drugs. In M.A.R. Kleiman & J.E. Hawdon (Eds.), *Encyclopedia of drug policy.* (Vol. 2, pp. 801–802). Thousand Oaks, CA: SAGE Publications.

Stolberg, V.B. (2014). Issues in mental health assessment. In A. Scull (Ed.), *Cultural sociology of mental illness.* (Vol. 1, pp. 49–53). Thousand Oaks, CA: SAGE Publications.

Stolberg, V.B. (2016a). Clinical trials. In S.E. Boslaugh (Ed.), *Encyclopedia of pharmacology and society.* (Vol. 1, pp. 384–389). Thousand Oaks, CA: SAGE Publications.

Stolberg, V.B. (2016b). Controlled Substances Act. In S.E. Boslaugh (Ed.), *Encyclopedia of pharmacology and society.* (Vol. 1, pp. 416–419). Thousand Oaks, CA: SAGE Publications.

Stolberg, V.B. (2016c). *Painkillers: History, science, and issues.* Santa Barbara, CA: ABC-CLIO.

Storebo, O.J., Ramstad, E., Krogh, H.B., Nilausen, T.D., Skoog, M., Holmskov, M., . . . Gluud, C. (2015). Methylphenidate for children and adolescents with attention deficit hyperactivity disorder (ADHD). *Cochrane Database of Systematic Reviews,* doi:10.1002/14651858.CD009885.pub2.

Su-Je, C., & Kwang-Sun, C.B. (2017). Using a multicomponent function-based intervention to support students with attention deficit hyperactivity disorder. *Journal of Special Education* 50(4), 227–238.

Tewar, S., Auinger, P., Braun, J.M., Lanphear, B., Yolton, K., Epstein, J.N., . . . Froelich, T.E. (2016). Association of Bisphemol A and attention-deficit/hyperactivity disorder in a national sample of U.S. children. *Environmental Research* 150, 112–118.

Thapar, A., Langley, K., & Owen, M.J. (2007). Advances in genetic findings on attention deficit hyperactivity disorder. *Psychological Medicine* 37(12), 1681–1692.

Wang, L.-J., Huang, Y.-S., Hsiao, C.-C., & Chen, C.-K. (2017). The trend in morning levels of salivary cortisol in children with ADHD during 6 months of methylphenidate treatment. *Journal of Attention Disorders* 21(3), 254–261.

Wender, P.H. (2000). *ADHD: Attention-Deficit Hyperactivity Disorder in children and adults.* Oxford: Oxford University Press.

Wiener, J., & Daniels, L. (2016). School experiences of adolescents with attention-deficit/hyperactivity disorder. *Journal of Learning Disabilities* 49(6), 567–581.

Wilens, T.E. (2004). Attention-deficit/hyperactivity disorder and the substance use disorders: The nature of the relationship, subtypes at risk, and treatment issues. *Psychiatric Clinics of North America* 27(2), 283–301.

Wilens, T.E. (2006). Action of agents used in attention deficit/hyperactivity disorder. *Journal of Clinical Psychiatry* 57(Sup. 8), 32–38.

Zeigler Dendy, C.A. (1995). *Teenagers with ADD: A parents' guide.* Bethesda, MD: Woodbine House.

Index

About the Author

VICTOR B. STOLBERG, EdM, MA, MS, MA, MSEd, MAT, MAH, MALS, MA, is an assistant professor and counselor at Essex County College, Newark, NJ, where he previously directed both the Office of Disability Support Services and the Office of the Substance Abuse Coordinator. He is the author of *Painkillers: History, Science, and Issues*, another book in the Greenwood series The Story of a Drug. He has authored, or coauthored, 49 scholarly articles, 87 encyclopedia articles, 6 chapters and contributed papers, and 63 miscellaneous other publications. He also has several publications currently in press; these include seven entries for the upcoming ABC/CLIO *Environmental Health in the 21st Century: From Air Pollution to Zoonotic Diseases* and six for the *Encyclopedia of Sex and Sexuality: Understanding Biology, Psychology, and Culture*. He has delivered hundreds of professional presentations in over 20 states consisting of papers, workshops, panel discussions, and such at state, national, and international venues. He serves on the editorial board of the *Journal of Ethnicity in Substance Abuse*. In addition to his substance abuse and disability experience, he is as trained archaeologist and historian. Current research interests include historical and cross-cultural studies of substance use and abuse, and college student issues.